British Politics and European Elections 1999

British Politics and European Elections 1999

David Butler
Emeritus Fellow
Nuffield College
Oxford

and

Martin Westlake
Head of Unit for Institutional Relations
European Commission
Brussels

First published in Great Britain 2000 by
MACMILLAN PRESS LTD
Houndmills, Basingstoke, Hampshire RG21 6XS and London
Companies and representatives throughout the world

A catalogue record for this book is available from the British Library.

ISBN 0–333–77078–1 hardcover
ISBN 0–333–77079–X paperback

 First published in the United States of America 2000 by
ST. MARTIN'S PRESS, INC.,
Scholarly and Reference Division,
175 Fifth Avenue, New York, N.Y. 10010

ISBN 0–312–23377–0

CIP information is available from the Library of Congress

This book is printed on paper suitable for recycling and made from fully managed and sustained forest sources.

10   9   8   7   6   5   4   3   2   1
09   08   07   06   05   04   03   02   01   00

Printed and bound in Great Britain by
Antony Rowe Ltd, Chippenham, Wiltshire

BUTLER & WESTLAKE: *BRITISH POLITICS AND EUROPEAN ELECTIONS 1999*

ERRATUM

Pages 189 Lines 5–7

Neither Mr Stevens nor Mr Donnelly was offered nor did they seek a candidacy on the Conservative Party's North West list. Nor were they offered places on any other lists outside their own region of the South East.

Contents

List of Tables and Boxes

Tables

Boxes

List of Cartoons

Acknowledgements

Although this book has two principal authors, many people have helped in its making. We would like to thank the Warden and Fellows of Nuffield College, both officially and personally, for once again supporting an election study. We are grateful to the Nuffield Foundation for its generous, and vital, support. We would also like to place on record our gratitude to the European Commission and the European Parliament; in particular the Secretary-General, Julian Priestley, and the Head of the London Office, Chris Piening. As always, we would like to make it clear that any opinions expressed are entirely personal.

We would like to thank those in the political parties who were generous with their time and their thoughts. Clearly, a study of an election would be impossible without the full cooperation of the participants. We have been helped most comprehensively by the candidates, the MEPs (both old and new), MPs, ministers and frontbench spokesmen, and a very large number of party activists, as well as by the journalists who followed the campaign. To them go our grateful thanks.

Those who contributed named sections to this study were punctual and perceptive. Our grateful thanks go to the polling organisations and to the cartoonists who have authorised us to reproduce their work here.

Chris Ballinger gave us invaluable research and editorial help. Andreas Arvanitakis, Marc Chasserot, Candida Jones and Marie Seren were generous with research and administrative help. Ian St John helped greatly with his editorial skills.

The authors are grateful to Martin Range, who did much of the statistical work. Thanks are also due to Steve Bell, Peter Brookes, Dave Brown, Steve Fricker, John Kent, Kenneth Mahood, Steve O'Brien and Chris Riddell for permission to reproduce cartoon material.

Last and never least, our grateful thanks go to our wives, Marilyn and Godelieve.

Nuffield College   David Butler
November 1999   Martin Westlake

Notes on Authors and Contributors

David Butler, Emeritus Fellow of Nuffield College, Oxford, has been associated with the Nuffield election studies since 1945 and has been the author or co-author of each one since 1951. His most recent publications include *Twentieth-Century British Political Facts 1900–2000* (with Gareth Butler) and *The British General Election of 1997* (with Dennis Kavanagh). He is well known for his election commentaries on television and radio and has written widely on British, American and Australian politics.

Martin Westlake has served in a number of European institutions and currently works in the European Commission, where he is responsible for institutional relations. He has published widely on the European institutions and British politics. His most recent publications include *The European Union beyond Amsterdam* (1998) and *Leaders of Transition* (1999). He is a Visiting Professor at the College of Europe, Bruges, and an Associate Member of the Centre for Legislative Studies at the University of Hull.

Chris Ballinger is a politics research student at The Queen's College, Oxford.

John Curtice is Professor of Politics, University of Strathclyde, and Deputy Director of the ESRC Centre for Research into Elections and Social Trends (CREST).

John Fitzmaurice is Professor, Free University in Brussels, and Head of Unit at the European Commission.

Paul Hainsworth is Senior Lecturer in Politics, University of Ulster at Jordanstown.

James Kellas is Professor of Politics, University of Glasgow.

Zig Layton-Henry is Professor of Politics, University of Warwick.

Lord Norton of Louth is Professor of Government, University of Hull.

George Parker is a political correspondent for the *Financial Times*.

Michael Steed is Hon. Lecturer in Politics and International Relations at the University of Kent at Canterbury.

Dafydd Trystan is a Lecturer at the Institute of Welsh Politics, University of Wales, Aberystwyth.

List of Abbreviations

AEA	Association of Electoral Administrators
AEEU	Amalgamated Engineering and Electronic Union
AP	Alliance Party
BSE	bovine spongiform encephalopathy ('Mad Cow Disease')
BNP	British National Party
CAP	Common Agricultural Policy
CJD	Creutzfeldt-Jakob disease (human disease similar to BSE)
CDU	*Christlich Demokratische Union* (German Christian Democratic Union Party)
DUP	Democratic Unionist Party
EC	European Community
ECB	European Central Bank
ECLP	Euro-Constituency Labour Party
ECOFIN	Economic and Finance Ministers Council
ECSC	European Coal and Steel Community
EDC	European Defence Community
EDD	Europe of Democracies and Differences (Group)
EDU	European Democratic Union
EEC	European Economic Community
EFTA	European Free Trade Association
ELDR	European Liberal, Democrat and Reform (Party)
EMU	(European) Economic and Monetary Union
EP	European Parliament
EPLP	European Parliamentary Labour Party
EPP	European People's Party
ERM	(European) Exchange Rate Mechanism
EU	European Union
EURATOM	European Atomic Energy Community
GFA	Good Friday Agreement
GM	genetically modified
GMO	genetically modified organisms
HL	House of Lords

IGC	intergovernmental conference
IRA	Irish Republican Army
MEP	Member of the European Parliament
MSP	Member of the Scottish Parliament
NAFTA	North American Free Trade Area
NATO	North Atlantic Treaty Organization
NEC	National Executive Committee (Labour Party)
NFU	National Farmers' Union
NHS	National Health Service
NI	Northern Ireland
NL	Natural Law (Party)
NUS	National Union of Students
OFT	Office of Fair Trading
OMOV	one member, one vote
OSCE	Organization for Security and Co-operation in Europe
PC	Plaid Cymru
PEB	party election broadcast
PES	Party of European Socialists
PPB	party political broadcast
PR	proportional representation
PUP	Progressive Unionist Party
QMV	qualified majority voting
RPR	*Rassemblement pour la République* (French Gaullist Party)
SDP	Social Democratic Party
SDLP	Social Democratic and Labour Party
SLD	Social and Liberal Democrats
SLP	Socialist Labour Party
SNP	Scottish National Party
SOLACE	Society of Local Government Chief Executives
SPD	*Sozialdemokratische Partei Deutschlands* (Social-Democratic Party of Germany)
STV	single transferable vote
TUC	Trades Union Congress
UKIP	United Kingdom Independence Party
UKUP	United Kingdom Unionist Party
UUP	Ulster Unionist Party

1
Background

Expectations and reality

Since 1979 there have been five sets of direct elections to the European Parliament. The first three had little impact. The 1994 Euro-elections were rendered significant by the sudden death of John Smith and the rise of the Blair phenomenon. But in 1999 the European elections broke fresh constitutional ground in the UK – they were to be the first nationwide contest fought under proportional representation. In the run-up to the elections there was much speculation about how the new system would affect the political parties and what sort of results it would generate.

Normally, the Labour government should have suffered from a traditional mid-term electoral slump, but Tony Blair was no ordinary Prime Minister and the situation in Kosovo had transformed the British political atmosphere. Labour expected to lose some seats, but with its leader still riding exceptionally high in the opinion polls, the party believed it would not suffer as much as in past electoral cycles.

The Conservative Party seemed as deeply divided as ever over European integration, and particularly over William Hague's anti-single currency stance. The UK Independence Party lay to Mr Hague's right, the Pro-European Conservatives to his left. Given that the Euro-elections would be fought under proportional representation (PR), would the Conservative vote split three ways? Would the Conservative Party itself suffer schism as the pro-Europeans left in search of more hospitable territory?

Paddy Ashdown had announced his intention of standing down as Liberal Democrat Leader after the Euro-elections. Squeezing the concession of PR for the Euro-elections out of the Prime Minister was

1

one of Mr Ashdown's proudest achievements; *now* the wasted vote argument was eliminated and the Liberal Democrats could show their true strength.

The Pro-Euro Conservatives had been encouraged by private polling to believe that under PR they stood a real chance of realising their primary aim – to deal Mr Hague a body blow, triggering a leadership election which, they hoped, would elevate the former Tory Chancellor, Kenneth Clarke.

The UK Independence Party, although encouraged by the opportunities offered by PR, privately felt that winning a seat would be beyond it. The calculations of the British Greens, on the other hand, had led them to believe that one seat was realistically within their grasp. The Scottish National Party was aiming for three seats. Encouraged by its excellent results in the 6 May Welsh Assembly elections, Plaid Cymru believed it could take two seats. The system was also expected to enhance the performances of other, smaller, political parties, though no one could predict with any certainty how, for example, Arthur Scargill would perform in London, or the Alternative Left Alliance in the North-West, or the Scottish Socialist Party in Scotland.

One of the most extraordinary aspects of the 1999 Euro-elections was that none of these expectations and predictions came true. Some parties – the Conservatives, the UK Independence Party, the Greens and Plaid Cymru – did far better than had been expected. Others – Labour, the Lib Dems, the Pro-Euro Conservatives, the SNP – did worse. In particular, Labour's Strasbourg representation was more than halved, and yet Mr Blair and his government continued to ride high in the opinion polls. The UK Independence Party and the Greens fared much better than they had hoped, but no other smaller parties made any electoral impression. Turnout was always low in European elections, but the dismal, record low of 23 per cent was worse than even the gloomiest of pundits had predicted.

There were deeper consequences. Doubts were raised about the government's commitment to a referendum on the single currency and about its ability to win such a plebiscite. The possibility of the government introducing PR for national elections was postponed to the next Parliament. Beneath these, there were consequences for Mr Blair's 'project' to create a new, radical, centre-left force in British politics. In late May, the polls found Tony Blair and Labour to be riding as high as ever. The polls found the same result in late June. In between, the glistening Millbank machine of new Labour lost an election and William Hague's vulnerable leadership not only survived but was consolidated. How could this be?

The purpose of this book is to describe what happened.

Britain and Europe

Britain has always seemed the odd man out in Europe (see Boxes 1.1 and 1.2), but particularly since the 1939–45 war. The post-war years can be divided into four distinct periods. During the 1940s and the 1950s, the British government championed an intergovernmental approach. The Western continent's first political organisation was the Council of Europe (set up on 5 May 1949), derived from an earlier and narrower five-power defence agreement, the 1948 Brussels Treaty. France and Belgium wanted the Council to be a supranational body, but Britain successfully insisted on an intergovernmental structure. When Britain was invited (1950) to take part in the negotiations leading to the creation of the European Coal and Steel Community (ECSC), with its revolutionary concept of pooled sovereignty, it declined. A year later (1951) Anthony Eden made it clear that British Army units would not participate in the envisaged (and ultimately ill-fated) European Defence Community (EDC). When the EDC project failed (1954), Mr Eden championed the creation of the confederal Western European Union. In 1956, Britain declined to participate in the talks that would lead to the creation on 25 March 1957 of the European Economic Community (EEC) and the European Atomic Energy Community (EURATOM). Instead, it instigated the negotiations which led to the creation on 3 May 1960 of the alternative European Free Trade Association (EFTA).

The second period, the 1960s, has been described as Britain's 'slow adjustment to reality' (George, 1990). In the immediate post-war period, the arguments for deeper British involvement in supranational experiments had been basically political. By the 1960s there were increasingly powerful economic arguments for British accession to the EEC. These led Britain (and Denmark and Norway) to apply for membership in the summer of 1961. But General de Gaulle, doubtful about the depth of British commitment, stalled the accession negotiations and effectively vetoed the British application (14 January 1963). Britain applied again in 1967 but, after the 1967 devaluation of sterling, a still doubtful President de Gaulle refused to allow negotiations to go ahead.

The third period began with Britain finally negotiating entry (1970–72) and acceding to the Community (1 January 1973), just as the EEC's most successful and prosperous period was ending, and as a prolonged recession began. Moreover, by then the Community had developed in ways which were bound to suit the original six Member States better than any new arrivals. In 1974–75, Britain sought to renegotiate its terms of membership. This led to the 1975 referendum and, later, to the

1979–84 negotiations over the size of Britain's budgetary contribution, culminating in the agreement reached at the June 1984 Fontainebleau European Council. As Prime Minister, Margaret Thatcher signed up to the Single European Act (1986) and membership of the Exchange Rate Mechanism (1990), but she was an instinctive Euro-sceptic and naturally adversarial in relations with her Continental counterparts. Her successor, John Major, famously wanted to be 'at the heart of Europe', but in the 1992 General Election won only a small majority and thereafter became increasingly beholden to the wrecking tactics of a minority of Euro-sceptic backbenchers. As he sought to drive the Maastricht Treaty through the Commons, Mr Major was beset on one side by his own backbenchers and on the other, by a Labour Party determined to exploit the situation and bring the government down. Mr Major survived, but his government became increasingly Euro-sceptical in tone and in practice, perhaps most notoriously characterised by the 1996 policy of non-cooperation in the Council of Ministers following the European ban on British beef (Westlake, 1997).

The fourth period began in 1997, with the election of a naturally pro-European Prime Minister with (perhaps just as importantly) a crushing majority. The new approach of the Blair government is described below. To Continental politicians it seemed at last that the United Kingdom might be undergoing a sea change in its attitudes towards European integration and the European Union. Mr Blair's promise of PR for European elections, together with the constitutional changes introduced by the Amsterdam Treaty, presaged a new departure in the European Union's development.

Box 1.1 Chronology of Britain and Europe, 1948–94

19 Nov 46	In Zurich speech Winston Churchill calls for a 'United States of Europe', later explaining that he sees Britain as being 'with but not in' such an entity
17 Mar 48	Brussels Treaty signed (Belgium, France, Luxembourg, the Netherlands and UK defence agreement)
4 Apr 49	North Atlantic Treaty signed
5 May 49	Council of Europe established
3 Jun 50	Britain declines participation in the Schuman Plan
18 Dec 51	Britain says it won't send army units to the planned EDC
24 Jul 52	ECSC established – without British participation

continued

Box 1.1 continued

10 Sep 52	ECSC Parliamentary Assembly meets for the first time
30 Aug 54	EDC plans abandoned
23 Oct 54	Western European Union established
2 May 55	Messina Conference opens. Britain again declines to take part.
25 Mar 57	Treaties of Rome signed. European Economic Community (EEC) established
19 Mar 58	European Assembly meets for the first time
3 May 60	European Free Trade Association (EFTA) established. UK a founder member
14 Jan 63	De Gaulle vetoes Britain's first application to join the EEC
29 Jan 66	Political crisis leads to Luxembourg Compromise
29 Nov 67	De Gaulle vetoes Britain's second application
30 Jun 70	Britain reopens negotiations to join the EEC
22 Jan 72	Britain signs the Treaty of Rome
4 Oct 72	Labour decides not to participate in the European Parliament until the terms of entry have been satisfactorily renegotiated
1 Jan 73	Britain's accession to the EEC
16 Jan 73	First British MEPs (Conservative and Liberal) take their places in the European Parliament
10 Dec 74	Paris summit agrees to the principle of direct elections for 1978
28 Feb 74	Labour government elected on platform which includes promise to renegotiate terms of entry
1 Apr 74	British government opens renegotiation of entry terms
11 Mar 75	Renegotiations completed
5 Jun 75	British referendum on continued EEC membership – 67.2 per cent vote 'Yes'
18 Jun 75	First Labour delegates take their places in the European Parliament
17 Feb 76	Government Green Paper on direct European elections
20 Sep 76	Council of Ministers signs European Assembly Elections Act
22 Mar 77	Lib–Lab pact
1 Apr 77	Government White Paper on direct elections
5 May 78	Royal Assent to European Assembly Elections Bill
10 Mar 79	European Monetary System established. Britain declines participation
3 Jun 79	General Election returns first Thatcher government
7 Jun 79	First European elections (Con 60 seats, Lab 17, Lib 0, others 4)
17 Jul 79	First directly elected European Parliament meets in Strasbourg
1 Oct 80	Labour Party Conference votes for British withdrawal from the EC
10 Nov 80	Michael Foot beats Denis Healey to become Labour Leader
26 Mar 81	SDP launched
1 Oct 81	Labour Party Conference votes to withdraw from the EC without a referendum

continued

Box 1.1 continued

9 Jun 83	General Election returns second Thatcher government
1 Oct 83	Neil Kinnock elected Labour Party Leader. Labour abandons outright opposition to EC membership
14 Feb 84	European Parliament adopts draft Treaty establishing European Union. Despite Thatcher's instructions to the contrary, 21 Conservative MEPs voted for the draft Treaty; 6 abstained and 28 were absent from the vote
14 Jun 84	Second European elections (Con 45 seats, Lab 32, Lib 0, others 4)
25–26 Jun 84	Fontainebleau European Council resolves the five-year running dispute about Britain's budgetary rebate
7 Jan 85	The first Delors Commission takes office
28–29 Jun 85	Milan European Council decides, with Britain opposing, to convene an intergovernmental conference on treaty reform
2 Dec 85	The IGC completes its work at the Luxembourg European Council
17 Feb 86	The twelve Member States sign the Single European Act
11 Jun 87	General Election returns third Thatcher government
1 Jul 87	Single European Act comes into force
3 Mar 88	Social and Liberal Democrat Party launched
27–28 Jun 88	Hanover European Council establishes Delors Committee on Economic and Monetary Union
8 Sep 88	Jacques Delors address TUC
20 Sep 88	Margaret Thatcher's Bruges speech
6 Jan 89	The second Delors Commission takes office
15 Jun 89	Third European elections (Lab 54 seats, Con 32, SLD 0, others 4, but Green Party wins 15 per cent of the vote)
27 Jun 89	Thatcher agrees to EMU IGC at Madrid
1 Jul 90	First stage of EMU, not requiring treaty amendments, begins
17 Jul 89	Austria applies for EC membership
11 Nov 89	Berlin Wall falls
3 Oct 90	German unification
8 Oct 90	Sterling unilaterally joins the European exchange rate mechanism (ERM)
28 Oct 90	EMU IGC's terms agreed despite British opposition
20 Nov 90	Thatcher 204, Heseltine 152. Thatcher withdraws on 22 November
28 Nov 90	John Major elected new leader of Conservative Party and hence becomes Prime Minister
15 Dec 90	Rome II European Council opens two IGCs with John Major's agreement
8 Jan 91	Britain publishes 'hard ecu' proposals
1 Jul 91	Sweden applies for EC membership
10 Dec 91	Maastricht Treaty agreed, with British 'opt-out' on Social Chapter and 'opt-in' on EMU

continued

Box 1.1 continued

18 Mar 92	Finland applies for EC membership
9 Apr 92	General Election returns Major government
2 Jun 92	Danish referendum rejects Maastricht Treaty by 50.7 per cent to 49.3 per cent
1 Jul 92	UK Presidency of the EC begins
18 Jul 92	John Smith elected Labour Party Leader
16 Sep 92	'Black Wednesday'. Sterling forced out of the ERM
20 Sep 92	French referendum approves Maastricht Treaty by 51 to 49 per cent
5 Nov 92	Britain postpones parliamentary ratification of the Maastricht Treaty
25 Nov 92	Norway applies for EC membership
11–12 Dec 92	Edinburgh European Council adopts subsidiarity, transparency and openness package designed to help Danes
31 Dec 92	British Presidency ends
1 Jan 93	Single European market comes into being
6 Jan 93	Third Delors Commission takes office
1 Feb 93	Enlargement negotiations begin with Austria, Finland and Sweden (and Norway on 5 Apr)
18 May 93	Second Danish referendum approves Maastricht Treaty by 56.8 to 43.2 per cent
20 May 93	Commons approves Maastricht Bill by 292 to 112
2 Aug 93	Britain deposits instruments of ratification the day the ERM collapses
1 Nov 93	Maastricht Treaty comes into force
1 Jan 94	Stage 2 of EMU, including the creation of a European Monetary Institute, comes into force
1 Mar 94	Enlargement negotiations concluded with Austria, Finland and Sweden (Norway 16 Mar)
27 Mar 94	Blocking minority row leads to Ioaninna compromise
4 May 94	European Parliament assents to accession of Austria, Finland, Norway, and Sweden
25 Jun 94	Britain vetoes Dehaene as President of the Commission

---

Box 1.2 Chronology of Britain and Europe, 1994–99

9 Jun 94	European Parliament elections. Lab 62, Con 18, Lib Dems 2. Lib Dems win Eastleigh by-election
15 Jul 94	UK agrees to Jacques Santer appointed Commission President
21 Jul 94	Blair elected Lab Leader. Prescott Deputy Leader

continued

Box 1.2 continued

18 Sep 94	At Lib Dem conference Paddy Ashdown urges 'common cause' with Lab
13 Oct 94	Swedes vote to join EU
20 Oct 94	Lab Shadow Cabinet reshuffle. Cook to Foreign Affairs; Straw to Home Affairs
21 Oct 94	Norwegians vote against EU membership for second time
28 Oct 94	31 Labour MEPs sign 'Save Clause Four' document
28 Nov 94	Government wins confidence vote on Maastricht Treaty 330–303. Whip withdrawn from eight Con rebels
1 Jan 95	Austria, Finland and Sweden join EU
24 Apr 95	Whip restored to eight Con Euro-rebels
29 Apr 95	Lab membership endorses new Clause Four
4 May 95	Local elections. Conservatives lose 1,800 seats
22 Jun 95	John Major resigns to seek re-election as Conservative Leader
26 Jun 95	John Redwood resigns from Cabinet to fight Major
4 Jul 95	Major re-elected Leader 218–89 (22 abstaining)
10 Oct 95	Con Conference; Portillo attacks EU and affirms independence of UK defence policy
27 Nov 95	Sir James Goldsmith launches Referendum Party
15 Feb 96	Scott report on 'arms to Iraq'
26 Feb 96	Govt escapes Scott censure 319–318
20 Mar 96	Link between BSE and CJD admitted. EU and worldwide bans on British beef
11 Jun 96	78 Con MPs support referendum on Europe
17–19 Jun 96	Amsterdam European Council meeting
20 Dec 96	Following resignation of Lord Plumb, Con MEPs elect pro-European Tom Spencer as leader by two votes
20 Jan 97	Cabinet publicly agrees EMU entry in 1999 'unlikely'
20 Jan 97	Brown accepts Con spending limits for next two years
27 Feb 97	Lab Win Wirral South by-election
18 Mar 97	General Election announced
25 Mar 97	40th anniversary of the signing of the Treaty of Rome
1 May 97	Labour wins General Election with landslide, 419 MPs to Con 165 and Lib Dem 46, Major resigns Con Leader
6 May 97	Blair hails 'new era' in Britain's relations with Europe, promises to sign Social Chapter. Chancellor of the Exchequer transfers interest rate management to a committee of the Bank of England
13 Jun 97	In *New Statesman* interview Robin Cook says he is unsure whether the next Euro-elections will be held under PR
16–17 Jun 97	Amsterdam European Council adopts draft Amsterdam Treaty
19 Jun 97	Hague elected Conservative Leader
11 Jul 97	Several Labour MEPs reportedly rebellious over Millbank attempts to impose a new code of discipline. 'Charge sheet' reportedly compiled against Hugh Kerr, MEP

continued

Box 1.2 continued

16 Jul 97	Blair declares PR will be used for 1999 Euro-elections
19 Jul 97	Euro-sceptic French MEP and UK Referendum Party founder Sir James Goldsmith dies
21 Jul 97	Labour Party and Liberal Democrats agree to set up a cross-party Cabinet-level committee to discuss common concerns
11 Sep 97	Scottish referendum – 74.3 per cent for proposed Parliament
16 Sep 97	Hugh Dykes switches from Con to Lib Dem over Europe
17 Sep 97	Edward McMillan-Scott, moderate pro-European, elected leader of the Conservative MEPs by one vote
18 Sep 97	Welsh referendum – 50.3 per cent for proposed Assembly
27 Sep 97	Share prices surge to record high following rumoured government decision that UK would join the single currency as soon as possible after 1999
22 Oct 97	Four rebel MEPs suspended from EPLP over refusal to accept new NEC code of practice. Four MEPs meanwhile consult EP President as to whether code is compatible with EP rules
28 Oct 97	Chancellor of the Exchequer states that there is no constitutional barrier to joining the single currency. Sterling will join when conditions are right, probably early in the next Parliament
29 Oct 97	Government announces it will table a proposal for a closed-list PR system for 1999 Euro-elections
1 Nov 97	Curry resigns from the Shadow Cabinet over Hague's euro-policy
5 Nov 97	Suspension of four rebel Labour MEPs lifted
6–7 Nov 97	Following Helmut Kohl's initial offer, Canary Wharf summit between British and French governments confirms European Central Bank seat will be 'kept warm' for UK
10 Nov 97	Gordon Brown presents proposals for making British business 'euro-friendly' by 1999
12 Nov 97	Commons approves Amsterdam Treaty after Hague imposes three-line Whip against
1 Jan 98	UK EU Presidency begins
8 Jan 98	Two Labour MEPs – Ken Coates and Hugh Kerr – expelled from the Labour Party
14 Jan 98	Conservative MPs endorse Hague's proposals for new rules for Conservative Party leadership elections
27 Feb 98	The 15 Member States formally file their statistical reports which will become the basis for deciding membership of the single currency
12 Mar 98	European Standing Conference on Enlargement in London brings together leaders of 26 countries
17 Mar 98	EU Agriculture Ministers approve a partial lifting of the 1996 export ban on UK beef (Germany and Belgium vote against)
17 Mar 98	Gordon Brown unveils his second Budget

continued

Box 1.2 continued

18 Mar 98	EU Commission unveils a blueprint for a drastic overhaul of EU spending, in preparation for future enlargement of the EU
25 Mar 98	European Commission reports that eleven countries should adopt the euro from 1 January 1999, based on statistical data; UK and Denmark have opt-outs, Greece and Sweden fail to meet the criteria
28 Mar 98	William Hague announces that his reforms to the Conservative Party have received 80 per cent support in a postal ballot of party activists
30 Mar 98	EU enlargement talks open
2 Apr 98	German Federal Constitutional Court upholds adoption of the euro
8 Apr 98	Spanish fishermen win a UK High Court ruling over fishing quotas
22 Apr 98	French National Assembly votes in favour of adopting the euro
1–3 May 98	EU Heads of Government meet in Brussels at a special summit on EMU. Wim Duisenberg appointed Head of the ECB for eight years, but reportedly 'signalled his willingness' to step down in 2002
6 May 98	Government announces plans to bring forward opening of Scottish Parliament from January 2000 to July 1999
7 May 98	Local elections produce modest gains for the Conservatives
11 May 98	First euro coins minted
22 May 98	62 per cent of Irish voters endorse Amsterdam Treaty
27 May 98	Partial lifting of ban on UK beef exports
28 May 98	Danish voters narrowly approve Amsterdam Treaty by 55.1 per cent to 44.9 per cent
1 Jun 98	Shadow Cabinet reshuffle. Ann Widdecombe and David Willetts brought in; Francis Maude becomes Shadow Chancellor
9 Jun 98	Silvio Berlusconi's Forza Italia joins the European People's Party (EPP) Grouping in the European Parliament
15 Jun 98	UK deposits instruments of ratification of Amsterdam Treaty
15–16 Jun 98	EU Heads of Government meeting at Cardiff
16 Jun 98	Alan Donnelly elected Leader of the EPLP
30 Jun 98	UK EU Presidency ends. Inauguration of the European Central Bank, Frankfurt
1 Jul 98	Austria takes over the Presidency of the EU
8 Jul 98	Government publishes its 'Strategic Defence Review'
27–28 Jul 98	Government reshuffle. Cunningham becomes 'enforcer', Mandelson becomes Trade Secretary. Harman, Strang, Clark, Richard and Field are out.
27 Sep 98	The SPD wins in Germany's Federal General Election and enters into a governing coalition with the Greens

continued

Box 1.2 continued

5 Oct 98	Conservative Party members approve of William Hague's proposal to rule out membership of the euro at the next election by 84.4 per cent on a 59 per cent turnout
6 Oct 98	Formation of an independent anti-fraud unit is announced by EU Commission President Jacques Santer after allegations of corruption in the administration of the EU budget
7 Oct 98	EU Commission sets out for the first time details of each country's net contribution to the EU budget. Alternative options for financing the EU are discussed
9 Oct 98	Italy's first centre-left coalition government, under Romano Prodi, collapses
14 Oct 98	Baroness Jay, the Leader of the House of Lords, announces the introduction of a Bill to terminate the rights of hereditary peers to sit and vote in the Lords
27 Oct 98	Ron Davies, the UK Secretary of State for Wales, resigns, following a 'moment of madness' on Clapham Common
27 Oct 98	Gerhard Schröder formally elected as German Federal Chancellor
29 Oct 98	The Jenkins Commission on electoral systems publishes its report, recommending a system of 'AV top-up'
4 Nov 98	EU Defence Ministers meet for the first time in EU framework
10 Nov 98	EU opens formal enlargement talks. Poland, Hungary, the Czech Republic, Estonia, Slovenia and Cyprus seek membership
17 Nov 98	Report on EU fraud presented to European Parliament
22 Nov 98	Finance Ministers of eleven centre-left EU governments launch *The New European Way – Economic Reform and the Framework for Economic Monetary Union*, a manifesto for a socialist Europe
26 Nov 98	In the Scotland North-East European by-election, the SNP retains the seat with 48 per cent of the vote and an increased majority (33,701) on a much lower turnout (20.5 per cent)
2 Dec 98	Hague dismisses Viscount Cranborne as Conservative Leader in the House of Lords. Deal announced with peers to ensure European Elections Bill becomes law in time for June elections
4 Dec 98	Anglo-French St Malo summit reaches agreement on new European defence initiative
11–12 Dec 98	Vienna summit meeting of EU Heads of Government to mark the end of the Austrian presidency
23 Dec 98	Peter Mandelson resigns as Trade and Industry Secretary
31 Dec 98	EU Finance Ministers meet to set conversion rates for currencies joining the euro
1 Jan 99	The euro comes into being – minus sterling. Exchange rates between the eleven are irrevocably fixed. Notes and coins will circulate in 2002. Germany takes up EU presidency

continued

Box 1.2 continued

14 Jan 99	European Parliament and European Commission clash over allegations of fraud and mismanagement. Censure motion against Commission defeated by 293 votes to 232
14 Jan 99	The European Parliamentary Elections Bill receives the Royal Assent after the Lords had rejected it for an unprecedented sixth time and the government had invoked the Parliament Act for the first time since 1991
20 Jan 99	Paddy Ashdown announces that he will step down as Lib Dem Leader after the Euro-elections
18 Feb 99	Strasbourg European Court of Human Rights rules that Gibraltarians should be able to vote in Euro-elections
23 Feb 99	Blair announces national changeover plan to the euro
1–2 Mar 99	Milan European Socialist Party Congress adopts common manifesto
2 Mar 99	Lords Owen, Healey and Prior launch 'New Europe' Group which is pro-European but anti-euro
11 Mar 99	Oskar Lafontaine resigns from the German government. Registrar of Political Parties authorises Pro-Euro Conservative Party title
12 Mar 99	Alex Salmond announces 1p 'tartan tax'
13 Mar 99	At Con Reading Spring Conference Hague talks of new 'kitchen table' politics
15 Mar 99	Following publication of wise men's report, European Commission resigns *en masse*
22–29 Mar 99	Gallup poll for *Eurobarometer* shows only 2.8 per cent of British respondents were aware of the date of the Euro-elections
23 Mar 99	Order given to initiate NATO airstrikes against the Former Republic of Yugoslavia
24–24 Mar 99	Berlin European Council nominates Romano Prodi as next President of the European Commission. Blair successfully defends UK budgetary rebate and wins regional funds for N. Ireland and Highlands and Islands
29 Mar 99	Salmond attacks the government's Kosovo policy
30 Mar 99	France's legislature ratifies the Amsterdam Treaty
18 Apr 99	Italian referendum narrowly fails to introduce first-past-the-post electoral system
20 Apr 99	Celebrations of twentieth anniversary of Margaret Thatcher's first general election victory. Peter Lilley makes speech urging Conservatives to accept that the free market has only a limited role
23–25 Apr 99	Summit of NATO leaders in Washington DC to mark NATO's 50th anniversary. Possibility of NATO ground invasion of Kosovo discussed
26 Apr 99	EU imposes oil embargo in Yugoslavia

continued

Box 1.2 continued

28 Apr 99	Berlin Congress of European Liberal, Democrat and Reform Party (ELDR) presents common Euro-manifesto
1 May 99	Amsterdam Treaty enters into force
3–7 May 99	Last Strasbourg plenary session of outgoing EP
5 May 99	EP approves Prodi 392 : 72 : 41 with some British Lab and Con MEPs voting against. Parliament rejects Council draft legislation on MEPs' statute and on their pay
6 May 99	Scottish Parliament and Welsh Assembly and English local elections. In Scotland, SNP fares worse than expected. Lab wins a majority but must enter coalition with Lib Dems. In Wales Plaid Cymru makes unprecedented gains in Islwyn and Rhondda Valley. In England, Hague's Cons win 1,200 seats back
11 May 99	Derek Fatchett dies, triggering Leeds Central by-election
12 May 99	Blair in agreement with Prodi nominates Neil Kinnock and Chris Patten as UK's European Commissioners
13 May 99	Donald Dewar elected Scottish First Minister
14 May 99	Blair Aachen speech and Charlemagne Prize. Affirms his 'real' intention to enter the euro-zone and desire to resolve UK ambivalence towards Europe once and for all. Hague University of Budapest speech calls for 'mix and match' European integration. Lab and Lib Dems sign coalition deal in Scotland
17 May 99	European elections campaign gets underway with Lib Dem manifesto launch
3 Jun 99	Milosevic accepts terms of Ahtisaari–Chernomyrdin peace plan. K-For troops enter Kosovo on 11–13 June
10 Jun 99	European Parliament elections and Leeds Central by-election
11 Jun 99	Leeds Central by-election result announced
13–14 Jun 99	Election results announced

The European Parliament

The EEC's 'founding fathers' had seen direct elections as the key to the evolution of the European Parliament and the democratic development of the EEC itself. But progress towards a direct and uniform system was almost immediately stymied by General Charles de Gaulle's 1958 accession to power. Throughout the 1960s, the Parliament remained an inconsequential institution, with only the feeblest of consultative powers, whilst the Commission and the Council were fast consolidating their roles and powers. Walter Hallstein's 1965 attempt to reform the Community's finances and give the Parliament a say over them was similarly crushed by General de Gaulle. His departure in 1969 led to renewed talks about finance, culminating in the creation of the Community's 'own resources'. The April 1970 Luxembourg Treaty first granted the Parliament budgetary powers, later consolidated by the July 1975 Brussels Treaty, but the Parliament did not have the political muscle to explore these powers until after the first direct elections in June 1979.

Chapter 2 details the negotiations which ultimately led to those first elections. After 1979, the Parliament, initially aided and abetted by Court rulings and sympathetic institutions, was able to evolve into a major player in the Community system. Above all, the succesive implementation of the Single European Act (1987), the Maastricht Treaty (1993) and the Amsterdam Treaty (1999) gave the Parliament far-reaching legislative powers and created a far more even balance between it and the Commission and the Council. Those who had seen the close vote on Jacques Santer's nomination in July 1994 as a prelude to a more politicised future were not to be disappointed.

From the very outset, the Parliament had had one very powerful weapon; it could censure (effectively sack) the Commission. For a long time the power was considered too powerful and indiscriminate in its effects, and in any case the Parliament lacked the democratic legitimacy to use it. However, the cumulative effect of direct elections and of the three major bouts of constitutional reform in the 1980s and 1990s produced between the two institutions something far more akin to a classic Western European style of Parliament–Executive relationship. Increasingly, the Parliament held the Commission to account, and the treaty changes gave it the tools to do this. One of these was the temporary committee of inquiry. The 1994–99 Parliament established two such committees, one on tax fraud in transport, and one on the BSE crisis. After the latter had reported, the Parliament came very close to using its censure powers for the first time, but chose instead to impose a 'conditional censure' upon the Commission.

Another tool was the obligation on the Parliament to grant the Commission discharge for (that is, approve) its implementation of each annual budget. Over the years, the Court of Auditors had consistently signalled shortcomings in budgetary implementation, but the Parliament had generally stopped short of adopting serious sanctions. However, in 1998 the Parliament's Budgetary Control Committee decided that the Court's allegations in regard to the implementation of the 1996 budget were sufficiently serious to warrant further investigation. The rapporteur on the 1996 discharge was a British Conservative MEP, James Elles, a longstanding proponent of budgetary reform. Increasingly vociferous parliamentarians argued that a number of Commissioners should take responsibility for the administration's wrongdoings and resign. But the named Commissioners protested their innocence and President Santer staunchly defended the Commission's collegiate nature – it was all or none. On 17 December 1998, after a protracted series of negotiations between the two institutions and the revelations of a 'whistleblower', Parliament refused to grant the Commission discharge. On the eve of the vote, President Santer had issued a 'back me or sack me' ultimatum to the Parliament. Pauline Green, leader of the Parliament's socialists, supported the Commission but now felt obliged to table a censure motion. It was intended, she argued, as a sort of confidence motion since no other mechanism existed through which the Parliament might assert its support.

On 14 January 1999, the Parliament duly voted on the censure motion. A majority of Mrs Green's group voted against censure, but a majority of the Christian Democrats, together with most German MEPs and a large number of MEPs from other groups, voted in favour. The motion was defeated by 293 votes to 232. The Santer Commission had – just – survived, but it had been badly wounded. The Union now faced a full-blown constitutional crisis.

In what was effectively an attempt to ward off the crisis and buy time, the two institutions agreed to the establishment of a committee of experts, dubbed 'the committee of wise men'. Jointly appointed by the two institutions, the experts were given three months in which to investigate eight specific allegations which had been made against the Commission in general and several members of the Commission in particular. On 16 March 1999 the Committee published its report. Virtually all of the allegations against individual members were found to be unjustified. On the other hand, the report argued that a number of more general charges of maladministration against parts of the Commission's administration were well founded. But the experts had appended a set of general conclusions to their report (See pp. 235–8), and this included the fatal phrase, 'it is difficult to find anybody in the Commission with any sense of responsibility'. It was the Santer Commission's deathknell. Within hours, Pauline Green had announced that the Group of the Party of European Socialists would vote in favour of censure. The same evening the Commission decided on collective resignation.

Thereafter, matters became confused. Commissioners were entitled to resign but, under the provisions of the Treaty, they were legally obliged to stay in place until their replacements had been named by the Heads of the Member States. At the same time, the Member States needed time to find replacements, not to mention a new President, with unanimity a necessary condition. Matters were further complicated by the imminent implementation of the Amsterdam Treaty, which would alter the Parliament's powers over the appointment of the new Commission. In yet a further complication, two members of the outgoing Commission, including Jacques Santer himself (the other was Emma Bonino), were selected to stand in the June European elections. All of these considerations militated in favour of leaving the resigned Commission in place until the Amsterdam Treaty had been implemented and until after the European elections.

Table 1.1 UK elections to the European Parliament, 1979–94 – Votes by party

	1979	*1984*	*1989*	*1994*
Great Britain				
Labour	4,253,207	4,865,261	6,153,661	6,753,881
Conservative	6,508,493	5,426,821	5,331,098	4,268,539
Liberal Democrat[*]	1,691,531	1,358,145[‡]	944,861	2,557,887
Scottish National	247,836	230,594	406,686	487,237
Plaid Cymru	83,399	103,031	115,062	162,478
Green[†]	17,953	70,853	2,292,718	494,561
SDP		1,233,490[‡]	75,886	
UK Independence				150,251
Natural Law				96,554
Liberal				100,500
Other	71,433	24,678	41,295	220,834
Total	12,873,852	13,312,873	15,361,267	15,292,722
Northern Ireland (first preference votes)				
Democratic Unionist	170,688	230,251	160,110	163,246
SDLP	140,622	151,399	136,335	161,992
Ulster Unionist	125,169	147,169	118,785	133,459
Sinn Féin		91,476	48,914	55,215
Alliance	39,026	34,046	27,905	23,157
Ulster Independence Movement				7,858
Conservative			25,789	5,583
Workers Party	4,418	8,172	5,590	2,543
Natural Law				2,291
Other	92,316	22,264	11,383	4,523
Total	572,239	685,317	534,811	559,867

[*] SLD in 1989/Liberal SDP Alliance in 1984/Liberal Party in 1979.
[†] Ecology Party in 1979 and 1984.
[‡] The Liberal/SDP Alliance total = 2,591,635.

Table 1.2 UK elections to the European Parliament, 1979–94 – UK MEPs by party

		1979	1984	1989	1994
Great Britain					
Labour	*(Number)*	17	32	45	62
	(% of UK MEPs)	21%	40%	56%	71%
Conservative	*(Number)*	60	45	32	18
	(% of UK MEPs)	74%	56%	40%	21%
Liberal Democrat					2
Scottish National		1	1	1	2
Total		78	78	78	84
Northern Ireland					
Democratic Unionist		1	1	1	1
SDLP		1	1	1	1
Ulster Unionist		1	1	1	1
Total		3	3	3	3
Total UK		81	81	81	87

This complicated set of events (Box 1.3) left a strange sense of anticlimax and, among many members of the European Parliament, a feeling of frustration. The Commission had resigned, but it had not gone. The Parliament might have forced the Commission to resign, but it had been cheated of the chance to sack it. Worse, in several Member States the media concurrently ran stories about alleged corruption or excess in the European Parliament. MEPs feared that the image of the Parliament would be subsumed in the more general perceptions of sleaze. The Parliament's image seemed further undermined by a perceived failure to vote through reforms to the statute and pay of MEPs (see p. 42–3).

The story of the Commission's resignation also overshadowed the 1994–99 Parliament's many substantial achievements in legislative and other fields. The Parliament had long sought to influence the Commission's draft legislation through annual legislative programmes and by amending draft legislation. The Maastricht Treaty introduced a new legislative device, the co-decision procedure, which promoted the Parliament to the status of co-legislature, together with the Council. The 1993–99 period saw the Parliament exercise its new legislative powers with considerable skill and ingenuity over a wide range of policy proposals, from food additives to tobacco advertising, from consumer protection to telecom liberalisation. The 1994–99 Parliament was also able to use its right to assent to the appointment of the ECB President, Wim Duisenberg, in order to force him and his institution into a

---

Box 1.3 The Parliament, the resignation of the Santer Commission, and the appointment of the Prodi Commission (chronology)

17 Dec 98	European Parliament refuses to approve Commission's accounts for 1996 budgetary year. Pauline Green tables a censure motion
14 Jan 99	Censure motion rejected, 293 to 232. Committee of wise men established to investigate allegations
15 Mar 99	Wise men's report published, including fatal phrase, 'it is becoming difficult to find anyone who has even the slightest sense of responsibility'
16 Mar 99	Santer Commission, including Neil Kinnock, resigns en masse but stays on, exercising caretaker functions, until 15 Sep 1999
23 Mar 99	Berlin European Council nominates Romano Prodi as new Commission President
5 May 99	European Parliament approves Prodi 392 : 72 : 41, with some British Lab and Con MEPs voting against
12 May 99	Tony Blair nominates Neil Kinnock and Chris Patten as UK members of the Commission
20 Jul 99	Prodi presents new Commission to the Parliament
30 Aug–7 Sep	Parliamentary hearings of individual nominees to the Commission
15 Sep 99	European Parliament confirms Prodi Commission 404 : 154 : 37. All British Lab MEPs vote in favour
17 Sep 99	Prodi Commission takes oath before European Court of Justice
18 Sep 99	Prodi Commission holds first official meeting

---

continuous political dialogue with the Parliament (Westlake, 1998). In addition, the Parliament made further progress in its traditional concerns such as human rights, equal opportunities, aid and development, and environmental concerns.

The 1994–99 Parliament met for the last time in Strasbourg in May 1999. As Patrick Smyth of the *Irish Times* put it, there were 'INTIMATIONS OF POLITICAL MORTALITY' in the air (8 May 1999). The careers of a larger than normal number of members of the European Parliament were coming to an end, not least among the British delegation. Among familiar figures retiring or at least withdrawing were Lord Plumb (Con), a former President of the European Parliament; Ken Collins (Lab), a longstanding Chairman of Parliament's powerful Environment Committee; and Tom Spencer (Con), a former leader of the British Conservatives and outgoing Chairman of the Foreign Affairs Committee. All three were first elected in 1979.

But Patrick Smyth was also referring to other forms of political mortality. It was a time, he argued 'for many to reflect on where the

Parliament is going politically' (*ibid.*). The new Parliament would have its full, post-Amsterdam panoply of powers. It would hold the fate of the newly nominated Commission in its hands. Shortly after the Euro-elections, a new intergovernmental conference would begin. How would the Parliament react to these new circumstances?

The 1994–99 period in the UK

To borrow from footballing parlance, the 1994–99 period in the United Kingdom was very much a 'game of two halves'. In the first half (1994–97), John Major's increasingly beleaguered Conservative government fought to overcome repeated resignations over sleaze and maladministration and to fend off the demands of an ever more insistent Euro-sceptic minority within the parliamentary party. In the second half (1997–99), Tony Blair appeared as the all-conquering hero, with his new Labour administration enjoying the longest honeymoon period with the British electorate in 40 years. Mr Blair's extraordinary personal popularity led the *Observer* newspaper to ask 'CAN BLAIR WALK ON WATER?' (2 May 1999). The first Labour Prime Minister since 1979 came to power with an ambitious political and constitutional agenda, including devolution and reform of the House of Lords and an open mind towards electoral reform in general and a later promise (16 July) of PR for the Euro-elections in particular. Behind these changes, political commentators increasingly identified Mr Blair's 'project' to create a new, radical, centre-left force in British politics, as epitomised by the creation on 21 July of a cross-party Cabinet level committee on constitutional issues between Labour and the Liberal Democrats.

At the European level, Mr Blair declared his determination to end the traditional adversarial stance of British governments. His election was welcomed by Commission President Jacques Santer in a special *Economist* article (10 May 1997). 'Britain's place', Mr Santer argued, 'is at the heart of the European Union.' Early indications came with the government's rapid (6 May) declaration that it would be signing up to the Social Chapter and the Chancellor of the Exchequer's (6 May 1997) announcement that the Bank of England would henceforth be independent in setting interest rates (central bank independence being an essential condition for membership of the single currency). Mr Blair sought a change to the 'mood music' of Britain's relations with the European Union. Ministers were, for example, instructed to be less aggressive and more conciliatory in their dealings with their Continental counterparts. In Strasbourg, Pauline Green led the Group of the Party of European Socialists, the largest in the Parliament, while British Labour MEPs were prominent in chairing important committees and authoring important reports.

The 1993 Maastricht Treaty had provided for a fresh intergovernmental conference to take place, and this new conference was nearing completion when the Labour government came into power. Mr Blair was happy to inherit much of the negotiating work which had been accomplished by his Conservative predecessor (though in fact largely done by the Foreign Office), but made a conspicuous point of accepting a number of points – integration of the Social Chapter into the body of the treaty, extensions of the co-decision procedure and extension of qualified majority voting – which had been sensitive or unacceptable for Mr Major. (Labour's IGC positions were derived from a paper which had been jointly drafted by frontbench spokesmen and leading MEPs and endorsed by the party conference.) The new Prime Minister, architect of Labour's landslide victory, was still bathing in the glow of his electoral prowess. He even 'won' a bicycle race organised by the Dutch hosts in Amsterdam before the signature of the new draft treaty (16–17 June 1997). The contrast could not have been greater; where Mr Major's government had struggled for over a year to win parliamentary ratification of the Maastricht Treaty, Mr Blair had no difficulty in getting Commons approval for the Amsterdam Treaty by 12 November 1997.

Another marked contrast concerned the euro. Where his predecessor, the man who had won the UK's opt-out at Maastricht, had been increasingly sceptical about the single currency, Mr Blair seemed genuinely favourable towards it. During the election campaign, Mr Blair had promised a referendum before sterling could enter the euro. But the government very quickly took steps which made it clear that, as far as Mr Blair and his Chancellor were concerned, the question was no longer 'if', but 'when'. On 27 October 1997, following on from the early declaration of the Bank of England's independence, Gordon Brown stated that there were no constitutional barriers to sterling joining the single currency. Having enumerated five conditions, he said that sterling would join when those conditions were right, probably early in the next Parliament. On 10 November 1997, Mr Brown presented proposals for making British business 'euro-friendly'. Thereafter, the government reportedly worked quietly towards the informal deadline of the year 2002, when notes and coins were scheduled to come into circulation. Most notably on 23 February 1999 (the single currency having come into being on 1 January 1999), Mr Blair announced a national changeover plan for the euro.

The then German Chancellor, Helmut Kohl, was so impressed by the sea change that he promised to keep a seat free for a British representative on the board of the European Central Bank, and the promise was backed by the French government at the 6–7 November 1997 Anglo-French Canary Wharf summit. But it was not all plain sailing. The French government was at the forefront of calls for the creation of a special Council of Ministers, dubbed the 'Euro-X', to take economic and monetary decisions related to the euro-zone. Despite Gordon Brown's efforts, the British government was excluded from the body.

On 1 January 1998, the Labour government was given another early chance to demonstrate its new approach when it took over the six-monthly Presidency of the Council of Ministers, culminating in the 15–16 June 1998 Cardiff European Council meeting. The Presidency was generally adjudged to have been a sound managerial success. But there was one hiccup. A landmark 3 May high-level meeting of the Council, chaired by Tony Blair, was supposed *inter alia* to appoint the first President of the European Central Bank. The usual preparatory diplomacy appeared to have failed, and Mr Blair had to keep his Continental counterparts waiting until late in the evening before a deal between the French President and the German Chancellor finally cleared the way for Dutchman Wim Duisenberg to be appointed.

Tony Blair was soon pointing to the benefits of his pro-European approach – a sort of solution was found to the BSE crisis, for instance – and the benefits were clearly cumulative. At the 23–24 March 1999 Berlin European Council, for example, the British budgetary rebate was not only saved but entrenched; and, in the context of reform of the EU's structural funds, special funding was won for Northern Ireland and the Highlands and Islands.

Mr Blair also sought practical ways to put flesh on his vision of British leadership in Europe. Early, clumsy, attempts to bypass the Franco-German axis gave way to more structured initiatives, particularly in the defence area, a policy field where the UK had strength and expertise. These culminated in an Anglo-French agreement at St Malo on 4 December 1998 which, by arguing that the European Union 'must have the capacity for autonomous action', clearly envisaged the creation of an EU military capability outside the NATO framework.

There were more general aspects to the changed 'mood music'. Mr Blair spoke French and took holidays in Italy and France. He wrote articles for *Le Monde* and other European newspapers and, on 24 March 1998, he was the first British Prime Minister to address the *Assemblée Nationale*. The new German Chancellor, Gerhard Schröder, was a fan of Mr Blair's 'Third Way' concept and controversially sought to introduce it in Germany. Bilateral summit meetings with European leaders became a regular occurrence and Mr Blair was at pains to cross old ideological barriers, meeting, for example, with the Spanish *Partido Popular* Prime Minister, José-Maria Aznar.

Mr Blair's approach reached its zenith in Aachen on 14 May 1999, on the eve of the Euro-elections campaign. Following in the footsteps of Winston Churchill, François Mitterrand and Helmut Kohl, he was given the Charlemagne Prize by the town's mayor, rewarding him for his 'contribution to European unity'. He was only the third Briton to receive the prize. In his acceptance speech, Mr Blair spoke about 'a new Europe' being transformed into a 'global force for good'. He said: 'I have a bold aim: that over the next few years Britain resolves once and for all its ambivalence towards Europe.' French Prime Minister Lionel Jospin replied by pointing out: 'Whatever detours are taken, whatever the pace, Britain always ends up back on the European road. But for the past two years what has struck us is that the detours have become less frequent and the pace has speeded up' (*The Times*, 14 May 1999).

On the same day, Mr Hague delivered a very different sort of mood music at Budapest University in Hungary. Mr Hague's predecessor as leader had struggled with increasing difficulty against the demands of a small number of Conservative backbenchers. But the minority had influenced a previously agnostic majority so that, by the time of Mr Hague's election as leader, the Conservative Party's parliamentary membership had become far more Euro-sceptical. Mr Hague was said naturally to be more Euro-sceptical than Mr Major had been. Perhaps more importantly, he knew that the party's divisions over Europe would continue unless he could somehow lance the boil. His chosen device was a plebiscite of the party's membership. Though much derided on the Pro-European wing of the party, the referendum was a *fait accompli* which enabled Mr Hague to build from an essentially Euro-sceptical base. With Mr Blair resolutely occupying much of the Conservatives' former political terrain, the party had to distinguish itself from Labour somehow, and Mr Hague was convinced the distinctive element could be the two parties' differing attitudes towards the single currency. In particular, his promise of no entry into the single currency during the life of the next Parliament bought him valuable political breathing space in which to attempt to fashion a viable opposition.

Thus, while Mr Blair was being honoured in Aachen for his contribution to European unity, Mr Hague was talking in Budapest ('No to a Federal Europe') about the need for a 'flexibility clause' amendment to the EU Treaties that would enable Member States to opt out of any developments not linked to the core areas of a single market and free trade:

new members should have the right to accept some EU policies on a selective basis in perpetuity ... existing members, too, should be free to develop a mix and match approach.

In Aachen, meanwhile, Mr Blair was warning that:

If we wish Europe to be guided by the common sense part of our character, we must also use our creative vision to see that only by participating can we shape and influence the Europe in which we live.

The tone of the forthcoming European elections had been set – or so it seemed.

2
Framework

The switch to a proportional representation system was undoubtedly the great novelty of the 1999 Euro-elections in the UK. The introduction of PR shifted the UK significantly closer to Continental electoral systems, although the creation of a truly uniform system for European elections, as envisaged over 40 years ago, still eludes the European Union.[1]

Direct and uniform elections

The 1957 Treaty of Rome had provided that 'The Assembly shall draw up proposals for elections by direct universal suffrage in accordance with a uniform procedure in all Member States' (Article 190). The EC's 'founding fathers' saw a directly elected assembly as an integral part of the Community they wished to establish and expected direct elections to take place soon after the Rome Treaty entered into force. The European Parliament made various attempts at drafting such a uniform procedure (see Box 2.1), first adopting a full-blown draft convention on 10 May 1960. The convention was blocked by Charles de Gaulle, and it was not until his departure in 1969 that the European Parliament, encouraged by the December 1969 Hague summit, could again consider seriously the concept of a uniform system of direct elections. Little progress was made.

By 1973, it was clear that the May 1960 draft convention was hopelessly out of date. The European Parliament decided to produce another, culminating in the January 1975 adoption of the Patijn report. This embodied a revolutionary approach, separating off the problem of uniformity from the problem of directness. The 1960 draft convention had proposed a transitional period during which only part of the Parliament's membership would be directly elected. Patijn borrowed the concept of a provisional period, proposing that, since it was uniformity rather than directness that was more problematic, the Parliament could be directly elected during a transitional period, leaving a uniform system to be negotiated later. The Patijn report led directly to the breakthrough which enabled the first direct elections to go ahead in 1979, some 20 years later than originally envisaged.

Box 2.1 Chronology of direct and uniform elections, 1957–99

15 Mar 57	Treaty of Rome signed. EEC comes into being
29 May 58	President de Gaulle comes to power
Oct 58	EEC Parliamentary Assembly establishes working party to draft convention – Article 138(3) – now Article 190
10 May 60	Parliamentary Assembly adopts draft convention (Dehousse report)
20 June 60	Convention forwarded to the Council of Ministers
Nov 61	First Fouchet Plan
Jan 62	Second Fouchet Plan
30 May 62	European Assembly decides to call itself 'European Parliament'
Mar 69	Parliament 'reminds' Council of its duties
28 Apr 69	President de Gaulle resigns
2 Dec 69	Hague summit decides to give 'further consideration' to the question of direct elections
1 Jan 73	UK accedes to the EC
Jun 73	Parliament decides to redraft its convention
10 Dec 74	Paris summit announces wish that Council should act in 1976, with a view to holding of direct elections 'in or after 1976'
14 Jan 75	Parliament adopts Patijn report, which distinguishes between uniformity and directness and sets target date of May 1978
5 Jun 75	UK referendum votes 67 per cent 'Yes' for continued EC membership
17 Feb 76	UK government publishes Green Paper
13 Jul 76	Brussels European Council reaches agreement on number and distribution of seats
Aug 76	Commons select committee expresses preference for first-past-the-post
20 Sep 76	European Assembly Elections act signed. It sets May–June 1978 as period for first direct elections
23 Mar 77	Lib–Lab pact

continued

Box 2.1 continued

1 Apr 77	Government publishes White Paper – Cabinet favours regional list system
13 Dec 77	Commons votes in favour of first-past-the-post (with STV for Northern Ireland)
8 Apr 78	Copenhagen European Council recognises delay and sets 7–10 June 1979 as period for first direct elections
5 May 78	UK Direct Elections Bill receives Royal Assent
9–12 Jun 79	First direct elections
10 Mar 82	Parliament adopts Seitlinger report, which calls for PR in multi-member constituencies. Council fails to act
14–17 Jun 84	Second direct elections
28 Feb 85	Bocklet report on a uniform system adopted in committee, but Parliament ultimately unable to adopt new convention
15–18 Jun 89	Third direct elections
10 Oct 91	First de Gucht report adopted (rules out identicality)
10 Jun 92	Second de Gucht report adopted (recommendations on number and distribution of members)
10 Mar 93	Parliamentary resolution abandons uniformity in favour of principle of 'general guidelines'
19 May 93	Plant Working Party on electoral reform recommends PR for Euro-elections
30 Sep 93	Shadow Home Secretary Tony Blair promises reform of Euro-elections system if Labour comes to power
1 Nov 93	Maastricht Treaty enters into force. Article 190 amended to give Parliament assent (veto) powers over draft convention
9–12 Jun 94	Fourth direct elections
21 Jul 94	Tony Blair elected Labour Party Leader
5 Mar 97	Firm agreement reached by joint Labour–Liberal Democrat Consultative Committee on a regional list system for Euro-elections
1 May 97	Labour's landslide General Election victory
11 Jun 97	Home Office minister Lord Williams declares government has no plans to introduce PR for 1999
1 Jul 97	Tony Blair and Paddy Ashdown reportedly reach agreement on PR for 1999 Euro-elections during flight back from Hong Kong handover ceremony
15 Jul 97	Euro-Parliament adopts Anastassopoulos report. Draft convention foresees common system for 2004 Euro-elections
17 Jul 97	Home Secretary Jack Straw announces that time will, after all, be found to legislate for PR during first parliamentary session
29 Oct 97	European Parliamentary Elections Bill published, providing for PR and closed regional lists
19 Nov 98	Registration of Political Parties Act receives Royal Assent

continued

Box 2.1 continued

14 Jan 99	European Parliamentary Elections Act receives Royal Assent
28 Apr 99	European Parliamentary Regulations come into force
1 May 99	Amsterdam Treaty enters into force. Article 190 amended so as to foresee uniformity or 'principles common to all Member States'
10–13 Jun 99	Fifth direct elections

Agreement on the number and distribution of seats was reached at the July 1976 Brussels European Council, and in September 1976 the 'Act Concerning the Election of the Representatives of the European Parliament by Direct Universal Suffrage' was signed. The Member States reaffirmed their desire to see the first direct elections take place in the May–June period in 1978. The Act built on the Parliament's detailed preparatory work. The Parliament was to be elected for a five-year term. Dual mandates were permitted, but the Act listed a number of offices, such as ministerial posts or membership of the European Commission, that would be incompatible with parliamentary membership. The Member States would each fix the date for their European elections, but would agree on a common Thursday-to-Sunday period within which all would have to take place. Votes would not be counted until after the close of polling in all Member States. Article 7(1) of the Act provides that 'the European Parliament shall draw up a proposal for a uniform electoral procedure', and Article 7(2) provides that, 'Pending the entry into force of a uniform electoral procedure and subject to the other provisions of this Act, the electoral procedure shall be governed in each Member State by its national provisions.'

The problems in finding a uniform electoral system were as old as the provision itself, but the 1973 accession of the United Kingdom, with its *sui generis* first-past-the-post electoral tradition, exacerbated matters. Nevertheless, different British governments signed up to the full provisions of the 1957 Treaty of Rome and the 1976 Act. Since other Member States' systems were broadly similar, it was clear that the United Kingdom would sooner or later have to make some obeisance to the Continental PR tradition.

In February 1976, the British government published a Green Paper on direct elections which avoided making any detailed proposals on possible systems. In May 1976 a House of Commons Select Committee was established, and in its first report (August 1976) it opted firmly for the traditional first-past-the-post system. On 22 March 1977, the minority Labour government entered into a 'pact', a weak arrangement falling short of a governing coalition, with the Liberal Party. One of the conditions imposed by the Liberal Party for its cooperation was that legislation for direct elections should be put to the House during the summer, with a free vote on proportional representation. On 1 April 1977, the government published a White Paper on direct elections which left open the choice between an open regional list approach, the single transferable vote, and first-past-the-post. Two weeks earlier, the Cabinet had opted for a regional list system. Thereafter, the bill to establish direct elections fell prey to various political forces and parliamentary filibustering. It contained two proposals, one for the regional list system, and the other for first-past-the-post. On 13 December 1977, the House voted by 319 to 222 in favour of the first-past-the-post system. On 5 May 1978, the bill received the Royal Assent.

The April 1978 Copenhagen European Council recognised that the initially envisaged 1978 date for direct elections had become unrealistic (in addition to the UK, the Netherlands was also badly behind schedule), and set a precise period, 7–10 June 1979, for the first direct elections. These duly went ahead, with each Member State adopting its own particular system. However, all, with the exception of mainland Britain, used some form of proportional representation (because of its particular cicrumstances, STV was used in Northern Ireland).

The June 1979 UK European elections provided immediate proof of the potentially distorting effects of first-past-the-post; the Conservatives won 60 of the 78 mainland seats to Labour's 17. Although they secured 12.6 per cent of the vote, the Liberals won no seats, and their absence from Strasbourg after the elections was all the more remarked since an appointed delegation of Liberal MPs and peers had sat in the European Parliament from 1973 to 1979. However, the main perceived distortion was the size of the Conservative contingent. The British Conservatives alone (with three token Danish Conservatives) displaced the Liberal Group (with representatives from eight of the nine Member States) as the third-largest Group within the Parliament, and gave the centre-right (with 216 MEPs) a majority over the left (with 156 MEPs). The perverse and disproportionate effects of the British first-past-the-post system continued to affect the political balance of the Parliament until June 1999. By then, it was the Labour Party which enjoyed over-representation, with 62 MEPs to the Conservatives' 18. The Liberal Democrats and other parties continued to be under-represented. Continental political parties, on all sides of the political divide, increasingly resented the distorting effects of the United Kingdom's idiosyncratic electoral system. They also resented the way in which it blocked agreement on a uniform system.

Soon after the first direct elections, the Parliament began work on drafting a new convention on uniform direct elections, culminating in the March 1982 Seitlinger report. No substantial progress was made in the Council, primarily because of British resistance. The 1984–89 European Parliament made a fresh attempt at drafting a convention, but the Bocklet report itself became embroiled in political controversy and remained unadopted by the time of the 1989 European elections. Thereafter, the Parliament opted for a new approach, illuminated by the debate over the subsidiarity principle. The rapporteur on this occasion was a Belgian Flemish Liberal, Karel de Gucht. With great ingenuity (reminiscent of Patijn's approach), de Gucht distinguished between the principle of the single-member constituency link on the one hand, and the problem of proportionality on the other. In its 10 March 1993 resolution, the Parliament argued in favour of 'general guidelines' rather than a uniform electoral system. As he put it, de Gucht tried to make it 'as difficult as possible for the UK to say no', even extending to provisions which would have allowed for the traditional over-representation of Scotland and Wales. The Parliament followed up its March resolution with a more detailed report (17 November 1993) but, yet again, little substantial progress was made in the Council, and the 1994 European elections were therefore held under the same diverse conditions as the 1979, 1984 and 1989 elections. However, a wind of change was blowing, at both the European and the domestic level.

New developments

A first development was an amendment to Article 190 by the 1993 Maastricht Treaty, granting the European Parliament assent powers (that is, the veto right) over any draft Council decision for a uniform procedure. Henceforth, the Parliament would be master of its own destiny.

A second, and highly significant, development was the German government's tabling to the Amsterdam intergovernmental conference of a proposal on a uniform electoral procedure which reproduced several key aspects of the European Parliament's 10 March 1993 resolution. The proposal, which was sympathetically viewed by a number of Member States, was not taken up in the 1999 Amsterdam Treaty, but there was, again, an important amendment to Article 190. This now provided for the European Parliament to draw up a proposal for elections by direct universal suffrage in accordance with a uniform procedure in all Member States *or* 'in accordance with principles common to all Member States'.

The Amsterdam Treaty would not come into force until 1 May 1999 but, encouraged by this new departure, the 1994–99 European Parliament again resolved on drafting a new resolution and convention. This time the rapporteur was an archly pragmatic Greek Christian Democrat and Vice President of the European Parliament, Giorgios Anastassopoulos. His report was adopted by a large majority on 15 July 1997 and forwarded to the Council in anticipation of the entry into force of the Amsterdam Treaty. The draft convention, which Parliament wished to see introduced for the 2004 European elections, set out in just eleven articles a number of basic principles, none of them incompatible with the probable evolution of the British system (see below). The basic provision was for a PR list system. Dual mandates would no longer be possible. The accompanying resolution suggested that the date for Euro-elections be shifted forward to May, and that voting should be held, at most, on two consecutive days (rather than over four days as is currently the case). The Council again set up a working party to examine the provisions of the Anastassopoulos report. This time, there seemed to be a fair wind, and at the time of writing there is a generalised expectation in Brussels and Strasbourg that in 2004, almost half a century after the Treaty of Rome entered into force, the provisions of the much-amended Article 190 will at last be fully implemented.

There had also been significant developments on the domestic front. Neil Kinnock, Labour Party Leader until 1992, had personally come to favour PR. In 1990, under his impulse, the Labour Party (then still in opposition) set up a working party on electoral systems under the chairmanship of Raymond (later Lord) Plant, a Professor of Politics at Southampton University. The working party was to consider all elections. The Plant report was published on 19 May 1993 (an interim report was published on 16 July 1991). A majority of the working party recommended that a regional list system should be used for European elections. On 30 September 1993, Tony Blair, then Shadow Home Secretary, promised the Labour Party Conference: 'We will reform the voting system for the European Parliament.' On 21 July 1994, following John Smith's death, Tony Blair was elected Leader of the Labour Party.

On 5 March 1997, with a General Election looming, a joint Labour–Liberal Democrat Consultative Committee, jointly chaired by Robin Cook and Robert Maclennan, announced that firm agreement had been reached between the two parties on a regional list system for European elections. At a press conference, Robin Cook (who was himself an advocate of PR) explicitly stated that it was Labour's intention, if elected, to introduce PR in time for the 1999 Euro-elections. This would necessarily involve legislating during the first session of the new Parliament and therefore implied that PR for Euro-elections would be an early Labour priority. However, a month later Labour's General Election manifesto stated only that 'we have long supported a proportional voting system'. There was no commitment to timing. Political commentators pointed to the fact that the new Shadow Home Secretary, Jack Straw, was himself publicly unenthusiastic about PR.

The introduction of PR

Labour won the 1 May 1997 General Election by a landslide and therefore did not need to rely, as some had expected, on the cooperation of the Liberal Democrats. Since concessions were no longer necessary and the Liberal Democrats were not in a position of strength, PR was generally seen as an uncertain prospect, and in any event more likely for 2004 than for 1999. On 11 June 1997, Lord Williams of Mostyn, a junior Home Office minister, confirmed this impression when he stated: 'We have no plans to introduce legislation on PR for European Elections this session.' However, Tony Blair and Paddy Ashdown remained close and, notwithstanding Labour's strength in the Commons, the Prime Minister remained strongly attached to his vision of forging a new radical centre-left alliance in British politics. On 17 July 1997 the Home Secretary announced that, after all, time would be found to legislate for PR during the first parliamentary session. The key factor in this turnabout was widely attributed to a conversation between Tony Blair and Paddy Ashdown during a flight back from the 1 July 1997 Hong Kong handover celebrations. Mr Ashdown was rumoured to have impressed upon the Prime Minister how essential such a gesture was for the continuation of wider inter-party understanding. Following Blair's announcement of his commitment to PR, there was some disagreement on timing within the Cabinet, it being known that most MEPs wanted to wait until 2004.

The Home Office had not done much preliminary preparation, assuming until July that the first-past-the-post system would survive and conscious that much work had been done in 1977. The first problem in devising the legislation was to decide what 'regional' was to mean. The areas of the ten regional offices set up in 1994 were soon settled on (except that Merseyside with its two seats was merged with the rest of the North-West). There were objections to the smallness of the North-East region (four seats) and the largeness of the South-East (eleven seats); such diversity was bound to produce very varying chances for smaller parties.[2]

The allocation of seats to regions was fixed at the existing figures for Scotland (eight) and Wales (five). In England the numbers were decided by working out the average electorate per MEP and experimenting to find the allocation that left the smallest aggregate of regional residues, plus or minus. The result was virtually the same as would have been achieved by a more formal application of a d'Hondt or a Sainte Lagüe or Droop quota. (The last seats in the South-East and Eastern regions provided the only doubtful case.)

Back in 1996, the Boundary Commissioners had started work on adjusting the old Euro-constituencies to conform to the new Westminster constituency boundaries that came into force in 1997. After the switch to PR was announced, the Commissioners suspended their operations, believing them no longer to be necessary. Later, on 3 December 1998, they had to restart them briefly when it seemed quite likely that the *European Parliamentary Elections Bill* would not be enacted in time for implementation in June 1999 since it had become enmeshed in the whole controversy over the government's plans for the reform of the House of Lords.

The Bill was published on 29 October 1997. Its most controversial aspect was the use of the closed list system, under which voters could only support pre-prepared party lists. It had a mixed reception. Most of those who welcomed it wanted voters to have a larger say over who should be their MEPs. Opponents of PR complained about the dangers of party dictatorship in candidate selection. The Electoral Reform Society pointed to the illogicality of introducing closed lists for Britain while retaining the single transferable vote for Northern Ireland, and asked why the government should favour a system that would effectively put the choice of candidates in the hands of party apparatchiks. 'This', it argued, 'will be the first election in Great Britain where voters will be deprived of the right to vote for an individual candidate.' Charter 88, while welcoming PR, also expressed grave concern about a system which leaves 'power solely in the hands of the party machine ... This cannot be good for democracy' (*The Times*, 10 March 1998).

The Bill went slowly through Parliament. It was discussed at the same time as provision was being made for other forms of PR election in Scotland, in Wales, in London, and indeed in Northern Ireland. Its discussion also coincided with the work of Lord Jenkins' Commission to determine the alternative to first-past-the-post which should be offered in a referendum on elections to the House of Commons, promised in Labour's 1997 manifesto. There were wry comments on a government enacting so many different electoral systems in a single session; additional member systems for the elections to the Scottish, Welsh and London assemblies, single transferable vote (STV) for Northern Ireland, and closed regional list for the European elections. (Some Continental commentators also pointed to the irony of the UK introducing a PR system in the same period that Italy was considering shifting to a first-past-the-post system, though in the end it did not.[3])

Box 2.2 The fraught passage of the European Parliamentary Elections Bill

1997–98 Session

29 October 1997: First Reading in House of Commons
25 November 1997: Second Reading in House of Commons
24 & 26 February and 5 March 1998: House of Commons Committee Stage (Committee of the Whole House)
12 March 1998: Report Stage and Third Reading in House of Commons
13 March 1998: First Reading in House of Lords
9 April 1998: Second Reading in House of Lords
24 and 25 June 1998: Committee Stage in House of Lords (Committee of the Whole House)
12 October 1998: Report Stage in House of Lords
20 October 1998: Third Reading in House of Lords. Bill returned to House of Commons with amendments
27 October 1998: House of Commons considers Lords amendments and disagrees with amendments 1, 2, 3 and 4. Reasons reported and agreed to
4 November 1998: House of Lords insists on its amendments
10 November 1998: House of Commons considers Lords amendments and disagrees with them
12 November 1998: House of Lords insists on its amendments. Bill returned to Commons with reasons
16 November 1998: House of Commons rejects Lords amendments
17 November 1998: House of Lords gives reasons for insisting on its amendments. House of Commons rejects Lords amendments. House of Lords insists on its amendments and returns Bill to Commons
18 November 1998: House of Commons rejects Lords amendments. House of Lords insists on amendments and returns Bill to Commons. Government statement explains Bill now lost for 1997–98 session

1998–99 Session

27 November 1998: First Reading in House of Commons
2 December 1998: All House of Commons stages
3 December 1998: First Reading in House of Lords

continued

Box 2.2 continued

15 December 1998: Second Reading in House of Lords
14 January 1999: After rejection by the House of Lords on 15 December 1998,
   the Bill was, in accordance with section 2 of the Parliament Act 1911, presented
   for Royal Assent which was given on this date

Source: Explanatory notes to the 1999 European Parliamentary Elections Act.

The Bill provided for seats to be allocated in each region by the d'Hondt quota, a mathematical formula known to favour larger parties. At the Second Reading, on 25 November 1997, Jack Straw gave a learned exposition, citing academic studies, (P. Dunleavy *et al.*, 1998b) as to why he had been unpersuaded by the case for the fairer Sainte Lagüe quota. D'Hondt was the standard for most European countries and none used the unmodified Sainte Lagüe. Under pressure during the debate, the Home Secretary said that he was willing to look into the question of open voting again. The Home Office commissioned an NOP poll on how voters might react to different systems and also some research into the working of *panachage* under the Belgian regional list system. The main findings were that open list systems frequently created divisions within the contesting parties rather than between them, and that they could produce paradoxical results, with less preferred candidates prevailing over those with more support. On 9 March 1998, Jack Straw announced that the government was sticking with closed lists; it would oppose Conservative amendments endorsing the Finnish system and Liberal Democrat amendments endorsing the Belgian system. The Home Secretary said:

> In balancing the Belgian system against the closed list system, we must give great weight to the need for simplicity … The over-riding problem with the Belgian system is that apparent preferences do not translate into electoral success. (HC Deb 12 Mar 1998 c.785–6)

On 12 March 1998, during the Committee stage, Mr Blair was much teased for his citation of focus group evidence in defence of the closed list system when he could not cite representations specifically in its favour. He also had to withdraw his assertion that no divisors had been used in allocating seats to regions.

The argument continued over several months in the House of Lords, where Lord Mackay of Ardbrecknish, pressing the Conservative amendments, showed himself to be one of the few politicians with a real grasp of electoral systems. But the technical issue soon became entangled with the much bigger question of the reform of the House of Lords. Seeking a confrontation over the government's plans to take away the voting rights of hereditary peers, the House of Lords five times rejected the *European Parliamentary Elections Bill* on the ground that it did not provide for open list voting.

The Bill was reintroduced in the new Session, starting on 24 November 1998, and dealt with under a Guillotine motion in four hours on 2 December 1998, a rancorous debate ending with 13 divisions on straight party lines. Under the terms of the *Parliament Act*, if the Lords gave it a Second Reading and then delayed it in Committee, it could not be enacted in time to operate in June of the following year. The Conservatives made much of the open list principle, even though they had not supported it earlier on 24 June when a Liberal Democrat amendment only failed by 89 to 73, and although its adoption would have greatly exacerbated differences between the pro- and anti-European integration tendencies within the Conservative Party. However, following the compromise over some continuing hereditary peers sponsored by the crossbench peers (and after William Hague had dismissed Lord Cranborne, his Leader in the Lords, for seeking a similar compromise), the Lords denied the reintroduced European Elections Bill a Second Reading on 15 December; that cleared the way for it to receive the Royal Assent under the *Parliament Acts* of 1911 and 1949 on 14 January 1999. One casualty of this means of enactment was the loss of a Commons amendment promising a review of the system after the 1999 election; however, this amendment had been primarily conceived as a procedural device to keep the bill shuttling between the two Houses until the issue of reform of the House of Lords had been settled.

Regulations

The *European Parliamentary Elections Act 1999* was novel in envisaging a national limit on election expenses, with central headquarters collecting and reporting the party's regional expenses. However, the arrangements for this, together with many administrative details, were to be left to subsequent Home Office regulations. The European Parliamentary Elections Regulation (Statutory Instrument 1999 No. 1214) came into force on 28 April 1999. It set £45,000 per MEP as the upper limit for expenditure.[4]

In Northern Ireland, deposits were set at £1,000 and were forfeited by candidates failing to win one-quarter of the quota.

Significantly, the Regulation raised the amount of the deposit for candidates to £5,000. However, the Regulation also reduced the condition of forfeiture from one-twentieth (5 per cent) to one-fortieth (2.5 per cent) of the total votes cast. The figure was reportedly set low enough to give sub-regional parties a fighting chance. Deposits are primarily intended to discourage spoof candidates, but the broadsheets published a number of letters from readers complaining about the way such a high desposit requirement could act as a discouragement for potential independent candidates.

The Home Office commissioned studies on the best form of ballot paper. Should the parties be listed vertically or horizontally? Was there a bonus for the party placed at the beginning – or in the middle – of the ballot paper? Where should the boxes for the voters' crosses be placed? (See Hedges and White, 1999.) The Home Office authorised one innovation: a valid vote no longer required a cross to be placed within the right box – any mark would do. The Greens suggested that their supporters should draw in a smiling face – ☺. It is not known how many counters were greeted in this way.

Following the Neill report on party finance, the Act provided for regulations to be made setting limits to total party expenditure. The old focus on constituencies as the place where expenditure should be recorded and limited was plainly irrelevant with regional list PR. In fact, whatever the ceiling, no party was going to spend anything like as much as was allowed. But every party expressed dismay at conforming to the Home Office regulations on presenting accounts. What, for example, should be charged for continuing rent and salaries at central party head-quarters, where only part of the activity was directed to the Euro-election? The Home Office refused to give guidance beyond the words of the regulations.[5]

Much remained to be settled by the Regulation. The political parties were consulted over a period of four weeks after the final passage of the *European Parliamentary Elections Act* on 14 January 1999, but it was a hurried process. On the other hand, exact drafting would take time and the Regulation had to be put before Parliament by early April. In the event, the Regulation entered into force on 28 April.

Among the points that caused trouble was the decision to leave to the Regional Returning Officers' discretion whether to count and report the votes at the Westminster constituency level; in the end, perhaps with some encouragement following a letter in *The Times* (8 March 1999), all decided to do so. Party headquarters welcomed this, since it gave them information on party strength and activity and since the publication of the figures would provide Westminster MPs and candidates with an incentive to be busy in campaigning. Indeed, some MPs objected to this implicit pressure. Some party officials also complained that the counting system would enable mavericks to claim individual impact.

Another difficulty arose over the rules for recounts. These could only be demanded at the Westminster constituency level; by the time they were transmitted to the Regional Counting Centre voting figures would be irrevocable and unchallengeable, even though it was only then that anyone could know if a recount could make any difference to the final outcome. (In the end, there were very few recounts and none of the regional results were close enough for it to be likely that a recount would have changed the outcome – although in the South-East the Greens snatched the last seat from the Conservatives by 249 votes.)

Two lawsuits might have had implications for the campaign. The 20 March 1999 ruling that Fiona Jones was guilty of making a false declaration of election expenses after the 1997 General Election was overthrown on appeal. The case had depended on the legally undetermined question of when the campaign began. In the event, the very low spending registered for the Euro-elections (see Chapter 8) made this consideration irrelevant. Another point where the law seemed unclear arose from a February 1998 ruling of the Strasbourg European Court of Human Rights in the *Bowman* case, which concerned unauthorised anti-abortion propaganda during the 1992 General Election. The Court found that the confining of constituency campaign spending to the official agents of the candidates breached the Freedom of Speech clause of the 1950 European Convention on Human Rights. Some observers feared that the ruling might open the door to lavish expenditure by the very rich, perhaps on the anti-European, or anti-euro, side, but the 1999 Euro-election saw nothing of this kind.

Solace (the Society of Local Government Executives) and the Association of Electoral Administrators took the innovations very seriously and went to considerable lengths to ensure that the new arrangements worked smoothly. It ran a Euro-elections project, largely directed at local government officials, which included the organisation of full training sessions on the counting of votes and other matters, a constantly updated website, and a regular publication. The European Movement, for so long the pioneer pro-European organisation, played a less conspicuous part than in previous Euro-elections, although it joined together with a number of organisations and charitable foundations in organising a public-spirited campaign to instruct the public and to get out the vote ('use your vote'). Among those participating in the campaign were the Young European Movement, the National Union of Students, the British Youth Council, Rock the Vote, the Institute for Citizenship and the European Parliament's London Office, together with the youth and student groupings of the main political parties. Charter 88 and the Federal Trust were also active in encouraging the electorate to turn out and vote, the latter putting out educational information packs which included instructions on mock European elections for schools. The Institute for Citizenship itself tried to fire enthusiasm with a campaign of three national launches and eleven one-day regional seminars attended by over 1,000 local officials and opinion leaders. Ethnic communities expressed some concern about the granting by the British broadcasters of a European Elections Broadcast to the British National Party. Operation Black Vote again encouraged ethnic members of the population to register and to vote. Some local councils made special efforts, using the 'No Vote, No Say' slogan, notably in Halton, Barnet and the Cotswolds, and Barnet engaged in an experimental action to encourage the registration of postal votes (see p. 228).

Eligibility

All European Union citizens aged 18 or over, whose names appeared on the electoral roll, and who were in full possession of their voting rights in their state of origin were eligible to vote in the UK Euro-elections (in contrast to national elections, Members of the House of Lords (and the Queen) may vote in European elections). The right for any European citizen to vote in this way was an innovation in 1994. On that occasion the Home Office devoted some money to an information campaign. Few non-nationals were aware and fewer still availed themselves of their right.[6] In 1999 there was no information campaign.

The Registration of parties

An essential prelude to the new list systems for Scotland, Wales and Europe was the passage of the *Registration of Political Parties Act*, which went through Parliament uncontroversially and received the Royal Assent on 19 November 1998. Although, under the Act, application was voluntary, only registered parties could put forward lists of candidates for the regional list system of the Euro-elections. Only registered parties were eligible to be offered an election broadcast, although registration in itself did not confer the right to a broadcast (see Chapter 6). Parties could register up to three emblems, and only a registered party could have an emblem printed alongside the candidate's name on ballot papers. In addition, a registered party would be able to protect its name from use by unauthorised candidates at elections. A maximum of six words were permissible in a registered title.

The Act placed dilemmas on the shoulders of the Registrar of Parties, John Holden (whose main function was as the Registrar of Companies). Before he could add a name to the register, he had to decide whether the name was likely to be confused with one already registered. On the other hand, he had the possibility of registering parties with similar names where experience showed that voters were able to distinguish between them.

He ruled, for example, that the Scottish Greens had to fight under the same umbrella name, together with the English and Welsh Greens. More controversially, he also ruled, on 11 March 1999, that the Pro-Euro Conservative Party could use that title, despite the protests of Conservative Central Office. In cases of doubt, the Registrar was able to seek the advice of a committee of MPs, appointed by the Speaker. The only questions referred to the Speaker's committee in this way concerned the two varieties of Socialist label in Scotland; Tommy Sheridan's 'Scottish Socialist Party' and Arthur Scargill's 'Socialist Labour Party'. The committee advised that the term 'socialist' was so generalised that these were admissible, although the committee no doubt noted that the Scottish Socialist Party's full title included an additional three words in brackets – '(Convenor Tommy Sheridan)'.

By early May 1999, 77 parties had registered their names and emblems. Apart from the three main parties, Conservative, Labour and Liberal Democrat, and the nationalist parties in Scotland and Wales, the most significant others were the Greens and the United Kingdom Independence Party (UKIP). There were also seven parties with the word 'Socialist' in their title, five with 'Labour' and seven with 'Democratic'. Some were localised (Highlands and Islands Alliance, Hackney First, Morecambe Bay Independents), some were single-issue (Legalise Cannabis Alliance, Pro-Life Alliance, Rhuddlan Debt Protest Campaign), and some were just idiosyncratic (The Pink Elephant, Witchery Tour Party, Resistance). But in the end, only eighteen party names appeared on the European ballots in mainland Britain and eight in Northern Ireland. There were also ten individuals who stood as independents with their own unregistered labels such as 'Independent – Anti Value Added Tax' or 'Independent – Anti Corruption Pro-Family Christian Alliance'. The only independent candidate of electoral significance was Christine Oddy, who nominated herself at the last moment (6 May) under the title 'Independent – MEP Independent Labour'.

The symbols registered by parties provoked some interest and, in the case of Ken Coates' Alternative Labour List, a little amusement – the List's symbol showed a banned sheep under the slogan 'NO CLONES'. A number of Euro-sceptical parties made liberal use of the Union flag. The '£' sign for sterling was prominent in the UKIP's symbol, and the Pro-Euro Conservative Party's symbol consisted quite simply of the euro sign – '€'. Given that registered symbols appear alongside lists on the ballot paper, the use of such emotive symbols can be expected to grow in Euro-elections in particular.

By-elections

From 1979 until 1999 there were six European by-elections in the United Kingdom, with no less than three taking place in the 1994–99 period (see Table 2.1). European by-elections were generally considered an

Table 2.1 European by-elections in the UK, 1979–99

Parliament	Date	Constituency			
1979–84	20.09.79	London South-West			
Cause: Disqualification of Shelagh Roberts who, at the time of the election, held an office of profit under the Crown					
			Votes	*%*	*% change since 1979*
Shelagh Roberts	Con		41,096	41.2	–10.8
Tony Hart	Lab		32,632	32.7	+0.5
Christopher Mayhew	Lib		23,842	23.9	+10.7
	Others (2)		2,135	2.2	–0.4
	Majority		8,464	8.5	
	Turnout			19.4	
1984–89	05.03.87	Midlands West			
Cause: Death of sitting MEP, Terry Pitt (Lab)					
			Votes	*%*	*% change since 1984*
John Bird	Lab		59,761	39.2	–11.5
Michael Whitby	Con		55,736	36.5	–0.7
Christopher Carter	Lib/All		37,106	24.3	+12.2
	Majority		4,025	2.6	
	Turnout			28.2	

continued

Table 2.1 continued

Parliament	Date	Constituency		
1984–89	15.12.88	Hampshire Central		

Cause: Death of sitting MEP, Basil de Ferranti (Con)

		Votes	%	% change since 1984
Edward Kellett-Bowman	Con	38,039	49.0	–2.8
John Arnold	Lab	16,597	21.4	–2.6
David Chidgey	SLD	13,392	17.3	–6.9
Martin Attlee	SDP	5,952	7.7	
Sally Penton	Green	3,603	4.6	
	Majority	21,442	27.6	
	Turnout		14.1	
1994–99	12.12.96	Merseyside West		

Cause: Death of sitting MEP, Kenneth Stewart (Lab)

		Votes	%	% change since 1994
Richard Corbett	Lab	31,484	53.8	–4.6
Jeremy Myers	Con	12,780	21.8	+1.8
Kiron Reid	Lib Dem	8,829	15.1	+1.0
	Others (3)	5,448	9.3	
	Majority	18,704	32.0	
	Turnout		11.3	
1994–99	07.05.98	South Yorkshire		

Cause: Retirement of sitting MEP, Norman West (Lab)

		Votes	%	% change since 1994
Linda McAvan	Lab	62,275	52.2	–20.5
Diana Paulette-Wallis	Lib Dem	22,051	18.5	+10.6
Robert Goodwill	Con	21,085	17.7	+3.9
Peter Davies	UKIP	13,830	11.6	+9.0
	Majority	40,224	33.7	
	Turnout		23.4	
1994–99	26.11.98	Scotland North-East		

Cause: Death of sitting MEP, Dr Allan Macartney (SNP)

		Votes	%	% change since 1994
Ian Hudghton	SNP	57,445	47.6	+4.9
Struan Stevenson	Con	23,744	19.7	+1.1
Kathleen Walkershaw	Scot Lab	23,086	19.1	–9.3
Keith Raffan	Scot Lib Dem	11,753	9.7	+1.5
Harvey Duke	Scot Socialist	2,510	2.1	n.a.
Robin Harper	Scot Green	2,067	1.7	+0.5
	Majority	33,701	27.9	
	Turnout		20.5	

Source: House of Commons Library Research Paper 99/57, 2 June 1999.

embarrassment by the political parties and went largely ignored by the media. Turnout was accordingly low – as low as 11.3 per cent in Merseyside West in December 1996. For this reason, when General Elections threw up numbers of dual mandate MEP/MPs, as occurred in both 1992 and 1997, Labour and the Conservatives preferred to wait until the subsequent Euro-election to release one part of the mandate (rather than through resignation), even though theoretically they frowned on dual mandates. Under the new system, by-elections may still occur, but only if an independent MEP should resign, retire or die, or if the party list is exhausted. For MEPs elected from party lists, any vacancy is filled simply by taking the next candidate on the list willing to serve, subject to certification that she or he is still in good standing with the party. It should perhaps be added that, since all 1999 UK MEPs were elected from lists, it is already known that there should be no European by-elections in the 1999–2004 period.

A common statute

In the 1997–99 period the European Parliament was beset by a number of high-profile allegations of malpractice by its members. These led the Parliament's authorities to impose new rules, including the linking of the payment of allowances to participation in parliamentary votes, tighter rules on travel expenses, stricter obligations to register interests, and codes of conduct for lobbyists. The European Parliament has consistently pointed out that the root of the problem lies in the very different status and salaries of MEPs who, under the terms of the 1976 Act, are paid the same as an equivalent national MP. An informal system had evolved whereby those MEPs from Member States where national parliamentarians were paid less had traditionally sought to boost their income through the use of various European Parliament allowances.

In implicit recognition of this shortcoming, the draftsmen of the Amsterdam Treaty introduced a new and innovative provision whereby the Parliament, with the unanimous approval of the Council, should 'lay down the regulations and general conditions governing the performance of the duties of its members'. In anticipation of the ratification and implementation of the Amsterdam Treaty before the 1999 Euro-elections, the Parliament adopted a draft common statute for all MEPs on 3 December 1998 and forwarded it to the Council. Although media attention focused on the provisions regarding MEPs' salaries, the draft statute covered a wide range of subjects, including incompatible offices, rules to be applied when a seat becomes vacant, and parliamentary immunity.

On 26 April 1999, the Council adopted its own position on the draft statute. There were considerable divergences over fundamental issues, including the tax status of MEPs and retirement age. Many MEPs argued that the Council's preference for MEPs to pay national taxes rather than a flat-rate Euro-tax undermined the principle of equal treatment and status. On 5 May 1999, at its last plenary session before the Euro-elections, the Parliament reluctantly rejected the Council's amended draft as it stood and called for further negotiations on the basis of its own draft text. The vote, which followed hard on the heels of the Parliament's approval of Mr Prodi as the new Commission President, was taken in the full glare of publicity, and generated headlines such as 'EURO MPS KEEP THEIR GRAVY TRAIN ON TRACK' (*Daily Mail*, 6 May 1999).

British MEPs had been at the forefront of efforts to tighten up the Parliament's rules: Glyn Ford was rapporteur on the Parliament's report on lobbying; David Martin had chaired a working party on the common statute. As a quaestor, Richard Balfe was instrumental in changing the rules governing the payment of travel expenses. Edward McMillan-Scott, Pauline Green and Alan Donnelly had all consistently pushed for stricter rules. Mrs Green and Mr Donnelly had urged Parliament to avoid a public relations disaster and take on board the Council's amendments. After the vote, Pauline Green expressed 'disgust' at what had occurred. To some, it seemed the Council was trying to rush the Parliament into accepting a disadvantageous draft; to others, it seemed the Parliament had very publicly scored an own-goal. With all momentum gone, there was speculation that the implementation of a common statute could be delayed for up to ten years.

The election date

The 1976 Act establishing direct elections to the European Parliament laid down that for all Member States the elections should take place 'within the same period starting on a Thursday morning and ending on the following Sunday'. It was left to the Council to decide when that period should be. However, once it had been chosen, the Act declared that subsequent elections should take place in the 'corresponding period' thereafter. The Council settled for the second week of June, and all four sets of direct elections since 1979 have occurred in that same period. For 1999, they would take place between 10 and 13 June. In March 1998, the Portuguese government wrote to the British Presidency to point out that Portugal had important holidays on 10 and 13 June and to request that alternative dates be found. Portugal had not been an EU member when the June period was chosen and requested. The Council immediately decided that there could be no change for 1999, but a Council working party was asked to look into possible alternatives for 2004 (if there were no change, the elections would again fall in the 10–13 June period). A consensus gradually emerged for the second Sunday in May and the three days preceding it, but this caused various problems: the French had a holiday on 9 May; Britain had local elections in the first week of May and would not want to switch to the second week; Ireland did not want to move its local elections back from June. Nevertheless, it seemed increasingly likely that the Euro-elections in 2004 and 2009 would be held some time in May rather than June.

Information money

The European Parliament traditionally allocated funds to political groups to enable them to publicise their work in the European parliament. The amounts involved were calculated on the basis of a quota for each member of a group. Following various Court of Justice rulings, and in contrast to the 1980s, there was no direct subsidy for electioneering. On the contrary, the Parliament imposed strict rules on how the information money could be spent. Expenditure had to be accounted for in detail and could not be used for party propaganda.[7] These rules are enforced by systematic auditing, and where the auditor feels expenditure was inappropriate the MEP or party concerned may be asked to reimburse the sums involved. However, the Parliament's political groups are entitled to devise their own rules for the disbursement of the funds allocated to them. Most balance expenditure by individual MEPs with an amount held back for centralised use by both national parties and European Parliament political groupings.

In election years, Parliament imposes a cut-off date upon itself; one month before the elections all disbursement of information fund money must stop. Nevertheless, the amounts of money involved are cumulatively important. Access to information money and office allowances are significant benefits of membership of the Parliament, particularly for smaller political parties. The Labour Party devised new arrangements for the use of its entitlements after the 1999 Euro-elections. In particular, it was agreed that part of individual MEPs' resources should be pooled in their regional teams, in the hope that the funds involved could have more impact in the new electoral regions. The Conservatives also centralised a large proportion of their information fund allocation, and some of the information money allocated to the two Liberal Democrat MEPs was also spent centrally by party headquarters.

The European Parliament itself earmarked part of the money for a decentralised information campaign about the Euro-elections. The UK campaign made use of a hot-air balloon – provoking mixed reactions.

The Home Office made plans to educate the public about the new electoral system. The amount of £3.5 million was allocated for this, and was largely spent on advertisements and on leaflets sent to every household, showing specimen ballot papers. These were to cause considerable annoyance. Labour officials complained that the design inadvertently made them look like Tory leaflets. Most of the minor parties objected that they were omitted from the examples of ballot papers. They argued that this, together with the artificial names used, led people to assume that particular parties or candidates were not standing. The UKIP and the Greens reported that up to 50 per cent of the telephone enquiries they received during the campaign were provoked by the Home Office advertisements and the two parties jointly agreed a letter of protest, together with Michael Meadowcroft's Liberal Party.

Under Post Office regulations agreed with the Home Office, every party list was entitled to the free delivery of one leaflet to every address in each region. If personally directed to individuals, one could be sent to each elector. The Home Office negotiated a discount with the Post Office, which charged 72 per cent of normal second class mail for each delivery.

The election cost the Treasury about £55 million in all; press advertising, postal services (£25 million went to the Post Office), printing of ballot papers and returning officers' fees were the main items of expenditure.

The European Level

Altogether, some 298 million Europeans were eligible to vote on 10, 11 or 13 June 1999 (Box 2.3). There would be 10,362 candidates fighting on 303 lists, including 41 in the UK and Greece, 36 in Spain, 29 in

---

Box 2.3 1999 Euro-election polling days throughout the EU

Thursday, 10 June	United Kingdom, Denmark, the Netherlands
Friday, 11 June	Ireland
Sunday, 13 June	Austria, Belgium, France, Finland, Germany, Greece, Italy, Luxembourg, Portugal, Spain, Sweden

Belgium, 27 in Italy, 23 in Sweden, 22 in Germany, 20 in France, and 11 in Denmark. There would, as usual, be an in-built representational bias in favour of smaller countries (Table 2.2).

Table 2.2 The differing numbers of inhabitants per MEP

Member State	Number of MEPs	Inhabitants per MEP
Germany	99	820,000
United Kingdom	87	670,000
France	87	665,000
Italy	87	655,000
Spain	64	610,000
Netherlands	31	495,000
Greece	25	415,000
Belgium	25	405,000
Portugal	25	395,000
Sweden	22	390,000
Austria	21	370,000
Denmark	16	325,000
Finland	16	310,000
Ireland	15	240,000
Luxembourg	6	65,000

Source: European Parliament.

Among the significant internal changes which had taken place in the European Parliament since 1994 was an amendment to the provisions of its rules of procedure governing the formation of a political group. In the old Parliament, 20 representatives of a single Member State could form a political group among themselves, and this was what Silvio Berlusconi's *Forza Italia* MEPs initially did in 1994. But in March 1999 the European Parliament amended its rules so that MEPs from at least two different Member States were now required to form a group. In the new Parliament, a political group could be formed, at a minimum, by 23 MEPs from two Member States, 18 MEPs from three Member States, or 14 MEPs from four Member States or more.

As winter passed into spring, all of the parties were looking to the electoral season in the United Kingdom, but the focus was much more on May than on June. Politicians had only partially grasped the new problems posed by the change of the electoral system. On the whole, they did not see the Euro-contest as very important, nor allocate to it major resources, whether money or, more simply, energy.

Box 2.4 The Electoral systems in other Member States for the 1999 European Elections

Country	Constituency	Form of PR
Austria	National	D'Hondt. Electors have one vote which can be cast for either a list or a candidate on a list
Belgium	Regional	D'Hondt. Votes can be cast for either a list or a candidate on a list
Denmark	National	D'Hondt. Votes can be cast for either a list or a candidate on a list
Finland	National (but with four voting regions)	D'Hondt.
France	National	D'Hondt. Electors have one vote which is cast for a list only
Germany	Federal and Länd lists	Votes are counted at Federal level using the Hare-Niemeyer system
Greece	National	Electors have one vote which is cast for a list only. Votes are counted using the Hagenbach-Bischoff method.
Ireland	Regional – four constituencies	Single transferable vote
Italy	Regional – five constituencies	Votes are counted at national level using the Hare method. If a constituency list has not obtained the quota they are transferred to the constituency in which the party has obtained a relative majority of the votes cast.
Luxembourg	National	Each voter has as many votes as there are seats; votes counted using the Hagenbach-Bischoff method. Votes can be cast for a whole list or distributed among individual candidates.
Netherlands	National	D'Hondt.
Portugal	National	D'Hondt. Votes are cast for a list with a fixed order of candidates
Spain	National	D'Hondt. Votes are cast for a list with a fixed order of candidates
Sweden	National	Modified Sainte Lagüe method

Annex: Gibraltar

On 18 February 1999, in the *Matthews* v. *United Kingdom* case, the European Court of Human Rights in Strasbourg ruled that it was contrary to the provisions of the 1950 European Convention of Human Rights (to which the UK was a signatory) for the inhabitants of Gibraltar, a part of the European Union, to be denied voting rights in the European Parliament elections. Gibraltar had been excluded by the British government from the provisions of the 1976 Act establishing direct elections. In 1980, a group of six British MEPs, three Conservative and three Labour, was set up to represent Gibraltar in European matters. This informal arrangement was ratified by the House of Assembly in Gibraltar, but not by the Foreign Office in London or by the House of Commons. It was intended only as a stop-gap measure. For 20 years, the people of Gibraltar pressed for the right to elect their own MEP, or at least to be joined to one of the existing UK constituencies. The Foreign Office argued consistently that Gibraltar was an 'autonomous territory' – not part of the United Kingdom, with no representative in the Commons, and with its own legislature. There were also practical (the small size of the population) and political (from 1986 onwards Spain was an EU Member State) considerations. When the *European Parliamentary Elections Bill* was introduced, Gibraltarians and their supporters again pressed their case, and an amendment was introduced and subsequently rejected by the government.

After the Court ruling, the British government conceded the point; Gibraltarians were entitled to their vote. However, ministers underlined that the provision of such rights would be a matter for the EU as a whole. There was nothing that Britain could do unilaterally, though the government expressed the hope that the provisions could be enacted in time for the 2004 Euro-elections if Spain agreed.

Notes

1. The formal term, 'European Parliament', was only introduced by the 1986 Single European Act, but the European Assembly had called itself a Parliament since 30 May 1962. To avoid confusing the reader, we have used the term 'European Parliament' throughout. On 1 May 1999, the Amsterdam Treaty came into force, including its provisions on the renumbering of Treaty articles. We have used the new numbering throughout.
2. The number of votes going to smaller parties, it was soon to become apparent, could have significant effects on the threshold needed to win seats.
3. The Italian proposals narrowly failed to win a sufficient majority in a referendum. Meanwhile, on 2 July 1998, French Prime Minister Lionel Jospin

withdrew a proposal to divide the French territory into eight regions for the purposes of the European elections. The aim had been to bring the candidates closer to the electorate, but M. Jospin faced fierce opposition from all points of the political spectrum (*Agence Europe*, 3 July 1998). The changes would have brought the French system closer to the new British system.

4. This meant that a full slate of candidates in London, for example, could collectively spend £450,000, while a full national slate of 83 candidates could have resulted in a maximum of £3,735,000 – there was very little chance of this upper limit ever being reached.

5. On 27 July 1999, the government produced its response to the Neill Committee's proposals (4413/99). The White Paper effectively agreed with almost everything the Neill Committee had suggested on limits to political donations and transparency about them. The White Paper also agreed to the proposal of express limits to the amounts spent centrally and on elections and referendums, the limits for regional and Euro-elections being commensurately less. Perhaps most importantly, the draft bill proposed an Election Commission to oversee any administrative problems arising out of elections.

6. In Oxfordshire's six constituencies, for example, there were 5,867 European but non-British citizens on the register. Of these, 1,807 filled in the application form needed to be able to vote on 10 June.

7. By nominally joining the Greens in December 1998, just before the end of the accounting year, the dissident Labour MPs, Ken Coates and Hugh Kerr, were able to secure £58,000 to spend on advertising the European Parliament and their work for it. Ironically, by delaying their departure to January 1999, the two Conservative pro-European dissidents forfeited any such largesse.

3
Party Preparations

For every party the two years running up to the Euro-elections were a period of reorganisation and reconstruction, an often painful adjustment to the earthquake of 1 May 1997. Both Conservatives and Labour had to learn, after 18 years, how different it is to run a party in opposition and in government. The Liberal Democrats had to digest the limitations of their unexpected success and the coming change of leader.

The Conservative Party[1]

John Major announced his resignation on the day after the 1997 General Election and the Conservatives spent six weeks in the election of a new Leader in a campaign that was at times unseemly. Peter Lilley, Michael Howard and John Redwood were successively eliminated before, on 19 June, William Hague beat Kenneth Clarke by 92 votes to 70. Kenneth Clarke was too pro-European for the new parliamentary party; his chances were also damaged by his decision to enter into a Faustian pact for the support of John Redwood. William Hague, aged only 36, and with only two years of Cabinet experience, was the surprise victor.

Mr Hague rapidly made an impact on the party, demanding a basic rethink of structure and policy. He was a better speaker than most of his predecessors and he made effective thrusts during Prime Minister's Questions. But the appeal of his youth and of his well publicised marriage were offset by his appearance. The brutal cartoons of him as a foetus (following a bad-taste joke by Tony Banks at the 1997 Labour Party Conference) and mocking reports of his attempts to gain credibility among younger voters contributed to a depressingly low rating in the polls. Three months after his election, 12 per cent of the public were satisfied with his performance and 48 per cent dissatisfied. This deficit of around 30 per cent continued through to June 1999, and so did the 20 per cent deficit for the Conservatives in answer to the question, 'How would you vote if there were a General Election tomorrow?' His press officer did not survive these ratings and shortly before the Euro-election Amanda Platell, ex-editor of the *Sunday Express*, took over the image-making role.

William Hague engaged in a vigorous reorganisation of his party. On the day of his election he invited a former Chairman, Lord (Cecil) Parkinson, to come back to supervise the ruthless retrenchment needed in party headquarters and he appointed Archie Norman, the Asda supermarket tycoon (a new MP but also a former colleague of his at McKinsey's), to act as Chief Executive. In an effort at integrating control, Mr Hague moved his own operations each morning from the House of Commons to Central Office. He reorganised the rules for the election of the Leader and had his own election endorsed by 81 per cent of the party's membership in a March 1998 referendum. In September 1998, in another ballot, he secured an 84 per cent endorsement of his policy on the euro, earlier spelt out in his Fontainebleau speech of 19 May 1998, whereby the party gave a commitment not to enter the European single currency before the end of the next Parliament.

He presided over the merger between the National Union of Conservative and Unionist Associations and Central Office along lines set out in an 18 February 1998 document, *A Fresh Future*. The National Union had long prized its nominal autonomy from the absolute control which party leaders exercised over Central Office. After the merger, authority within the party was transferred to a fifteen-person board of which only five were direct nominees of the Leader (mostly *ex officio*).

The old Area structure was abolished and 40 County Areas were created under 25 Area leaders. There were some 180 full-time constituency agents covering about 215 seats. The ill-fated post of Director of Communications was not filled. Andrew Cooper became Head of Political Operations in November 1998. Daniel Finkelstein moved to Head of Policy from being Head of Research, where he was succeeded by Rick Nye. Significantly, all three had roots in the centre-right Social Market Foundation, a think-tank founded by David Owen (the peer, former Labour minister and joint founder of the ill-starred Social Democratic Party). Integration continued in Central Office as the Press and Research Departments worked together in a newly developed 'war room'. After 20 years the party turned sharply against the Saatchi style of advertising. It was not just shortage of money that made them reject any general deployment of posters in the 1999 campaigns. There was a generalised feeling that a new approach was needed.

The October party conferences of 1997 and 1998 provided successful endorsements of the new Leader and his policies. His ascendancy was enhanced by the departure of the old guard, who were removed, or removed themselves, from Shadow office. By the summer of 1999 Sir George Young and William Hague were the only members of the Conservative front bench who had sat in John Major's 1999 Cabinet. Even some of the new appointments did not last. Lord Parkinson passed on the Chairmanship to Michael Ancram in 1998 and Archie Norman yielded to David Prior as Chief Executive in 1999. Sir Tony Garrett was sacked as Director of Campaigning in 1998 and replaced by Stephen Gilbert. There were many other departures from Central Office.

Daniel Finkelstein, Andrew Cooper and Andrew Lansley played a large part in the arguments over how the Conservative Party should position itself in the new situation. How far was the record of the Conservative government to be defended? How bluntly should they apologise and move on? How far, given the centrist positions taken by new Labour, should the Conservatives move to the right to preserve the 'clear blue water' between the parties that Michael Portillo had insisted upon in 1996? After a massive 'listening exercise', consulting with the party faithful, William Hague powerfully endorsed the idea of 'kitchen table' politics, extolling the new strategy to the Shadow Cabinet on 3 March 1999. Set out in a strategy paper largely drafted by Daniel Finkelstein, drawing on the political vocabulary of the United States, and taking a leaf out of New Labour's book,[2] the strategy paper's central message was that the Conservative Party should concede and move on. The party should embark on a policy renewal process, with the aim of persuading people, by the time of the next General Election, that:

> The Conservative Party knows what people really think and has policies to deal with the things that really matter. In other words, we must become Kitchen Table Conservatives.

Mr Hague enthusiastically endorsed the strategy and ordered all members of his Shadow Cabinet to adopt the new approach. The underlying analysis reinforced his belief that under Margaret Thatcher, and especially under John Major, Conservatives had become obsessed with economics and abstract economic language. Mr Hague spelt out the new approach to the Conservatives' Spring conference on 13 March 1999. It was to be a new departure.

But it was not an altogether easy exercise. The Shadow ministers were often slow to adapt to their new situation. Peter Lilley, the Deputy Leader, who was charged with rethinking policy, had a hard time when, on 20 April 1999, he made a speech which emphasised that the Conservatives must not go too far in attacking the public services. His remarks, which might at any other time have been considered common sense, unfortunately coincided with celebrations of the twentieth anniversary of Margaret Thatcher's coming to power. They provoked vehement criticism in the right-wing press (and Peter Lilley did not survive the reshuffle that followed after the Euro-election).[3]

The party's income had fallen drastically and attempts to increase membership met with only limited success. The Treasurership was given to a billionaire expatriate, Michael Ashcroft, whose efforts at finding new subscribers, together with his own personal donations (allegedly £3 million), helped to give the party some financial stability, despite a vast overdraft.

In the local elections of May 1998, and still more in those of May 1999, the party made some recovery from the abysses of four years earlier. Indeed the feat of gaining 1,000 seats (the threshold political pundits reckoned Mr Hague would have to pass in order to avoid a threat to his leadership) and 25 councils in 1999 was a powerful tonic to Conservative morale as the Euro-elections approached. Though modest, they were also 'GOOD ENOUGH FOR HAGUE' (*Guardian*, 8 May 1999). But, Mr Hague knew that the result was a reprieve rather than a pardon. His leadership was still a matter of speculation, and it was therefore vital that he should use the Euro-elections in order further to consolidate his grip on the party.

However, the divisive issue of Europe still haunted the Conservatives. They tried to unite under the slogan 'Europe should do less but do it better'. 'Of course we want to stay in Europe, more or less', argued Mr Hague. 'But it will be a Europe where less is more' (*Independent*, 21 March 1999). But the most respected senior MPs, Michael Heseltine and Kenneth Clarke, made no secret of their unhappiness at the party's drift towards Euro-scepticism. The possibility of an open break exercised a restraint on the Hague camp, but there was an increasing feeling that the pro-Europeans had had their day. The Conservatives had a wider task, as they sought to define their domestic differences with an essentially centrist and moderate Labour government, often carrying out policies it had effectively inherited from the Conservatives, but Europe – particularly the single currency – kept on emerging as the defining issue. It was for

Daily Telegraph (31 May) (Steve Fricker)

The cross-pressuring of Conservative voters was perhaps exaggerated

this reason that Mr Hague had embarked upon his controversial referendum on the single currency in September 1998. As he put it:

> As long as our party is distracted by endless debates on the single currency, we will always have one hand tied behind our back as we fight this Government. (*Daily Telegraph*, 8 September 1998)

He was implicitly critical of Mr Major's more consensual, wait-and-see approach. 'I believe that unity comes through leading, not pleading. I believe it comes through consistency, through clarity, through certainty' (*ibid.*). But although the referendum killed the single currency issue at the Conservatives' Autumn conference, the divisive issue remained.

The Conservatives, like Labour, tried to organise for the elections of May and June 1999 as a seamless single effort and, with the freedom of opposition, they were relatively successful in doing so. As far as the European election was concerned, a manifesto committee was set up in September 1998, chaired by the Shadow Foreign Secretary, Michael Howard.[4] The committee met monthly through the winter and a draft was substantially completed by March 1999.

In a Cabinet meeting in the run-up to the 1997 General Election campaign, William Hague had reportedly invented a snappy phrase to summarise the party's policy towards the EU. The phrase, *'In Europe but not run by Europe'*, ultimately figured in the Conservative Party manifesto. Private polling on the slogan in 1998 and 1999 revealed it to be very effective, particularly after the word *'but'* was dropped, and it was decided that it should become the manifesto title and overall campaign slogan for the 1999 Euro-elections.

The manifesto, *In Europe, not run by Europe*, contained some vigorously Euro-sceptical rhetoric but its specific proposals for reform were more pragmatic. William Hague's introduction spoke of 'the case for a Europe that works, for a free-enterprise Europe'. The main text started: 'Europe has great potential but it needs to get its priorities right ... Conservatives will resist Europe's lurch to the left. And we will all oppose all moves towards a single European state. Beyond the single market, and core elements of an open, free-trading and competitive Europe, we will press for governments to have greater freedom in deciding what other aspects of the EU they intend to adopt.' But the key passage came later:

> Britain has the sixth largest economy in the world. In a competitive world, the flexibility afforded by having our own currency will enable Britain to flourish further. *We will oppose entry into the single currency*

at the next election as part of our manifesto for the next Westminster Parliament. This, in effect, covers the whole term of the European Parliament elected in June. Only Conservatives offer this pledge. [original emphasis]

A notable characteristic of the Conservative manifesto was that it was exclusively devoted to European themes – unlike almost all other Euro-manifestos, present or past.[5]

The campaign was managed by a strategy committee which met weekly from April.[6] Once the campaign began, this committee met daily and merged with the daily meeting which William Hague normally held in Central Office.

Andrew Lansley played a key role in managing the campaign. He had stayed aloof from the May elections to focus on the Euro-contest and he kept the campaign tightly along the planned war-book lines, with its unremitting emphasis on the slogan *Britain in Europe, not run by Europe.*

The Labour Party

The scale of their victory on 1 May 1997 surprised the Labour Party and they felt immensely proud of what the campaigning machine at Millbank had achieved (Butler and Kavanagh, 1997, pp. 224–43). In the aftermath, all the party's operations were moved from the old-style Walworth Road (its headquarters since 1980) to the altogether more modernistic Millbank Tower. But at the same time, 'Millbank' was denuded of its best talents, as Peter Mandelson and other New Labour high-fliers concentrated on their ministerial tasks and cherry-picked special advisers from the campaign team. The Excalibur computer, so essential to rapid response tactics, was partially decommissioned. Away from the centre, the party workers, deprived of the urgent goal of winning an election, were asked to give loyal support to a government that at times seemed centralising and arbitrary. The party was perhaps relieved that its 1998 membership at 392,000 fell so little from the 1997 peak of 405,000 (although it tumbled further as 1999 advanced).

Tony Blair had quickly established himself as an exceptionally strong prime minister. 'Nothing happens unless people think he's involved – and then everything happens.' Tony Blair gave his blessing to further development in the party organisation. The NEC authorised a transformation of structure and operations. The ideas were set out in the document *Partnership in Power* prepared before the 1997 election but published afterwards. This envisaged Labour having a two-year rolling programme, based on the findings of policy commissions. The National

Conference would remain supreme over policy but the old system of composite resolutions would be abandoned in favour of an agenda prepared by a strengthened National Policy Forum. The NEC would be largely stripped of MPs, except for the leaders, three frontbenchers and one backbencher; there would be, among others, six constituency Labour Party representatives and two from local government.

Despite these changes the leadership did not get everything its own way. Ken Livingstone defeated Peter Mandelson for the last place on the constituency section of the NEC in 1997 and four out of the six places in the constituency section went to a left-wing slate in 1998, although Tom Sawyer won one place back for the Blairites in 1999.

Tony Blair continued to use Philip Gould as a source of focus group information and strategic advice, and there is no doubt that Gordon Brown and Peter Mandelson, sometimes in an adversarial way, continued to play a large part in the Prime Minister's political planning.

The government stayed handsomely ahead in the polls. Minor embarrassments, such as the October 1997 Ecclestone affair (a week after a visit to Downing Street by the Formula One racing chief, Bernie Ecclestone, Formula One motor racing were granted an extension on tobacco advertising) and the December 1998 Mandelson resignation (when the Secretary of State was forced to resign from the Cabinet after the revelation of an undeclared loan of £370,000 from millionaire fellow minister Geoffrey Robinson), seemed to bring no hint of electoral retribution. But there was so much going on in the European Union, in Yugoslavia and in Northern Ireland (not to mention constitutional reform) that Tony Blair had little time to focus on the details of electoral strategy.

Margaret McDonagh had taken over from Tom Sawyer as General Secretary in September 1998 and assumed general charge of campaigning. David Gardner was made responsible for the candidate selection process but was later seconded to a position in the private sector. After a wide reshuffle of other posts, it was only early in 1999 that Nick Peccorelli emerged as Euro-election campaign director and Phil Murphy as the party's press and communications officer. Alan Barnard had been head of elections since 1997. The Labour Party reorganised itself into seven regions, based on the standard regions but merging East and West Midlands as well as Yorkshire and the North-East.

Millbank worked busily, trying to sustain party membership, producing cheerful literature and organising conferences and consultations. The contests in Scotland and Wales attracted particular attention. Although Labour, like the Conservatives, claimed to treat the 1999 elections – local,

The award of the Charlemagne Prize at Aachen   *Independent* (15 May) (Chris Riddell)

devolution and European – as a seamless whole, the European contest, five weeks after the others, assumed a low profile and was to become something of an anti-climactic afterthought.

Wales had traditionally been a Labour stronghold, but there were increasing indications that these 'Labour heartlands' resented the new Labour leadership's cavalier attitude towards their support. Matters first came to a head over the way in which Ron Davies MP was preferred to the locally more popular Rhodri Morgan as Labour's candidate for the Welsh premiership. After Ron Davies' 'moment of madness' in October 1998, the party leadership was again perceived to be pushing a preferred candidate, Alun Michael, in preference to Mr Morgan. Mr Michael's narrow victory, backed by trade union votes, was seen by many local Labour supporters as a 'fix' and by political commentators as a serious contribution to Labour's failure to secure a majority in the Assembly elections on 6 May and to the continued rise of Plaid Cymru.

In Scotland Labour faced a similar though lesser embarrassment. Denis Canavan, the populist left-wing MP, was denied a Labour nomination for the Scottish Parliament. His rejection was seen as the work of Blairite 'control freaks'. He stood as an independent and won handsomely. The damage was not enough to explain Labour's failure to secure a clear majority. Indeed, the party was pleased to keep the SNP in second place, although Gordon Brown was thought to have done well in his management of the Scottish campaign.

Table 3.1 6 May 1999 election results

	Con	Lab	Lib Dem	SNP/PC	Other	Total
Scottish Parliament			Turnout 58.9%			
Total seats	18	56	17	35	3	129
Direct vote	15.6%	38.8%	14.2%	28.7%	2.1%	100%
Welsh Assembly			Turnout 46.3%			
Total seats	9	28	6	17	3	60
Direct vote	15.8%	37.6%	13.5%	28.4%	4.7%	100%
Local Authority Elections			Estimated turnout 30%			
Elected	3751	4802	2607	409	1660	13243
Change	+1344	–1161	–75	+95	–215	
% vote (est.)	34%	36%	24%			

A campaign committee, with Margaret Beckett in the chair, was set up after the party's October 1998 conference, but it made no important strategic decisions and was not involved in the manifesto drafting exercise. Mrs Beckett was surprised to discover that there had been no post-mortem on the party's much-criticised 1994 Euro-campaign. Robin Cook and Alan Donnelly MEP headed the party's European operations, while Gordon Brown focused on the elections to the Scottish Parliament and Hilary Armstrong on local elections. Ann Taylor was charged with organising MPs into campaigning, and John Prescott was to tour the country enthusing the party faithful. But these were mostly busy ministers and matters tended to be left very much to the relatively inexperienced Millbank team.

The Labour Party decided not to produce a separate Euro-manifesto. Instead, the party relied on an omnibus manifesto for all of the spring elections. This included four pages of general reference to Europe. In addition, the party fully subscribed to a Party of European Socialists (PES) manifesto on which all EU socialist and social democrat parties would be fighting. A primary draft of the PES manifesto was the fruit of protracted, though always amicable, discussions between Robin Cook and Henri Nallet, the French Socialist Party's spokesman on Europe, in the autumn of 1998. The Labour Party's international secretary, Nick Sigler, had drawn up an initial draft, which Mr Cook took to the French, whose principal negotiator was François Hollande, first secretary of the French Socialist Party. Recalling the political capital its opponents had been able to make out of a manifesto commitment[7] to limit working hours in 1994, Labour was determined to avoid giving the slightest hostage to fortune. In the event, there were no serious differences,[8] and Labour was able enthusiastically to sign up to the common manifesto at the PES Congress in Milan on 1–2 March 1999. Later, during the 1999 Euro-campaign, a number of Conservative Party officials gleefully pounced on Labour's failure to adopt a national manifesto as a strategic blunder. But Labour's old campaign hands remembered how Labour candidates in 1994 had made much more use of the PES manifesto which, by its nature, was more restricted to consensual themes and upbeat, cheering photography.

In terms of strategy, Labour believed it had an interest in getting out its own vote without encouraging an energetic campaign. Insiders predicted that the campaign would be fought on national issues 'that people care about'. Labour would emphasise its record. As one official put it: 'We are delivering. Get the vote out. Be afraid of the alternatives.' The same official cheerfully predicted a turnout as low as 20–25 per cent. But there had been some debate in the campaign committee about how exclusively the campaign should focus on domestic issues. Off the record, party officials were happy to confirm that the party would be relying heavily on its most powerful weapon – Tony Blair. In a head-to-head contest between the two party leaders, Mr Blair would win hands down, and the relaxed confidence evident in Millbank seemed perilously close to the complacency Mr Blair had so frequently warned against before the 1997 General Election. Nobody seemed to have thought of the possibility that the conflict in the former Yugoslavia might continue and that the Prime Minister might be obliged to withdraw from the campaign until it was too late. Nobody seemed to have thought of the possibility that Mr Hague, relying on support from the Euro-sceptic press, might come up with winning short-term tactics. Nobody seemed to have thought of possible alternative strategies.

There would be a daily brief to candidates and a candidates' hotline, but there was to be 'no hyperactivity'. There would be no big media events, there being a fear in Millbank that such events, if not done right, could boomerang back as 'silly stunts'. In any case, the party had little money. Each Westminster constituency had been asked to donate £2,000 to the campaign cause, but nobody was counting on such largesse.

The Labour teams of candidates mostly worked well together. Those at the bottom were trying to win their spurs, but those at the top were potentially more of a problem, since they were certain of getting to Brussels. Nevertheless, all teams had regular meetings with the top candidates. Candidates were assigned to work on 6 May 1999. They were allocated policy functions within each region on the basis of their strengths and expertise. Candidates tried not to be geographic although they mostly had strong constituency bases. Campaigning had to be by approaching voters in their workplaces or wherever else they were concentrated. They wanted to decentralise ('High Street not Wall Street', was an internal mantra), though they accepted that the general thrust of the campaign would be national, focusing on Tony Blair. The slogan ultimately chosen for the campaign, *Leadership in Europe*, was of uncertain provenance, but it was designed to place the emphasis on Mr Blair's personal leadership qualities in contrast to those of Mr Hague. Plans were made to distribute a leaflet to every home. There was to be direct mail from the centre to 1.4 million known party voters. There were arrangements, later circumscribed by the *Data Protection Act*, to cold-call a large number of voters and play a personal message from Tony Blair.

As the campaign proper neared, pro-European activists within the party became increasingly disappointed. They had hoped that the Euro-elections and the introduction of PR could be used as a platform for displaying further evidence of the new departure in the UK's attitude towards the EU. But the leadership had other ideas.

The Liberal Democrat Party

In the 1997 General Election the Liberal Democrats won 46 seats. Their vote was slightly down on 1992 but their skilful and energetic targeting enabled them to achieve a result well beyond anyone's expectations. Despite the success, Labour's overwhelming majority (419 seats compared to 238 for all others) meant that Paddy Ashdown's hoped-for parliamentary leverage was limited. But the understandings with the Labour Party, established in the days when a coalition had seemed the only sure way of defeating the Conservatives, continued. Thinking far ahead, the Prime Minister cherished what was dubbed 'the project'; he had long wanted to consolidate a centre-left relationship that would block any return of the Conservative hegemony which had prevailed for so much of the century, and he had established a close rapport with Paddy Ashdown. A joint committee on constitutional matters, set up under Robin Cook and Bob Maclennan in 1996, reported in March 1997 with a promise of PR for Europe. After the election, to the irritation of some Labour MPs, Liberal Democrats were invited to serve on a Cabinet committee on constitutional issues. On these and other matters Paddy Ashdown stayed in close personal touch with Tony Blair. Some Liberal Democrats, notably Simon Hughes and some councillors from the Northern cities where Labour constituted the Liberal Democrats' principal opposition, expressed uneasiness at the Labour embrace. But there was no serious challenge to Paddy Ashdown's authority.

   The party had a moment of triumph in the Winchester by-election of November 1997, when a majority of two was transformed into one of 15,000, but Liberal Democrat support drifted down in the polls and the party's local government base was slightly dented. None the less, the party felt itself flourishing with the presence of so many MPs; it also delighted in the prospect of the enhanced representation that was to come with PR for Europe and Scotland and Wales – and perhaps, later on, for Westminster.

   Paddy Ashdown was elected Leader of the Liberal Party in 1988 and of the new Liberal Democrat Party in 1989. He seemed prominent and successful, but before the end of the next Parliament he would be 65. If he was not to carry on indefinitely, he felt he had to clarify his position before heading the Liberal Democrats' campaign in the Euro-election. If he was to announce his resignation after the contest, he might be accused either of pique at a bad result, or of deceiving the public if he led the party to a triumphant outcome. He and his advisers agreed that it was wise to announce his intended departure in January, but to put a ban on campaigning for the succession until the Euro-election was over (in this they were influenced by the example of the Labour party truce when John Smith died just at the start of the 1994 Euro-election). There was a faint hope of winning sympathy – 'a last tribute to Paddy'; there was also the thought that potential successors would be especially active in travelling around the country to campaign for the party and for themselves; and the pending leadership contest would help to keep the Liberal Democrats in the headlines. In practice the publicity was not always favourable. Although in the end only five candidates were nominated, half a dozen others toyed publicly with the idea of throwing their hats into the ring, despite the fact that few outsiders could see them as leadership material: 'Paddy and the 7 Dwarfs', said one cartoon. There was also the argument that, not knowing who would be leader, voters were being asked to buy a pig in a poke. It was also plain that, for good or ill, no Ashdown successor would be quite as close to Tony Blair, although closeness to Labour was one way of distinguishing the rival candidates.

In past times the Liberal Democrats had not always been happy with their Liberal colleagues in the European Parliament, who were considered to be mostly to their right. But by 1999 the policy differences had diminished and the UK Liberal Democrats' influence had increased. The changes were symbolised by the Liberal Democrats' subscription to a Euro-Liberal manifesto and to a manifesto of their own, both having been drafted largely by Andrew Duff, who was close to the leadership and a leading Euro-candidate. Drafting started in December 1998 and was finalised in April 1999. The drafting of the national manifesto was overseen by a Steering Group chaired by Menzies Campbell and composed of peers, MPs, and an MEPs' representative, Graham Watson.

Paddy Ashdown's high-profile involvement in the Yugoslav conflicts meant that he attracted headlines on Kosovo rather than European Union issues. Mr Blair made it known how much he valued Mr Ashdown's Balkans advice. Indeed, the Liberal Democrats, so long the most ostentatiously pro-European of parties, irritated some of their own supporters by concentrating on domestic issues and by not being more aggressively pro-EU and, indeed, pro-euro.

Nick Harvey, reputedly the most Euro-sceptic of Liberal Democrat MPs, was made Chairman of the Campaign and Communications Committee which planned the May and June contests. Like the other parties, the Liberal Democrats tried to work on the principle, 'Two polling days, one election'. Chris Renard, who had built up a great reputation in by-elections throughout the 1990s, was in charge of organisation and

The leadership question hung over all Liberal Democrat campaigning *The Times* (12 June) (John Kent)

campaigning. The veteran political correspondent, David Walter, was in charge of publicity. Paddy Ashdown would of course lead the campaign and Shirley Williams would play a prominent part.

The Liberal Democrats' manifesto, *Ambitious for Britain*, focused extensively but cautiously on Europe. Paddy Ashdown's introduction observed: 'We are not blind to Europe's faults. Our approach is simple. "Local where possible, Europe where necessary".' As the main text emphasised, 'Our determination to engage positively in Europe is matched only by our determination to reform Europe.' But the manifesto also gave space to the ordinary domestic issues, health, education, crime and the environment.

The Green Party

In the Euro-elections of June 1989, the British Green Party came close to achieving a historical breakthrough. The Greens took over 2.2 million votes – almost 15 per cent of the national vote – and drove the Social and Liberal Democrats (as they then were) into fourth place in every seat in England except Cornwall. Under a PR system, the Greens would have won up to 12 seats. Under the first-past-the-post system, they won none and the momentum they had achieved was subsequently dissipated, though largely through internal disputes. Despite considerable reform (including the creation of a separate Green Party for Scotland), in the 1992 General Election the Greens were able to contest only 256 of the 651 seats, and secured an average of just 1.3 per cent of the vote in the seats that they did contest. Though they fielded a full slate of 84 candidates in the 1994 Euro-elections, the party won won just 3.2 per cent of the overall vote, and nowhere could their candidates achieve anything better than fourth place. The only good news was that they had saved three deposits; their best individual performance coming from their joint leader, Jean Lambert, who polled 6.5 per cent of the vote in London North-East.

By 1999, the Greens had regrouped significantly. The party, which prided itself on its highly democratic organisation, had roughly 4,000 members drawn from fourteen UK areas. Its nine-member Executive met every six weeks. Its two principal speakers were Jean Lambert (a candidate again in London) and Mike Woodin, an Oxford Councillor. The party had a paid staff of four, including a press officer and a part-time agent. The Euro-election campaign would be organised nationally, but the candidates were selected regionally, by one member, one postal vote, after hustings (using the single transferable vote). In a move which caused vigorous debate, gender balance was not mandatory but was left to the regional organisations. In general, the divisions and personal feuds of 1994 were distant history and the party was once again in good spirits.

It was the introduction of PR for the 1999 Regional Assembly and Euro-elections which most gave the Greens fresh heart and created an almost heady atmosphere, particularly in the headquarters of the English and Welsh Party. (The Registrar insisted that the Scottish Green Party and the English and Welsh Party, normally distinct entities, should stand under a single banner in the European elections.) The Greens had been gradually establishing a substantial foothold in local politics, particularly in the South. In the 1998 local elections, the party polled 9.9 per cent across the South-East in the 47 seats in which it fielded candidates (the threshold for the South-East in the Euro-elections was calculated at 8.3 per cent). In the London region, where 9.1 per cent would be needed in the Euro-elections, the party averaged over 10 per cent in its 257 seats. Indeed London, where principal speaker Jean Lambert topped the list of candidates, was the party's second target (its first was the South-East).

The party had been developing local pockets of substantial support in the southern region, particularly in and around Oxford. It was fortuitous that the Green Party enjoyed its strongest levels of support in the very region where it needed the lowest share of the votes; this encouraged its leadership to dream of sending one, perhaps two, MEPs to Strasbourg. Moreover, the party's list-leader for the South-East region, Dr Caroline Lucas, was a personable and engaging 38-year-old Oxfam policy adviser, married with two children, and a former County Councillor – no echoes of David Icke there.

A January 1999 MORI opinion poll commissioned by the party showed that 16 per cent of electors would be more inclined to vote Green in the Euro-elections if they thought PR would give the party a chance to win a seat (*Financial Times*, 22 March). Mike Woodin, the party's other joint leader and principal speaker, said at the Greens' 20–21 March spring conference that, 'taking account of regional variations in this figure, it would only require half of these people actually to vote Green for the first British Green MEPs to be elected'. He told the conference that the party was 'sharpening up its act', but the *Financial Times* reported a 'decidedly shabby feel' about the meeting. 'People don't take us seriously', admitted longstanding member Isle Isbey. Adam Swallow, an election coordinator, added: 'We are seen as extreme because we are not generally seen and we are not generally seen because we are seen as being extreme' (*ibid.*). But the Greens remained confident that the growing salience of ecological issues, in combination with the new electoral system, would enable them to make significant electoral inroads.

The 6 May results gently confirmed the Greens' Euro-confidence. In both Scotland and Wales, the party's strategy was to stand only in the regional vote and hence to put forward no constituency candidates. The strategy paid off in Scotland, where Robin Harper was elected as an additional member in the Lothians with a 6.9 per cent share of the vote. It was the Green Party's first parliamentary seat in the UK. But in no other region did the party win over 4 per cent. In Wales, the party's regional shares of the vote were even lower. In the English Council elections, meanwhile, the party won 25 seats for an overall gain of 14 seats – the largest number of gains the party had made in a single round, and giving it a record high of 38 principal authority Councillors on 18 different Councils. On four of these there was no overall control and, in an omen of what was to come, all of the gains bar one were at the expense of the Labour Party. The Green Party was now represented on all types of principal authority – District, Unitary, Metropolitan Borough, County and London Borough Councils.

At the policy level, a number of factors seemed to play in the Greens' favour, particularly in the European context. Perhaps above all, their opposition to genetically modified (GM) food tapped into a growing concern in Britain about its potential disadvantages. This was combined with opposition to the European single currency – on the grounds that the national economy needed to retain the flexibility which would enable it to be moulded to local conditions. When combined, these two policy planks represented an idiosyncratic but potentially attractive electoral platform in an election where voters would be 'liberated' from the responsibility of choosing a government. Opposition to the euro might also serve as a distraction from a division in opinion within the party over EU membership itself.

Enthusiasm at home was reflected, at least initially, by encouragement abroad. In 1994, 23 Green MEPs had been elected to the European Parliament, and by 1999 this figure had drifted up to 27. By 1998, Green ministers occupied the environment ministries in Germany, France, Italy and Finland. In 1997, *Les Verts* broke into French national government by winning seven seats in the left's landslide General Election victory and were awarded with the Environment ministry. In the 1998 German Federal Election the prize was even grander, with Joshcka Fischer becoming Germany's first Green foreign minister. But, inevitably, power brings responsibility and therein lay the Continental Greens' Achilles' heel, particularly in Germany. The unfolding events in Kosovo, where the NATO allies' bombardments were having both humanitarian and environmental consequences, left Fischer in an increasingly awkward position.

The UK Greens were part of the Europe-wide Green Federation. A potential problem arose from the fact that most other member parties of the Federation were pro-single currency. However, the UK Greens were able to sign up to a common manifesto which avoided the problem through the simple expedient of not mentioning the euro. The UK Party additionally drafted its own manifesto and intended fighting on its own issues, though this, said insiders, would be more a matter of style than substance. Membership of the Federation provided support but no significant funding. The UK party was able to organise a 15–16 May training weekend for Green Party Euro-candidates and activists with some Continental backing.

Although similar events had been organised before, the training weekend was part of a general change in the party's campaigning efforts, with emphasis on a more professional approach. Altogether the party would spend about £200,000; £30,000 of this was intended for the production of a much-admired party election broadcast. They would target London, the South-East and the North-West as the largest areas where they had the best chance of winning more than the quota. 'Targeting' mainly meant more and better-quality leaflets. The media remained the party's main weakness, the conclusion being that the party had to seek out more photo opportunities if possible.

The UK Greens had had some contact with the UKIP and other minor parties and they had been represented at a February meeting of the anti-Maastricht/Amsterdam Congress for Democracy at Church House, London. There was no formal alliance. When Ken Coates and Hugh Kerr left the Labour Party, taking their EP information money with them, their approaches for some sort of loose alliance with the Greens were rebuffed.

In overall terms, the British Greens found themselves in a potentially popular position on genetically modified organisms, but a potentially awkward position on international affairs. It was perhaps a measure of the Greens' potential which led the Deputy Prime Minister, John Prescott, to unveil a White Paper on saving resources at the very start of the Euro-campaign and to dismiss Green pressure groups as 'whingers' for their sniping at the government's environment record (*Daily Mirror*, 18 May 1999).

The United Kingdom Independence Party

The United Kingdom Independence Party (UKIP) was founded in 1993 by Alan Sked, a lecturer in international history at the London School of Economics, and a former Liberal candidate. In the 1994 Euro-elections the party fielded 24 candidates who won, on average, 3.3 per cent of the vote, and the party's spoiling candidates cost the Conservative Party at least one seat, if not two (see Butler and Westlake, 1995, p. 267, Table 9.7). Dr Sked was a longstanding anti-federalist. His philosophy was to restore national sovereignty through withdrawal from the EU. The UKIP's quixotic 1994 manifesto promised that, if elected, the party's candidates would not take up their seats in Strasbourg. It was the only party to contest the 1994 Euro-election on a straightforward commitment to withdraw from the EU.

In 1997, after a power struggle, Dr Sked resigned from the party. A more permanent structure was established, with the creation of an elected National Executive and leadership. Michael Holmes, a retired publisher, was duly elected Leader; and Nigel Farage, a commodities broker, Party Chairman. The policy commitment of leaving the EU was embodied in the new constitution. Following the death of Sir James Goldsmith, the UKIP consciously sought to attract former members and supporters of the Referendum Party (see pp. 79–80). In its literature, the UKIP made much of the fact that in the 1997 General Election the two parties' candidates had together polled 'almost a million votes'. The UKIP claimed its membership had subsequently climbed from 4,000 in 1998 to 7,000 in 1999, while 40 per cent of its first- and second-placed 1999 candidates had stood under Sir James Goldsmith's banner two years earlier.

A London rally in April had assembled most of the party's 71 English candidates. The full slate had been an important precondition for an electoral broadcast. The UKIP broadcast had been prepared professionally and was designed to stress the sovereignty theme.

The party had few big names to support it. Leo McKern, an actor; Christopher Booker, a *Sunday Telegraph* columnist; and Bill Jamieson, economics editor of the same newspaper, were their most high-profile supporters. The party also made much of 'six peers' who had contributed to its funds. Though not excessively well-off, the party claimed to have received enough private contributions to be able to mount a serious offensive. In addition to the electoral broadcast, there would be a nationwide distribution of UKIP leaflets to every household. These would be prepared nationally, but with regional inserts. As in 1994, the party eschewed a full-length manifesto in favour of a four-sided broadsheet which stressed the party's commitments to withdrawal from the EU and the retention of sterling. It was drafted largely by John Whitaker, a lecturer at Lancaster University and specialist in economic and monetary affairs, and number one on the party's North-West list. The sterling sign also figured prominently in the party's registered symbol. The campaign itself would be organised regionally, with the party's candidates campaigning as teams.

The party suffered some bad publicity as a result of the objections of its former leader, Alan Sked, which culminated in a six-column article by Dr Sked in *The Times* (8 June). The party remained quietly confident for three reasons. First, in the 7 May 1998 South Yorkshire by-election, the party's candidate, Peter Davies, had taken a very respectable 11.6 per cent of the vote (to the Tories' 17.7) on a 23.4 per cent turnout. The party knew that PR would change the rules of the game and calculated that, if extrapolated to a region, 11.6 per cent support would probably win the party one MEP. Second, a March 1999 MORI poll gave the party an unprecedented 25 per cent support, on the assumption that the UKIP was the only party campaigning for 'Britain to retain the pound for ever'. Third, the doorstep support reported by the party's activists was encouraging, though it was a moot point as to whether the party's support would be undermined by William Hague's increasingly anti-euro stance.

The Scottish National Party

For the Scottish National Party (SNP), 1999 was, with two major electoral contests to come, a red-letter year. As *The Economist* put it, the 6 May 1999 Regional Assembly elections represented the 'culmination of a quiet revolution' (1 May 1999). For the SNP, the 6 May elections also represented the beginning of a new political era, one in which it could hope to take the centre of the Scottish political stage as a major player. Because of this consideration, the Assembly elections largely overshadowed the subsequent European elections, although these were also of great importance to the SNP. The major parties had made much of running 'One campaign, two polling days', and to a certain extent the SNP found itself caught up in this concept of a 'seamless' election campaign. In the event, there was more seam than campaign in May. More importantly, it was recognised that the Euro-election results in Scotland would be closely related to what occurred on 6 May.

Until 1975, the SNP was opposed to membership of the European Community and it was prominent in the 1975 referendum campaign, urging its supporters to vote 'No'. Thereafter, its views gradually changed in acknowledgement of the clear verdict of the Scottish people in the referendum. The party's President, Winifred Ewing, played a significant part in this transformation. Between 1974 and 1979 she was an SNP MP for Moray and Nairn (she had been MP for Hamilton, 1967–70). After the referendum, she was delegated to the European Parliament as the

SNP's representative on the British delegation of MPs. She was at that time a Vice-President of the SNP and, principally through her, the party began to reconsider its position on Europe. An indefatigable constituency MP and a fiery orator, she was effective at defending Scottish interests, such as fisheries and agriculture, in Strasbourg (earning herself the soubriquet, '*Madame Ecosse*'). During the 1980s, as the party became steadily more pro-European, it strengthened its representation in Brussels, though Winifred Ewing sat alone in the European Parliament until at last, in 1994, she was joined by the party's deputy leader, Dr Allan Macartney.

With Scotland still governed largely from Whitehall and Westminster, the SNP became increasingly attached to the concept of a devolved, confederal European Union in which 'regions' would become increasingly autonomous. The 1997 election of the Labour government, with a radical reform package including devolution for Scotland and Wales, radically reinforced the SNP's European vision. Not only would devolution centre a large swathe of power and politics in Scotland, but the breakthrough in the Northern Ireland peace process had created the prospect of a Council of the Isles, underlining Scotland's increased economic interest in the Irish Sea basin (and Scottish hopes of emulating the Irish Republic's boom economy).

Clearly, the SNP was well placed to build upon the mood of expectation and change in Scotland; opinion polls in the summer of 1998 had begun to suggest that the SNP could win control of the Edinburgh Parliament and thus, through a referendum, realise its goal of an independent Scotland. Following a controversy surrounding the alleged Scottishness of the Labour candidate, Ian Hudghton easily took Allan Macartney's old North-East Scotland seat in the 26 November 1998 by-election, and the SNP entered the New Year in good spirits. In a 16 February 1999 address to members of the Irish Institute for European Affairs in Brussels, party leader Alex Salmond gave a very upbeat view of Scotland's, and the SNP's, future in Europe. He spoke about Scotland as a European nation, in a 'Union of equals rather than an unequal Union.' As the party's manifesto put it, they sought *Independence within Europe*.

But the party ran a far from happy campaign in the run-up to the 6 May elections. In seeking to distance himself from the three other major parties, Alex Salmond made two controversial statements. First, on 13 March, Mr Salmond appealed to the Scottish people to forgo the Chancellor's promised 1p cut in income tax in favour of spending on public services. This was immediately dubbed the 'tartan tax' and gave the other parties a controversial policy to snipe at. Then, on 29 March,

Mr Salmond attacked the government's policy in Kosovo as 'unpardonable folly'. The *Observer* (11 April) later reported that Mr Salmond's 'gamble' that Scottish voters would see Brown's promised tax cut as a 'bribe' was prompted by private polling which showed that the SNP had reached a high-water mark on the issue of independence and that Labour voters tempted by the SNP wanted to see more proof of progressive policies. But the same newspaper reported that his 'unpardonable folly' remark had led to a 'dramatic drop' in Mr Salmond's ratings; an NOP poll carried out the previous week showed Mr Salmond on 33 per cent (as against 55 per cent for Labour's Donald Dewar). Mr Salmond, perhaps worried about scaring off floating voters, played the 'independence card' close to his chest, leading to criticism from the SNP's fundamentalist wing. The German Commissioner for regional affairs and structural funds, Monika Wulf-Mathies, inadvertently made an unwelcome intervention in the SNP's campaign by questioning whether it was right to encourage the creation of more nation states within Europe (*Sunday Times*, 25 April).

Initially, the SNP could console itself with the Labour Party's indifferent campaign, but the Chancellor of the Exchequer, Gordon Brown, stepped in to bolster it. He had already masterminded Labour's comeback strategy against the SNP and had himself drafted the intellectual case for regional government in Scotland (*New Scotland, New Britain*). In the closing stages of the campaign he took a high-profile stance and was in the forefront of Labour's attacks on the SNP's policy proposals, particularly on tax, leading to a series of flattering headlines; for example, 'CHANCELLOR OF THE EXCHEQUER PAVES WAY FOR BLAIR'S GLORY' (*Financial Times*, 5 May 1999). Polls showed the SNP's support waning as Labour simultaneously directed its fire at the nationalists and sought to woo its potential coalition partners, the Liberal Democrats. Despite an upward surge in the closing days and a strong call for independence on polling day by Mr Salmond, the SNP finished on a bleak note. What had been billed a year ago as an election to decide on the future of Scotland was now being seen as an election which would decide the future of Mr Salmond's leadership.

In the event, Mr Salmond's leadership was safe. Overall, Labour won 56 seats, the SNP 35, the Conservatives 18, and the Liberal Democrats 17. Although Labour received a few shocks, the results were largely as expected, and Labour went ahead to form the much-touted coalition with the Liberal Democrats. The SNP now turned to face the second electoral contest. With the prospect of a referendum on independence now entirely gone, the SNP had to gear down its campaign to the more modest level of representation under the current arrangements.

On 25 August 1998, the party had been rocked by the untimely death of Allan Macartney. A brilliant polyglot and academic, Dr Macartney was, genuinely, 'one of the most decent people in politics' (*Independent*, 27 August 1998). He was much-loved, both in Scotland and abroad, particularly in the European Parliament.

Strasbourg would also lose '*Madame Ecosse*' when, after 20 years' service as a directly elected member, Winifred Ewing announced that she would be standing as a candidate for election to the Scottish Parliament on 6 May and did not intend to stand for election to the European Parliament again.

Winnie Ewing and Allan Macartney had been two of the SNP's pillars of strength, but despite this and the uncertain campaign in April and May, the party went into the Euro-elections quietly confident that it would return to Strasbourg strengthened by the addition of a third MEP.

Plaid Cymru – Party of Wales[9]

Plaid Cymru had long dreamt of challenging Labour to become the principal Welsh party, but the new Labour government's commitment to devolution and the introduction of PR for the new Assembly and the European elections opened up fresh vistas. Plaid Cymru's fortunes were transformed. From a party that had never exceeded 12 per cent in a Principality-wide contest for Westminster, it was poised to leap over the Conservatives and the Liberal Democrats to become a serious rival to Labour.

It was still a small organisation with only three full-time staff in its Cardiff office, but under the long-standing leadership of Dafydd Wigley, MP for Caernarfon since 1974, its membership had risen to about 10,000. The party was also poor and was only able to contest the 1999 elections through the help of a generous bequest. Iuean Wynn Jones, the MP for Ynys Mon (who was accredited with having been a major force in committing the party to full Europeanism), acted as Director of Organisation. Jill Evans drafted the *Wales in Europe* policy document.

The campaign was to be managed by party officials. Plaid Cymru was enormously buoyed up by its successes in the elections to the Welsh Assembly on 6 May. Not only did it secure 28 per cent to Labour's 38 per cent, but it won sensationally in Westminster seats like Rhondda and Islwyn which it had regarded as beyond its reach. The party now had representation in every part of Wales and a pulpit in the Welsh Assembly. More than any other party, it was able to fulfil the general dream of 'Two elections, one campaign' and sustain the enthusiasm of its own troops in an effort to cap the May efforts with something even better in June. It also managed to some extent to use genuine European issues as effective campaign material, citing how the Treasury in Whitehall had blocked the receipt of Objective One subsidies to Wales. The Party's theme of 'A Voice for Wales' was seen as powerful, particularly after Millbank's heavy-handed interference in the selection of Alun Michael over Rhodri Morgan as Labour's leader. Meanwhile, Labour's anti-Plaid campaign propaganda had failed to dent the party in May, leaving activists quietly confident that it could repeat its success in June.

The Pro-Euro Conservative Party

The Pro-Euro Conservative Party was founded by two sitting MEPs, Brendan Donnelly and John Stevens, in February 1999. Mr Donnelly had first been elected as a Conservative MEP in 1994, Mr Stevens in 1989. Both had fallen foul of the Conservatives' new selection procedures, and both attributed this failure to the strong pro-single currency line they had taken at the London hustings. Mr Stevens, a successful City trader, had sat on the Parliament's economic and monetary affairs committee since his election and was a fervent believer in the single currency. Mr Donnelly had served as a political adviser to a former leader of the British Conservatives in the European Parliament and was an equally fervent believer in the euro. Both argued strongly that they would have had no trouble in being reselected under the old system. Their failure to get selected reinforced earlier doubts both had voiced about the closed list system, which they suspected (wrongly, as it happened) would be used to enforce the party leadership's increasingly Euro-sceptical stance. There was, argued Mr Donnelly, a 'profound paradox' involved in introducing PR with closed lists. At the Conservative Party's 6–9 October 1998 conference the two worked together in trying to convince pro-Europeans within the party to fight against the leadership's stance. They also wrote to constituency chairmen in the same vein. They conducted a private poll before the conference which strongly demonstrated the potential electoral appeal of a pro-euro party led either by Kenneth Clarke, the former Chancellor of the Exchequer, or Michael Heseltine, the party's former Deputy Leader. To borrow from Sir Bernard Ingham, the two were becoming 'semi-detached', and the Clarke/Heseltine poll reportedly brought them close to suspension.

In January 1999, the two 'went over the top' and resigned from the Conservative Party, though, significantly, both remained as allied members of the EPP Group in the European Parliament. A second private poll in February was similarly encouraging, and the two then decided to fight the elections through a new party. The Registrar's permission to use the title 'Pro-Euro Conservative Party' had been a considerable *coup*. The Registrar had written to say that he had problems, but Mr Stevens and Mr Donnelly had replied forcefully that there was sufficient distinction between the two parties and the Registrar had demurred (their chosen alternative would have been 'The European Party').

Mr Stevens and Mr Donnelly privately admitted that the party's success would probably hinge on their ability to convince a 'big hitter' from the Conservative Party to join them. There were newspaper reports of confidential meetings with, among others, Sir Leon Brittan, Michael Heseltine and Kenneth Clarke, but no defections. The party's founders increasingly focused on Mr Clarke, who had doughtily defended the Conservative Party's previous agnosticism on the single currency, and the new party's literature pictured Mr Clarke and quoted liberally from him. But an angry Mr Clarke refused either to leave the Conservative Party or to give his support to the new party. Nevertheless, the Pro-Euros campaigned on such slogans as 'A vote for us is a vote to get rid of Mr Hague and instal Mr Clarke'. Their main purpose, they argued, was to 'get the party back onto sane ground'. They proposed to do this by acting as spoilers in the Euro-elections, hoping that this would provoke a leadership contest which Mr Clarke could win. As to the euro, Mr Stevens said: 'We feel the party should be neutral on monetary union at the next general election' (*Financial Times*, 30 April 1999).

The party decided to run a full slate of candidates in order to qualify for an election broadcast. The broadcast – which was to prove controversial – was professionally made. Mr Donnelly managed the candidate lists (while Mr Stevens concentrated more on campaign issues). He did not see the deposit as being unduly high and remained sanguine about recouping most deposits. Candidate selection was done on an *ad hoc* basis, drawn from a pool of volunteers and those recruited by the two leaders. There were no big names. Among those of some prominence were journalist Marcelle D'Argy Smith (a former editor of *Cosmopolitan*), former Tory MEP Paul Howell, and Commission official and former MEP Andrew Pearce, who had defected from an unwinnable position on the Conservative's North-West list.

The party had no time to build up membership or a full organisational structure. Six staff worked from a small temporary office near Victoria Station, while much of John Stevens' campaign work was run from his own flat in Smith Square, two doors away from Conservative Central Office. There would be no national mailing. Mr Stevens and Mr Donnelly had commissioned a consultant to identify the most promising postal districts in terms of support, and these would be targeted. They claimed to have raised over £200,000 from private contributions and felt this was enough to compete directly with the Conservatives. Mr Stevens and Mr Donnelly themselves drew up the party's manifesto, a professional, glossy brochure entitled *Time to Decide*. Although it dealt with other issues such as Kosovo, human rights and free trade, the brochure's main thrust was to set out a strong argument in favour of the euro. It concluded: 'Our manifesto conveys an attitude and a philosophy that would otherwise not be available to voters on 10th June. We are a Conservative party which is pro-European.'

Ken Coates and the Alternative Labour List

Ken Coates was first elected as a Labour MEP in 1989. He came to the Parliament with a long record as an academic and labour historian, with over 20 publications to his name. He was also on the left of the party and a politician who believed in speaking his mind. Over the next ten years, Mr Coates concentrated on the interests of his Nottinghamshire North and Chesterfield constituency, with its abandoned coalfields, and specialised within the Parliament on human rights and employment-related issues (he had been the Parliament's rapporteur on a Temporary Committee on Employment). Growing disquiet at the new direction taken by the Labour Party under Mr Blair crystallised around the emotive issue of the reform of Clause Four of the party's constitution. Mr Coates was one of a majority of members of the EPLP who signed an appeal against its revision. Thereafter, relations deteriorated, with Mr Coates suspended from the party in the autumn of 1998. He was later reinstated (November) but was already so disenchanted with the party leadership that he began to think of taking a more independent stance. Mr Coates maintained that it had originally been his intention to retire from the Parliament in 1999, but he was so incensed with what he described as an 'Orwellian nightmare' (*Parliament Magazine*, 29 March 1999, No. 66, p. 26) that he decided to seek re-election on his own terms.

For Mr Coates, as for another left-wing rebel, Hugh Kerr, the crunch issue was entitlement to the European Parliament's information funds (see Chapter 2). For as long as Mr Coates remained a Labour member, the funds would be managed and divided by the Group of the Party of European Socialists, the European Parliamentary Labour Party, and the domestic party. Though this was standard practice, Mr Coates resented it, as he did the reports that Labour candidates would be required to devote some of their overall fund entitlement to new regional party offices. Under the Parliament's accounting rules, Group membership (and hence information fund entitlement) was calculated from the beginning of the calendar year. Since he had already been suspended once, Mr Coates had a strong suspicion that he might be dismissed from the party. As he put it, 'I didn't want them picking up my entitlement of information money and *then* throwing me out.' (However, individual MEPs are not entitled to information money. Rather, the quotas attributed to political groups are calculated on the basis of the number of members. It was only in that sense that Mr Coates and Mr Kerr could talk about 'their' entitlement.) In order to avoid falling foul of the Parliament's accounting rules, Mr Coates and Mr Kerr asked the Green Group in the Parliament to 'hold' their entitlement. The Labour Party promptly announced that Mr Coates and Mr Kerr had excluded themselves because they had joined the Greens. Mr Kerr had indeed made overtures to the Greens, arguing for a form of 'red–green coalition', and was to sit with the Group for the remainder of the 1994–99 Parliament. Mr Coates complained that, while he had always been very friendly with the Greens, he had never wished to join them. Ultimately, he joined the Confederal Group of the European United Left for the remainder of the Parliament, where he sat, notably, with the French Communists.

Mr Coates' sentiments, as set out in a number of publications and interviews (see, for example, 'Some are more equal than others', *Parliament Magazine, ibid.* and 'New Labour New Democracy', Independent Labour Network, 1998), were twofold: on the one hand, he felt that the new Labour Party had abandoned or neglected large parts of its traditional constituencies; on the other, he resented what he saw as an unjustifiable increase in centralised party power through the introduction of the closed list system. He therefore decided to fight the East Midlands region as an independent candidate, first for the 'Independent Labour Network', and then, for registration purposes, as a candidate of the 'Alternative Labour List Supporting Left Alliance' (the Registrar would not allow 'Independent Labour'). Mr Coates was close to kindred spirits in Yorkshire, particularly in the Leeds Labour Party and to five Hull Independent Labour Party councillors. In the end, the Alternative Labour List put up twelve candidates: five in the East Midlands and seven in Yorkshire and the Humber. Hopes of putting up allied candidates in London were not realised.

Mr Coates intended to run on his constituency record and concentrate on local issues, such as landfill, or widespread concerns, such as genetically modified organisms (the Greens were weak in his region). In terms of potential electoral performance, the Alternative Labour List was an unknown quantity. Candidates of other parties were apprehensive about Mr Coates' high local profile but were uncertain, as was Mr Coates himself, about how this would work out in the broader context of the electoral region.

The Scottish Socialist Party

In 1998, Tommy Sheridan, a veteran left-winger and Glasgow councillor formed the Scottish Socialist Party, with the intention of fighting both the Scottish Parliament and European elections. Its first electoral showing was in the 26 November 1998 North-East Scotland European by-election, where it took 2.1 per cent of the vote. Early in 1999, Mr Sheridan was formally joined by former Labour MEP Hugh Kerr, though it was clear that the two had been discussing political plans for some time (despite Mr Kerr's flirtation with the Greens). The party held its first annual conference in February 1999, bringing together a coalition of activists from Militant Labour, environment and community groups.

Both Mr Sheridan and Mr Kerr had reputations as maverick political firebrands. Tommy Sheridan was a well known figure in Glaswegian and Scottish politics. He led a famous crusade in Scotland against the poll tax, was imprisoned in Edinburgh for refusing to pay the tax, and ran an election campaign from his prison cell, winning a seat on Glasgow District Council. He was purged from the Labour Party in 1989. Though a Scot, Hugh Kerr won the Euro-seat of Essex West and Hertfordshire East in the 1994 European elections. Describing himself as an old-fashioned socialist, Mr Kerr did little to hide his contempt for the Blairite Labour Party and was ultimately expelled on 8 January 1999. Mr Sheridan and Mr Kerr believed the new party could profit from two considerations: first, the traditional belief that Scotland was more to the left than the English electorate; and, second, the interrelated feeling that the Scottish left resented the London-based 'control-freakery' of new Labour. According to them, the real significance of the North-East Scotland by-election was that the Labour Party had been beaten into third place (see Table 2.1).

The Scottish Socialist Party went into the elections fighting for a 'full-blooded socialist alternative', including legislation on drugs, an independent Scottish republic and a radical plan to nationalise most land. In the 6 May elections, Mr Sheridan stood as a candidate in his Glasgow patch, while Mr Kerr stood on the West of Scotland list. Altogether, the party ran 19 candidates and, to its joy, Mr Sheridan was elected as one of the 'top-up' MSPs. 'Scotland's fifth party has now been born', he announced; 'the Scottish Socialist Party is here to stay'. (*Independent*, 8 May). The party was further encouraged by the election of a Green MSP and of Labour renegade Dennis Canavan as an independent.

Although he had stood in the 6 May elections, Mr Kerr's primary objective was the Euro-elections, where he topped the Scottish Socialist Party's list, though he admitted this was an outside chance. Much of the party's slender resources had been concentrated on 6 May.

The Socialist Labour Party

Arthur Scargill, leader of the National Union of Mineworkers since 1975, formed the Socialist Labour Party in May 1996, in response to the Labour Party's decision to reform Clause Four of the party's constitution. Mr Scargill consistently rejected suggestions that his party might be in danger of splitting the left-wing vote at elections, arguing that the SLP was the only true socialist party. For the 1999 Euro-elections the SLP put together a national slate of candidates which enabled the party to qualify for an electoral broadcast. Mr Scargill himself headed the party's London list. The party was committed to withdrawal from the EU.

The Referendum Party

With the death of Sir James Goldsmith on 19 July 1997, the Referendum Party lost its founder-President and its chief source of finance. Once Tony Blair had promised a referendum on the single currency during the 1997 General Election campaign, it could also have been argued that the party had lost its principal *raison d'être*, though the party still insisted that there should be a more general referendum on the United Kingdom's continued EU membership. Over the next two years, in its own words, the party fought 'to survive and re-organise itself with an entirely voluntary administrative system'.

The Referendum Party's chief power in 1997 had been as a conditional spoiler in marginal Conservative constituencies, with the underlying aim of rendering the British electoral atmosphere ever more hostile to matters European. Such a role would still have been possible in the European elections, though on a regional scale, for, as the UKIP's performance was to show, there were not only votes but seats to be had for Euro-sceptical parties. But the Referendum Party's resources did not allow it to compete with the UKIP and its finances remained limited, and so, perhaps making a virtue of a necessity, the party boycotted the Euro-elections. A four-page manifesto was prepared (though it was only distributed on a limited basis). A key clause called upon voters to:

> Join the Referendum Party in boycotting these spurious elections. Refuse to endorse the lists of party nominees. Refuse to lend credibility to the pseudo-parliament by taking part in this mockery of an election. Abstain from voting, or spoil your ballot paper ...

The party's literature made much of its intention of building up to the next General Election, in which it would again call for a full referendum on British membership of the EU. But the ultimate success of the United Kingdom Independence Party in the Euro-elections and the likely predominance of the narrower issue of the single currency would make it difficult for the Referendum Party effectively to assert its distinctive political demands.

The Liberal Party

The Liberal Party was set up in 1989 by those Liberals who refused to merge with the then Social Democratic Party to form today's Liberal Democrat Party. The party was led by Michael Meadowcroft, who had been the MP for Leeds from 1983 to 1987. The party's strength lay in pockets in Yorkshire and Merseyside. Although its support was very limited, its candidates had at times confused the voter, perhaps making a crucial differnce in two seats in the 1994 Euro-elections. For the 1999 elections the party put up 43 candidates in 5 regions (London, the South-West, the Eastern region, the West Midlands, and the North-West). Michael Meadowcroft himself headed the party's list in the North-West. The party ran on an idiosyncratic platform, combining opposition to the single currency and nuclear energy with support for devolution and animal rights. The party's failure to put forward a full slate of candidates meant that it could not qualify for an election broadcast, and the party had virtually no national profile.

Others

The introduction of PR and the promise of an electoral broadcast encouraged the British National Party to field a full slate of candidates and contest the Euro-elections nationwide. The Natural Law Party, extolling the virtues of the Maharishi Mahesh Yogi's philosophy based on eternal laws, again fielded a full slate of candidates both in the UK and throughout the European Union.

Notes

1. The Nuffield General Election studies long ago adopted the practice of dealing with the major parties in alphabetical order. The same practice has been adopted here and in Chapter 4.
2. The paper quoted liberally and admiringly from Philip Gould's *Unfinished Revolution*.
3. Shadow Cabinet critics pointed out that the new approach and the date of Mr Lilley's speech had been sanctioned by Mr Hague.
4. Its members were Michael Ancram, Peter Lilley, Francis Maude, John Redwood, Liam Fox and Tim Yeo for the front bench; Edward McMillan-Scott, Caroline Jackson and John Corrie from the MEPs; Daniel Finkelstein and Peter Campbell (Secretary) from Central Office; and Anthony Teasdale from the Conservatives' European secretariat.
5. Given the strategic choice of concentrating on European issues, the committee was obliged to rely on the expertise of its MEPs and of Anthony Teasdale, the MEPs' officer within Central Office. The result was a manifesto text which was broadly acceptable to all MEPs, including the most Europhile.
6. Its members were Michael Ancram, Michael Howard and Andrew Lansley from the front bench; Daniel Finkelstein, Andrew Cooper, Peter Campbell (Secretary), David Simpson, Stephen Gilbert, Ceri Evans and George Osborne from the party staff, and Edward McMillan-Scott, Caroline Jackson, John Corrie and Anthony Teasdale from the Brussels side.
7. Non-existent, as it happened! (Butler and Westlake, 1995, pp. 127–30.)
8. Potentially tricky issues had included tax, working hours, majority voting, youth policy, women's rights and labour rights flowing from the new Amsterdam Treaty.
9. In 1998, Plaid Cymru officially changed its name to 'Plaid Cymru – the Party of Wales', and later formally registered the name.

4
Candidate Selection

The introduction of proportional representation, particularly at such short notice, presented all political parties with new problems over candidate selection. Each party solved its problems in a different way – but each sought to present a balanced ticket and each encountered trouble.

The Conservative Party[1]

The Conservatives had a relatively simple task in selecting their candidates. Only 18 Conservative MEPs had been elected in 1994 and four of these were retiring voluntarily (Lord Plumb, Sir Jack Stewart-Clark, Graham Mather and Anne McIntosh). The South-East was the only region where the party had more sitting MEPs than were likely to win seats. In the end, three of their MEPs jumped ship after reverses in the selection process and one withdrew because of personal scandal. Another two accepted unwinnable places. Only eight out of the fourteen seeking renomination survived high on the ticket and earned another term at Strasbourg.

After the Conservatives had lost the spurious battle over open lists in the House of Lords (spurious because victory could have proved deeply embarrassing, encouraging public scrapping between Euro-sceptics and Euro-enthusiasts), the party made a virtue of the relative openness of their selection process, based on one member, one vote (OMOV) among party supporters at open meetings.

An essential pre-phase in the selection procedure was the drawing up of an approved list of candidates. This was done by a vetting panel chaired by former Cabinet minister Lord (Roger) Freeman. Among those who failed to make it through to the final 200-strong list, announced on 5 April 1998, were former MPs Winston Churchill and Tony Marlow (Euro-sceptics both), and Edwina Currie (who had been a Euro-candidate in 1994). One high-profile former Cabinet minister who did make the cut was Norman Lamont. This gave rise to much speculation about the consequences if he were successfully selected and elected. Though Mr Hague denied it, pro-Europeans within the party suspected that Mr Lamont was a covert candidate for the leadership of the Conservative delegations. As one Tory MP put it, 'it would be difficult to have a man of his seniority in Strasbourg and not appoint him leader' (*Guardian*, 6 April 1998).

Conservative Central Office produced a document on 18 March 1998, laying down the procedure to be followed. The ground would be prepared by Regional Selection Colleges composed of the Chairs of the old Euro-constituencies and of all the Westminster constituencies in the area; that meant, in the South-East, a body of some 120 members. The Colleges chose a sub-committee of about 20 which drew up a 'long shortlist' of people to be invited to extended interviews by the whole committee. The names considered were drawn from those who had put themselves forward from the list of approved candidates described above. The Regional Selection College was instructed to treat all candidates equally: candidates were asked to give a short address and then to answer some basic agreed questions before voting took place on who should go forward to the final stage.

In the South-East, with 11 seats, 24 were interviewed and 12 were called to appear for final ranking. This was done by any subscribing Conservative who chose to come to the Regional Meeting, held on 30 May 1998 in the London Arena, a vast hall in London's Docklands. Two other meetings (Yorkshire and Humberside, and West Midlands) took place that day. Three more English regions met in late June and three in July (Eastern and South-West, 13 June; North-East, 20 June; London, East Midlands and North-West, 11 July), so that unsuccessful candidates could have a second or a third chance.

At these meetings, each candidate spoke for 10 minutes and faced 15 minutes of questions. At the end of the day, the faithful balloted to rank-order the candidates. There were complaints about the procedure. The rank-and-file did not see the CVs of the candidates till they arrived and there were no testimonials. The aim was to deter canvassing and disingenuous tributes that might intrude on objective judgement, but it opened the way for heckling and enabled planted questions to have a disproportionate effect.

The attendances were disappointing. The South-East, with over 100,000 Conservative subscribers, drew only 1,200 to take part in the choice. In other regions the selection was made by 300–500 enthusiasts willing to travel considerable distances and to give up a summer Saturday.

Those who came probably included a disproportionate number of party members with strong views on Europe either way, as well as many personal supporters of sitting MEPs. Many incumbents effectively bussed in their local activists. In the South-East, four of the top five slots went to incumbents. Although the official ban on canvassing was circumvented by such tactics, there was no suggestion that the selections were rigged. Some candidates emerged unexpectedly high on the lists simply by virtue of personality and eloquence: Daniel Hannan, the Euro-sceptic in the South-East, was an outstanding example; Theresa Villiers in London was another.

It was plain at the London arena that John Stevens and Brendan Donnelly dished their chances by being too open in refusing to endorse William Hague's 19 May Fontainebleau speech, with its commitment against accepting monetary union before the end of the next Parliament; they refused to take their chance in other regions and subsequently left to found the Pro-Euro Conservative Party. But in the same selection Tom Spencer was ranked second, even though his carefully crafted speech was very strongly pro-European. It was estimated that, of those in the 30 most winnable positions, only five could be considered strong Euro-sceptics. It did seem in some of the speeches that 'centre-right' was used as a code-word for 'Euro-sceptic'; however, in others, it seemed to signify 'mainstream'. As one candidate pointed out:

> by putting emphasis on the oral presentation they really handed an advantage to the sitting MEPs, since they were both knowledgeable about European affairs and used to trimming their language to suit a domestic audience. It would have been a different kettle of fish if they'd gone for a postal ballot.

Some famous names failed to be chosen; some failed even to be shortlisted. Lord Newton and Lord Lamont, two senior ministers in John Major's government, were among the casualties.

There was an alleged prejudice against older MEPs which was said to have cost James Moorhouse (74), Brian Cassidy (65) and Edward Kellett-Bowman (67) renomination at a winnable place. James Moorhouse, a Conservative MEP since 1979, subsequently joined the Liberal Democrats.

There was also some hesitation about choosing MPs defeated in 1997 who were seeking a European route back to office. None the less, twelve ex-MPs were chosen, seven for winnable positions. Four former MEPs were also given safe places on the ticket (Lord Bethell, Christopher Beazley, Lord Inglewood and Bill Newton Dunn). Others (Margaret Daly and Anthony Simpson) did not even make the shortlist. One more, Andrew Pearce, after being given a low place in the North-West, defected to lead the Pro-Euro Conservative Party list in that Region.

There was no positive discrimination in favour of women. Two did head regional lists (Caroline Jackson, an experienced MEP, in the South-West and Theresa Villiers, a young lawyer, in London) but the only other in a winnable position was Jacqueline Foster, who just got the last marginal place in the North-West. Bashir Khanbhai in the Eastern region and Nirj Deva, an ex-MP in the South-East, were the only candidates from ethnic minorities in apparently winnable positions.

The Labour Party

The Labour Party's problems, albeit self-inflicted by the change of system, were the greatest. In 1992, 62 Labour MEPs had been elected under the first-past-the-post system. In four regions the party held every seat. But under PR, even on the most optimistic assumptions, Labour could not hope to elect more than about 44 members. Only a few MEPs planned to retire. Which sitting members were to be denied a winnable place on the new lists? How could space be found for new blood? How was adequate representation to be ensured for women and ethnic minorities? And how much could be done to safeguard Blairite political reliability? Such considerations undoubtedly coloured Jack Straw's decision to opt for a closed list system.

After extensive internal consultations, the Labour Party adopted a highly complicated selection procedure which would inevitably leave scars and suspicions, although party officials argued that, given the circumstances, it was a reasonable solution. Three guiding principles had underpinned the process. First, the system had somehow smoothly to manage a reduction from 62 to at most 44 MEPs, including a significant shift in geographic presence from north to south. Second, the party set itself the objective of drawing up a high calibre and attractive list broadly representative in terms of gender, geography and background. Third, the party sought to involve members and local parties. The party also underlined that the system was intended as a transitional mechanism for 1999 only. An internal document pointed out that 'The procedures for this selection round are exceptional and unique in moving from a constituency-based system with very high but volatile representation, to another regional-based proportional system with lower, but more stable, representation.'

All those interested in being candidates had to fill in a standard, two-sided application form, indicating their preferred regions in order. For aspiring candidates, the choice and number of preferred regions already represented a difficult decision. To put down one or two might indicate attachment to a particular region – presumably a plus – but limited the chances of being nominated. To put down many might indicate greed and a lack of geographical attachment but would enhance a candidate's chances of being selected. (The great irony, though, was that candidates might anyway be shifted from their preferred region in the final round of the selection process.) Altogether, some 400 members registered an interest in seeking selection and completed the application forms. The party went to great lengths to ensure that the system was properly understood and its rules respected.[2]

The selection system thereafter consisted of four phases, with a variant for sitting MEPs who wished to stand again. The first was to win nomination. The completed application forms were distributed to all branches and constituency parties, affiliated Trade Unions and Fabian or Co-operative Societies in the regions for which candidates had expressed a preference. Each branch/union/society could nominate one candidate (though some, in confusion, believed they could nominate two). Party insiders thought most nominations could probably be put down to nominees being locally-known, though many nominating organisations relied simply on the application forms. For aspiring candidates seeking nomination outside their geographical base, the process of becoming sufficiently well-known locally to gain nomination could be a time-consuming and expensive business. Several candidates pointed out that the system gave unfair advantage to those who had understanding employers, generous resources and few family commitments. An unwaged or low-waged person would have great difficulty in mounting a campaign, even within a single European constituency.

In the second phase, nominated candidates were interviewed by the General Committee of the appropriate Westminster Constituency Labour Party. Each General Committee was to select two candidates, one male, and one female.

The third phase involved a one-member, one-vote ballot held at the old Euro-constituency level. Once again two candidates, one male and one female, were to be nominated. Separate ballots (alternative vote) were held for male and female candidates. The successful nominees were those who came top of their ballots. On 3 August 1998, the party announced that 59 men and 55 women had been nominated in this way. The results of the postal OMOV ballots showed much higher levels of participation than had been expected, averaging about 30 per cent. Because there had been no limitation on regional preferences, a number of candidates had received multiple nominations.[3]

All sitting MEPs who wanted to stand were guaranteed a place on the final lists and did not have to go through the first and second phases. Of the 62 sitting MEPs, 52 initially indicated that they wished to seek selection. Two MEPs subsequently announced their retirements on elevation to the Lords. Before the third phase, each Euro-constituency Party was consulted by a 'trigger ballot' on whether they wanted their MEP to continue as a candidate. All 50 MEPs were successful, with support reportedly in the range of 80–99 per cent. In a few cases, these votes may have affected MEPs' positioning on the final list (by indicating to the final selection panel how popular the member was). In one case, an 82 per cent endorsement was rumoured to have induced a decision to retire.

By late August 1998, therefore, the system had produced a pool of 164 candidates, composed of 50 sitting MEPs and 114 Euro-Constituency Labour Party (ECLP) nominees. Since all 50 sitting MEPs had been guaranteed a place on a regional list, only 34 places remained for the 114 other candidates.

All MEPs successful in their trigger ballot and all candidates selected to the national pool were sent seven-page application forms which had to be completed and returned by 31 August. At this stage, candidates could indicate up to three preferences for electoral regions and had to sign declarations that they would abide by the Selection Board decisions, the NEC guidelines, a memorandum of agreement for regional MEPs (including the aggregation, at regional level, of a proportion of their individual allowances), and the EPLP's Standing Orders. According to the party's internal document, the application forms were to be marked by 'a small team of professional advisers' and then 'validated' by members of the national selection board in Manchester on 12 September. The selection boards were given detailed instructions about how to assess the forms, with four categories (representational, knowledge, skills and personal statement) sub-divided into ten 'competences'. These application forms would count for 30 per cent of each candidate's final 'score', and it was rumoured that all had in fact been anonymously adjudicated by just one individual, David Gardner, Assistant General

Secretary – giving rise to jokes about 'Gardner's Question Time' (O'Neill, 1999, p. 79).

The fourth and final phase took place from 17 to 20 September 1998, at Stoke Rochford, a Lincolnshire country house belonging to the National Union of Teachers. Candidates appeared before a panel composed of five NEC members (Richard Rosser, Ian McCartney, Margaret Wall, Maggie Jones, John Allen), three representatives of the Regional Board concerned, one ethnic minority member (Gloria Mills), one member of the National Trade Union Liaison Committee (Mick Leahy) and the party's General Secretary, Tom Sawyer. According to an internal party document, these selection boards were to 'take account of the principles of managing the transition and quality and diversity within each regional list in determining the selection and ranking'. In so doing, they were to 'take account of the record of sitting MEPs, the application forms of candidates, and their performances during the interviews at shortlisting'.

The panels, who had been carefully trained, listened to a four-minute presentation by each nominated candidate on 'Why I would be a good MEP/candidate.' Those new nominees satisfying the selection board in their application and their presentation, together with all sitting MEPs who wished to stand again, then went forward to the next stage. For many of the new candidates who had got so far, rejection at this stage was a cruel blow. (One complained that members of the panel had yawned during the presentation.) But the selection board members had been advised to reduce the number of candidates going through to the last stage to the number of list places for that region plus half again. Clearly, for the smallest regions (North-East, 4; Wales, 5) this meant that there was very little room indeed for new candidates.

The 'survivors' went forward to a final ten-minute interview in press conference mode, with candidates fielding hostile questions from the panel. Again, the boards were given guidance on how to assess for experience, knowledge, presentational skills and personal vision, giving marks for various sub-categories. It was rumoured that some experienced MEPs had turned in comparatively poor performances at this stage. One sitting MEP was reported to have demonstrated a surprising lack of knowledge about the EU. Once the interviews were completed, all scores from selection board members were aggregated and candidates ranked in five bands, from A to E, following guidelines on suggested percentages laid down by Millbank.

It was only after this highly complicated procedure had been completed that the choice of candidates and the ordering on the regional lists could be done. The regional selection boards met again, in the order of the most competitive region (that is, the region with the highest concentration of MEPs seeking selection to winnable seats) first. The boards had to take account of *all* candidates/MEPs expressing a preference for their region/country, and not just those expressing a first preference. Thus, at this final stage, the selection boards were able to move candidates, including sitting MEPs, from their first- to a lesser-preferred region. The boards were also obliged to take account of *all* the party's established criteria: performance (as reflected in the overall banding), diversity (gender, race, geographical), and the need to manage the transition. Boards had also to increase the number of black MEPs and seek to ensure that at least five of the eleven regions were headed by women candidates. Finally, the selection boards were asked to specify first and second reserves, in case a selected candidate withdrew. The overall decisions of the selection boards were announced on 22 September 1998, after their approval by the NEC. The party and the selection boards had been faced with a thorny and thankless task but could justifiably claim that they had followed the procedure to the letter.

Of the 62 sitting Labour MEPs in the 1994–99 Parliament, two with left-wing pedigrees, Ken Coates and Hugh Kerr, decided not to put forward their candidatures, in the suspicion that the system would almost certainly have denied them a winnable position. (Both later stood for other parties, though Mr Coates claimed he had initially had no intention of standing again.) Another sitting MEP, Christine Oddy (Coventry), fought as an independent and was to poll strongly in her old Euro-Constituency. John Tomlinson and Christine Crawley announced their retirements from the Parliament and were later elevated to peerages. Wayne David announced that he would be standing for the Welsh Assembly and therefore would not seek re-election to the Parliament. Three MEPs were shuffled between regions. Glyn Ford (Greater Manchester East) was moved to head the list in the South-West. Richard Corbett (Merseyside West) crossed the Pennines to be number three in Yorkshire and the Humber. Lyndon Harrison (Cheshire West and Wirral) was given the number three spot in Wales. Though he was Welsh by birth, the move pushed a local sitting MEP, Joe Wilson, into an unwinnable position. Amid the growing resentment in the Welsh party against 'control freakery', the move provoked so much controversy that Mr Harrison nobly withdrew (and was compensated with a working peerage in the June 1999 list). Ken Collins, a veteran MEP first elected in 1979 and a longstanding Chairman of the Environment Committee, announced his retirement. Two other 1979 veterans, Alf Lomas and Tom

Megahy, also retired. A further five MEPs, all on the left – Peter Crampton, Alexander Falconer, Michael Hindley, Stan Newens and Alex Smith – did not put their names forward, perhaps because they had seen the writing on the wall.

That left 45 MEPs in the field as well as some strong non-MEP contenders. Thirteen MEPs fought on with difficult or unwinnable positions (Gordon Adam, Tony Cunningham, Michael Elliot, David Hallam, Veronica Hardstaff, Mark Hendrick,[4] Hugh McMahon, Clive Needle, Barry Seal, Shaun Spiers, David Thomas, Peter Truscott and Sue Waddington). A further seven in marginal positions were to be struck down by the June landslide (Roger Barton, Angela Billingham, Anita Pollack, Mike Tappin, Carole Tongue, Ian White and Joe Wilson).

Just five outsiders clambered through to winnable positions. Michael Cashman, a former *EastEnders* television star emerged as number two in the West Midlands and Claude Moraes, a leading campaigner for ethnic rights, as number two in London. Three others, locally prominent women, were given a good chance: Neena Gill (number three in the West Midlands); Mo O'Toole (number three in the North-East); and Catherine Taylor (number three in Scotland).[5]

Thus, of the 60 Labour MEPs elected in 1994 (or their by-election successors), three left the party and stood against it, three went to the Lords and only 24 survived to serve in the 1999 Euro-Parliament, where they were joined by five neophytes. If Labour had done as well as originally expected, winning an extra seat in every region, there would have been 34 ex-MEPs in the total of 40. Ten other ex-MEPs would still have languished lower down the tickets.

The ordering of the candidates provoked some surprise. Why was Carole Tongue only allotted the marginal number five slot in London? Why was the veteran Gordon Adam pushed to an unwinnable fourth in the North-East? Why was Ian White, Labour's sole South-West MEP, only given the doubtful second slot?

The pre-eminence of ex-MEPs provoked some disillusion among outside aspirants. They had slaved hard to secure nominations, travelling extensively to address constituency parties and to brief themselves about the scene. They had given up weeks or months of their lives in a vain pursuit and in some cases spent considerable sums of money. If they made the shortlist to Stoke Rochford, they were judged on the basis of an application form, a four-minute speech, and an aggressive, quick interview. What were Labour's Five Pledges? When would Britain join the single currency? Why be an MEP? In the end, only MEPs and celebrities made it to winnable positions. There were dark rumours about the extent to which the rank-order had been fixed in advance. One minister boasted to the authors months ahead: 'I know how the candidates will be listed in my region; they don't.' Such allegations provoked firm denials from the honourable participants in the Stoke Rochford process, but they were still largely repeated and believed by many in the party.

Whatever the rumours, there was an 'evident statistical pattern of age discrimination':

> It was as though someone had gone through the list of MEPs and systematically excluded from 'winnable' positions most men born before 1945. (O'Neill, 1999, p. 78)

New Labour
New Democracy
Ken Coates MEP
and others

Leader All
One Member, One Votes

The analogy between Labour candidate selection and the cloning of sheep was cited by left-wing MEPs

Guardian (13 November 1998)
(Steve Bell)

For O'Neill, the primary issue was not so much Old Labour being excluded as *elderly* male Labour. But there was also much speculation about a 'purge of the Left'. No less than 31 of Labour's 60 MEPs (over 50 per cent) had signed a 1994 statement opposing Tony Blair's ultimately successful campaign to ditch the Clause Four commitment to public ownership. At a subsequent meeting of the EPLP, the Prime Minister was heckled, and was said to have been 'furious'. O'Neill's statistical analysis shows that 54 per cent of MEPs in the 'drop zone' signed the statement, and that only two MEPs born after 1945 who signed the document were allotted 'safe' positions (Joe Wilson and Richard Balfe), and one of these (Wilson) was to fall foul of Labour's poor electoral performance (*ibid*., p. 79). O'Neill concludes that, for there to have been a systematic exclusion of 'Old' (and elderly male) Labour, it could most easily have been done through the marking of candidates' application forms, and he claims to have found evidence that this was indeed the case. David Gardner himself argued that the process had produced a set of candidates who would be 'a credit to the party, first-class representatives upholding the highest standards in public life who will sustain a Labour Government' (*Tribune*, 16 October 1998).

The NEC was so alarmed by media coverage of the increasingly vociferous signs of disquiet about the party's new selection systems that on 23 March 1999 it adopted a new code of practice under which candidates and party members were required to refer any complaint or observation about the party's selection procedures to the party's General Secretary, Margaret McDonagh (or, where appropriate, the company supervising the particular ballot in question). Anyone voicing complaints or concerns about selection/election procedures would be open to disqualification. Although the new code of practice had been designed primarily in reaction to criticism of the NEC and Welsh Assembly selectoral/electoral systems, it would clearly have implications for future Euro-contests as well.

The darker rumours clearly fed off the resentment about so-called Millbank 'control-freakery'. But many pointed out that the system was an almost inevitable consequence of the decision to switch to PR. Certainly, most Labour MEPs wished openly that use of the PR system could have been postponed to 2004. One said furiously: 'If, as we all suspect, this was a gesture to the Liberal Democrats, they didn't need to do it until 2004.' Most were confident that they could have secured renomination and election under the old constituency system. Many had invested heavily in building up their constituency links and they valued the relationship, however tenuous, between an individual member and his or her own part of the country.

However, once PR had been decided upon, the party managers did face a real difficulty in sorting out in an orderly way the natural claims of sitting members to continue their work. As one MEP commented: 'It was like trying to get a quart into a pint pot' (O'Neill, 1999, p. 81). Party officials argued with some passion that, notwithstanding the task that initially faced them, they had managed to produce a strong and balanced team of candidates which was to result in an equally strong and balanced team of MEPs.

The Liberal Democrat Party

The Liberal Democrats employed the most open electoral system, agreed at their 21 September 1997 Eastbourne Conference, with 65 per cent support. Potential candidates were asked to fill in a single-page statement of their qualifications and position. Regional Committees drew up shortlists and the candidate statements were circulated to all the party members in the region. Candidates could stand in more than one region. A number of hustings meetings were held in each region but the final order of candidates was decided by postal vote (STV). About 40 per cent of Liberal Democrat members cast ballots.

The Liberal Democrats also discussed gender balance at their Eastbourne conference and, though a 'zipping' procedure, did most to ensure equitable representation of the sexes. The two sitting MEPs in the South-West were male and in the strongest Liberal Democrat region. Because of this, the next region, in terms of Liberal Democrat strength in 1997, was to have a woman at the top of the list. The other regions, ranked by 1997 percentage, were to alternate between a man and a woman at the head. The party ended up with an equal gender division among their ten successful candidates. Those who had some prior political prominence were at an advantage. Apart from the sitting MEPs in the South-West there were three regions where an ex-MP headed the ticket and one other came second as the top male.

Candidates were required to promise in advance that, wherever they came on the list, they would campaign equally vigorously, even though it was plain that in most Regions not more than one candidate had any hope. Not all lived up to this ideal but there were no signs of any serious scars being left by the Liberal Democrat selection process.

The Green Party

The Greens made their selection by postal ballot among their 5,000 members, the latter deciding both the candidates and the list order. Selection began very early, in autumn 1997, and with an initial candidate announcement in June 1998. Selection was left to the regions; in some areas there was little competition but in the South-East, in London, and in the South-West there were hustings meetings and a close-fought race. The issue of gender balance was left to each region to decide upon. Only three regions took active decisions (East Midlands and Yorkshire went for 'zipped' lists; London for a top female candidate). As it turned out, women headed seven out of eleven lists, and their two victors, Jean Lambert and Caroline Lucas, were women.

The United Kingdom Independence Party

The party put together a full slate of candidates. In its areas of strength, particularly the South-East and South-West, there was strong competition for the higher-ranked positions. These were decided by postal ballot. In other regions, where candidatures were less likely to be successful, the party leadership was able to rank volunteer candidates without going through full-blown selection procedures.

The Scottish National Party

The party's selection system was devised by Dr Allan Macartney, the party's Deputy Leader and an MEP since 1994. A one member, one vote system had initially been contemplated but, aware that its membership lists were not sufficiently up to date, the party instead opted for a system involving delegates and a multiple choice vote. The system was adopted at the SNP's 5–6 June 1998 special conference in Perth.

The party first drew up a list of 'approved possible candidates'. To be considered, candidates had to be nominated by at least two constituency associations. Nominees would then go forward to regional primary selection meetings (one for each region). Each regional primary selection meeting could nominate just one candidate. As the system was initially devised, the resulting list of eight candidates was supposed to have been issued to the party at large on 1 September 1998, with party branches and constituency associations subsequently meeting to discuss the possible ranking of candidates. But on 25 August, Dr Macartney suddenly died and the carefully scheduled system was thrown into disarray. A by-election had to be held under the old first-past-the-post system. This, in turn, required the selection of a candidate. Ian Hudghton, who had been Dr Macartney's constituency agent, was duly selected and went on to win the seat with a large, and increased, majority (see Table 2.1). Though he had not been on the initial list of approved possible candidates, Mr Hudghton was now brought into the selection contest. At the party's 24 September 1998 Inverness conference, Mr Hudghton emerged with first place on the overall list of eight candidates. A local man, and a former councillor and member of the EU's Committee of the Regions, Ian Hudghton was a strong and popular list leader. He was followed in the potentially winnable positions on the list by Neil MacCormick, an Edinburgh-based law professor; Dr Anne Lorne Gillies, a Glasgow-based singer, writer and TV producer; and at fourth position, Dr Gordon Wilson, a Dundee-based solicitor and former MP (1974–79) and National Convenor of the Party, 1979–90. The party believed it had created a strong and balanced list of candidates, and realistically hoped to take three seats in the June contest.

Plaid Cymru – The Party of Wales

Plaid Cymru's National Executive appointed panels to vet applicants. The selection was carried out by Plaid's 250-strong National Council. In the end, twelve candidates were questioned. The National Council then ranked the male and female candidates on separate lists before establishing a ranking order for a single national list that was not gender-based. The five successful candidates were well known within the party and experienced in European affairs. The list leader, Jill Evans, was a local councillor and party activist who had served as national chair of the party from 1995 to 1997. She had also been an alternate member of the EU's Committee of the Regions. The number two, Eurig Wyn, was also a local councillor and currently a Plaid Cymru representative on the Committee of the Regions.

The Pro-Euro Conservative Party

The pro-European Conservatives had had to act arbitrarily in putting together a full national slate at the last minute. Several former MEPs and MPs were cajoled into putting forward their names and in five regions headed the ticket.

In elections candidates matter far less than parties. Voters enjoy the illusion of personal choice but what the label stands for is much better known than the actual qualities of the individual or individuals who are seeking votes. In 1999, faced with a new electoral system, the British political parties attacked the problem of candidate selection in very different ways. Almost all endeavoured to enlist the opinions of party activists and almost all produced a more balanced slate than before, at least in terms of gender and ethnicity. But none were wholly satisfied with their procedures. Even if the electoral system stays the same, candidate selection will be different in 2004.

Notes

1. The Nuffield General Election studies long ago adopted the practice of dealing with the major parties in alphabetical order. The same practice has been adopted here and in Chapter 3.
2. The party's constitutional unit issued an information pack for candidates seeking selection, an information pack for European Constituency Labour Parties and (Westminster) Constituency Labour Parties on the selection procedures, and procedure guidelines for regional directors and NEC designated representatives. The guidelines had been the subject of extensive consultation with the European Parliamentary Labour Party.
3. One candidate had five nominations from three regions; another had three from three; two had two from two; two had four from one; four had three from one; and ten had two from one. However, these multiple nominations were not necessarily an advantage. Of the five candidates who made it through to safe places on the lists, two had four nominations from one region, two had two nominations from one region, and one had just one nomination from one region.
4. It was rumoured that Mr Hendrick would have got a winnable position in the West Midlands but that he refused to leave Lancashire.
5. Three candidates, not in really winnable positions, had to withdraw because, being on hospital boards, they were technically in 'offices of profit under the Crown' and therefore ineligible.

5
The National Campaign

The 1999 European elections campaign in the United Kingdom was a non-campaign. Consider the first week. It is then that the political parties by tradition set out their stalls and try to impart momentum to the campaign, that the major themes are established, party political differences emphasised, and the media's appetite whetted. In the second half of May 1999, none of this happened.

The first week

In some Member States the Euro-elections campaign would not get under way until the end of May. In the United Kingdom, nominations had closed on 13 May 1999, and campaigning proper started on Monday, 17 May 1999, when Paddy Ashdown and his foreign affairs spokesman, Menzies Campbell, launched the Liberal Democrats' manifesto, *Ambitious for Britain*. With the Euro-elections being portrayed as his swansong, Mr Ashdown asserted that the party's carefully achieved balance – between Euro-enthusiasm and calls for reform – would send record numbers of Liberal Democrat MEPs to Strasbourg. Under the slogan 'Local where possible, European where necessary', the Liberal Democrats argued that they were best placed to work for an 'open, democratic and decentralised' European Union. The manifesto's basic requirements included a rapid referendum on the single currency, a written European constitution and a strengthened European Parliament. Mr Ashdown argued that, 'We have a government sitting on the fence and a Conservative party that is saying "please stop the world, we want to get off."'A Conservative spokesman later accused the Liberal Democrats of 'steering a path towards a federal Europe', while Labour more pragmatically pointed out that, under PR, tactical votes for the Liberal Democrats were no longer necessary (*Guardian*, 18 May).

For all its upbeat message, the Liberal Democrat launch barely made the evening news bulletins, which were dominated by the story of a victory for the Labour Party in Israel. Closer to home, Mr Blair's Labour Party stole the Liberal Democrats' thunder in two ways. First, the news bulletins described the Prime Minister's front bench mini-shuffle, following Donald Dewar's appointment as First Minister in the Edinburgh Parliament. Second, the Party ran its first party political broadcast immediately after the evening bulletins. Under the slogan '*New Labour making Britain better*', the broadcast spliced part of an old broadcast about progress on education and employment on to scenes of Mr Blair receiving the Charlemagne Prize in Aachen the previous Thursday. Mr Blair, it claimed, had brought leadership to Europe. In addition, he had found a solution to the BSE crisis, had defended the British budgetary rebate and won new holiday rights for British workers as well as gaining new money for British regions. It was thus already clear that Labour intended to put the Prime Minister's stature, achievements and sustained popularity – if not the Prime Minister himself – to the forefront throughout the campaign.

The next morning saw the Labour Party making the news in a different way. After an all-night Commons debate on the government's controversial welfare reform and pensions bill, the government whips postponed the ensuing vote to avoid humiliation in the division lobbies. The threat followed vociferous criticism from rebellious backbenchers that proposed means-tests and restricted entitlements were Treasury-driven.

By lunchtime, the 'flap' was over and news bulletins led with stories about genetically modified organisms and images of a visit by Mr Blair to a refugee camp in Macedonia. Far down the pecking order came the Conservative Party's official campaign launch that morning at Smith Square. Mr Hague, accompanied by Mr Ancram, Mr Howard and Mr McMillan-Scott, launched the Party's manifesto, *In Europe, not run by Europe* (see p. 55 on the genesis of this title). The manifesto's central planks included fighting fraud, opposing the single currency for the lifetime of the next Parliament, opposing fiscal harmonisation, reducing the EU's budget and the UK's budgetary contributions, and a 'mix and match' form of integration. 'Many people who do not normally vote Conservative have indicated that, on the issue of Europe, they support our approach,' Mr Hague argued. By making the euro a key to the campaign Mr Hague risked a political backlash from Europhiles within the Conservative Party, but he believed it was the one issue where he could show clear blue water between the Tories and Labour.

Unhelpfully for Mr Hague, news bulletins also reported the UKIP's manifesto launch, with the potential for confusion over very similar policy messages. Claiming itself to be 'Euro-realist' rather than 'Euro-sceptic' (a term its spokesmen argued had 'hand-wringing and negative connotations'), UKIP, too, ran on an anti-euro, anti-fraud platform, though, in addition, it favoured immediate withdrawal.

A campaigning Paddy Ashdown meanwhile returned to Sheffield to celebrate the Liberal Democrat victory in the 6 May local elections. With the Kosovan tragedy clearly playing on his mind, and with speculation growing that he would be appointed as an EU envoy to the region after he stepped down as leader, he stressed the need to bolster Europe's military potential and for the EU to spend more on defence.

The Green Party announced that it was planning to seek an injunction to prevent publication of government publicity material for the Euro-elections. Leaflets prepared for distribution in England by the Home Office included a dummy ballot paper for the South-West region. Although the Greens had hopes of picking up one of the seven South-West seats, the dummy form featured only the three mainstream parties, together with a number of fictitious parties and independents. (See Chapters 2 and 8.)

Tuesday night saw the Conservatives' first Euro-election broadcast. In contrast to Labour's decidedly patrician approach, the broadcast followed the Tories' new trend, borrowed from America, of a 'soap' docu-drama involving an 'everyday' couple who worried about the euro.

The headlines on Wednesday 19 May embraced a disparate series of themes. Among the tabloids, only the *Daily Express* featured a European story on its front page, continuing a series of 'exposures' of MEPs' alleged malpractices (it had run a story based on allegations against Pauline Green the previous week), devoting most of its front page and a two-page inner spread to allegations made by the former assistant of a Labour MEP, Glyn Ford.

News on the Euro-elections was largely restricted to diminutive articles in the inner pages. Among the broadsheets, the *Daily Telegraph* sported a front-page article, 'BLAIR BACKS SOCIALIST EUROPE', flagging up Labour's manifesto. At the other extreme, the *Guardian*'s front page concentrated on NATO splits, GM food research, and the arrest of Manchester United captain Roy Keane.

The morning's main event was the official launch of the Labour Party's omnibus manifesto and campaign, *Elections 99*, by the Prime Minister. Mr Blair was surrounded by Labour's 84 candidates who were, as the BBC's Robin Oakley reported, 'marshalled like film extras', though MEPs Pauline Green, Alan Donnelly and Glenys Kinnock were much to the fore.

Inevitably, journalists homed in on Labour's policy towards the euro and believed they had detected something new in the Prime Minister's pronouncements. The government had never publicly agreed on a referendum timetable, but its preferred option was widely understood to involve the holding of a vote shortly after the next General Election. Answering questions, Mr Blair declared that he would not be pushed into setting an 'arbitrary time limit' on joining the euro: 'We are making the preparations necessary, so early in the next parliament we can hold a referendum, but I'm not saying we will hold a referendum early in the next parliament irrespective of the economic conditions … .' He denied being ambivalent: 'We have resolved questions of principle in relation to the single currency.' But, 'the economic conditions have to be right.'

Mr Blair said that Labour would be fighting the elections as the party of enterprise and business. He said that the Conservatives' 'extreme European position made them incapable of representing British business'. He accused the Tories of committing a historic mistake on Europe – 'half-in, half-out'. The Prime Minister also made an appeal to Labour voters not to stay at home: 'So I say to voters: Europe matters, the European Parliament matters, this election matters.'

In the evening, the Liberal Democrats ran their first Euro-election broadcast. It continued with their established use of a mock news bulletin, 'News from the Liberal Democrats'. The first two items featured Paddy Ashdown – criticising the government's record on schools and hospitals; a third reported 'civil war' between two East Midland Tory candidates, Euro-sceptic Roger Helmer and Europhile Bill Newton Dunn; and a fourth featured Charles Kennedy, as the party's agriculture and food spokesman, arguing the euro's advantages for consumer price transparency.

Once again, on Thursday 20 May, the front pages covered a variety of themes, notably the reported desertion of Serb soldiers in Kosovo, but the Euro-election campaign was nowhere to be seen.

On the inside pages of the *Daily Mail* Tony Blair wrote about his 'cancer crusade'. It was only on page 10 that the paper reported, very briefly, on the launch of the Labour campaign. The *Daily Express*, continued with the Glyn Ford story, and the *Guardian* also reported that Ford's future was in doubt. The *Sun* ran a 'poll guide to party policies', juxtaposing the supposed positions of Labour and the Conservatives, and an editorial broadly supporting Mr Hague's approach.

Among the broadsheets, it was Tony Blair's subtle message on the single currency which attracted most comment. As Peter Riddell wrote in *The Times*, it was 'hard to credit Labour's single currency strategy', because the government wanted to have the best of both worlds – certainty on the principle, but ambiguity on the timing. In the *Daily Telegraph*, George Jones reported: 'Blair drops first hint of delay on euro referendum.' An accompanying article contrasted the reserved and conditional nature of Labour's manifesto on the single currency with the positive and unreserved position of the PES manifesto, *The New Europe*.

The Times published a passionate article by John Stevens, leader of the Pro-Euro Conservative Party. 'The issue', he concluded, 'is leadership. Those who want Blair to be bold and Hague to go should vote for the Pro-Euro Conservative Party on June 10.'

In the evening's television news bulletins, Plaid Cymru's upbeat campaign launch, following hard on the heels of the party's successes in the 6 May Assembly elections, merited a few seconds' coverage far down the order. At the top of the same order came the expected revolt by the Labour government's backbench rebels over the welfare reform bill, which was passed, but with 65 Labour MPs voting against and 39 abstaining.

Front-page headlines on the morning of Friday 21 May concentrated on the conviction of a serial rapist and former DJ (*Daily Mail*, *Daily Express*, *Daily Telegraph*, *The Times*, *Guardian*) and, among the broadsheets, Labour's backbench revolt over welfare reform (*Daily Telegraph*, *The Times*, *Guardian*) and the continuing repercussions of the Kosovo crisis.

There were a large number of independent approaches, as the papers sought more newsworthy angles to their Euro-elections reportage. *The Times* and the *Daily Express*, for example, reported that Mr Blair had been 'forced onto the backfoot' after being challenged to a live television debate by William Hague and Paddy Ashdown.

The *Daily Telegraph* reported Liberal Democrat allegations that a BBC news bulletin the previous day had bowed to Labour pressure. According to the allegations, a midday bulletin's coverage of Labour's manifesto launch had picked out four main points, 'all highlighting government plans to cede more power to Brussels. When the launch was covered in the early evening news they had been substituted with less contentious pledges.' The Liberal Democrats' campaign chairman, Nick Harvey, argued that the BBC had bowed to pressure – a charge the BBC denied strenuously.

The Times also revealed that the General Secretary of the Pro-Euro Conservative Party, 24-year-old Andy Mayer, had been a Liberal Democrat since 1991. John Stevens and Brendan Donnelly were said to be 'aghast' at the news, which they feared would deter Tories uneasy with William Hague's stance on the euro from switching their support. The Liberal Democrats were said to be equally appalled. An insouciant Mr Mayer claimed he had left a message on their answering machine but that he still received Liberal Democrat literature: 'I suspect the Liberals will kick me out now.'

The Times and the *Daily Mail* ran substantial pieces on Mr Hague's claim that Europe's pension funds were facing a 'ticking time bomb' and that sterling's adhesion to the single currency would diminish British immunity to this malady.

The Times ran a full-page comparison of the party manifestos, concluding that, on all of the relevant issues, the main parties' positions were very similar.

An *Independent* article, 'TORIES SIGN PRO-EURO DECLARATION', highlighted the European Democratic Union's common statement to which Tory MEPs had signed up. Michael Howard said: 'Although we agreed with that document and don't resile from anything in it, we have put our own Conservative Party manifesto to the British people in these elections ... It is not a question of tailoring the message differently ... .' In fact, the EDU text had been drafted largely by the Conservative Party's International Secretary.

On Friday evening the Pro-Euro Conservatives' Euro-election broadcast went out in Wales and Scotland (it was broadcast three days later in England). Mr Hague was depicted as 'a political tramp', an 'aggressive beggar providing a running commentary from his patch of Little England' (*Daily Express*, 21 May). The punchline was: 'Turning your back on Europe will put your future at risk.' In England, meanwhile, the British National Party ran its Euro-election broadcast. The party's leader, John Tyndall, filmed in front of the Cenotaph, argued that the country's war dead 'deserve something better' and appealed to the nation's 'fighting spirit'. Nick Griffin elaborated the argument in favour of complete withdrawal from the EU.

There was virtually no coverage of the Euro-elections in the weekend's newspapers. An exception was the *Sunday Times*, which ran a banner headline and front-page article entitled 'JAGUAR GAVE LABOUR LEADER HALF-PRICE CAR', plus a back-page article entitled 'CAR INDUSTRY REWARDED ITS

FRIENDLY MEP', accompanied by a large photograph of Alan Donnelly, leader of the EPLP. The *Observer* carried an editorial on the same story. Mr Donnelly, it was alleged, had failed to declare in the MEPs' register of interests his use of a Daimler car at a special lease rate. Mr Donnelly argued that he had done no wrong and, as in the case of the allegations against Glyn Ford (see p. 99), the matter was referred to the Parliament's Secretary-General for adjudication (see also p. 188).

Emerging trends

It is important to underline that, as far as the general public was concerned, the beginning of the campaign was virtually invisible. As the first week drew to a close, the Euro-elections remained resolutely on the inside pages of the newspapers and, to the extent that they figured at all, far down the television and radio news bulletins. The major political parties, reacting to very sparse attendance, began to cancel some of their scheduled national press conferences, and there was very little sense of involvement by either frontbench political figures or, more significantly, the parties' activists. With this substantial caveat entered, a number of trends had become apparent.

Kosovo

The first, and most important, were the ramifications of the continuing conflict in Kosovo. This had been expected to be a short, sharp affair. Certainly, nobody in the government had believed it would continue so far into May, let alone June. The Foreign Secretary, who had been intimately involved in the drafting of the Labour/PES Group common manifesto, was completely absorbed by the war. So, too, was the Prime Minister, who had clearly come to see a successful completion to the Allies' bombardment as a personal crusade. Millbank let it be known that the Prime Minister felt it inappropriate to engage in a partisan campaign for as long as the conflict continued. However, Mr Blair's absence from the campaign tore the heart out of Labour's strategy, which had been predicated on the Prime Minister's personal popularity and his perceived strong leadership.

Mr Blair's presidential distance also left the field clear for Mr Hague to develop his Euro-sceptic and anti-euro tactics. Though the basic tenor of Mr Hague's campaign theme had been decided in advance, the absence of effective opposition encouraged him to take his tactics further. This begs the question as to whether such effective opposition could not have been mounted by Labour's other big guns. The indefatigable Deputy

Prime Minister was locked into two gruelling regional tours (for which he was rewarded with scant media coverage), but what of the Chancellor of the Exchequer? Gordon Brown had imposed his authority on Labour's Scottish election campaign to great effect, and was to make several interventions in the Euro-election campaign, but none on the matter of the single currency. Indeed, one of the mysteries of the 1999 Euro-election campaign, considered in more detail on pp. 204–27, is why Mr Brown did not play a more prominent role in countering Mr Hague's tactics.

The continued conflict in Kosovo also had an effect on the Liberal Democrats' campaign. Military affairs and the Balkans were Mr Ashdown's forte, and it was known that he had the Prime Minister's ear. Not unnaturally, journalists sought out his views on the Balkan crisis. But the result, especially given Mr Ashdown's pre-eminence within his party, was to swamp the Liberal Democrats' planned campaign, which was supposed to concentrate on domestic issues and, in a PR election, critically to differentiate the party from its new Labour ally. Nor did the *sotto voce* leadership campaign generate the sort of headlines some activists had hoped for. On the contrary, the sporadic press reports did little more than mock the profusion of little known candidates.

Lack of engagement

A second clear trend was the general lack of practical commitment by the major parties. The *Financial Times* ran a detailed analytical piece about how 'LACK OF FUNDS HITS EUROPEAN ELECTION CAMPAIGNS' (5 June). Indeed, disgruntled candidates later complained that their party headquarters had sought to take money *out* of the campaign. Certainly, there was a lack of the logistical support in depth which generally characterises major electoral battles. Perhaps the worst sinner – anecdotally, at least – was the Labour Party, which gave the impression of having embarked on nothing more than a holding operation. There were few signs of the fabled electoral machine which had transported the party to undreamt-of electoral heights in 1997. Rather, there were strong hints of the complacency which Mr Blair had then been so intent on eschewing. The Liberal Democrats' national campaign gave a similar sense of complacency, with many activists apparently confident that the new electoral system would reward the party with ten seats in addition to the two it already held. Mr Hague's Conservatives, buoyed by their local election successes (measured in terms of avoidance of failure), were the least complacent of the big three. But even Mr Hague's tactics depended on a tight, centralised message which, to his delight, was enthusiastically taken up by a compliant Euro-sceptic press, rather than the commitment of major party resources. In all three cases there was no impression of a 'continuous campaign' embracing local, Scottish and Welsh and European elections and, indeed, the prior expenditure of scarce electoral resources, from activists' energy to expenditure on polling and posters, was a major factor behind the lack of practical commitment.

Few policy differences

A third trend was, with one exception, the absence of major policy differences between the political parties. The *Sun*, *The Times* and the *Evening Standard* all published comparisons of the parties' manifestos, and all came to the conclusion that, whatever their rhetoric, little distinguished them. (The Greens confirmed the impression by publishing the identical voting records of the MEPs of the 'big three' in Strasbourg on what the Greens argued were crunch ecological issues – *Green World*, Summer 1999 edition; see also, for example, *Daily Mail*, 8 June). The broad themes of the party manifestos are set out in Table 5.1.

Judging from similar questions asked at the parties' national press conferences, journalists were puzzled by the dissonance between party rhetoric, with its traditional adversarial references to left–right opposition, and the policy reality. In previous Euro-elections, the combination of the Strasbourg Parliament's consensual working methods and the oppositional Westminster model had highlighted this dialectic, but PR seemed to underline the dissonance even more.

An evident consequence was media bemusement about how to present the elections. The first week saw a number of 'sleaze' articles about the alleged misdoings of MEPs – particularly Labour MEPs – but these stories soon faded away, presumably because there was little in them. There were also a number of 'gravy train' articles about MEPs' allowances, but these, too, soon died out. Perhaps more profoundly, over the previous six months the media had presented the European Commission as the corrupt branch and the Parliament as a righteous scourge; presenting the Parliament now as a similarly corrupt institution led to all sorts of analytical and presentational difficulties.

Sparse media coverage

A fourth trend, product of the above three, was the extraordinary profusion of 'front-page' stories covered by the media. On the rare occasions when Kosovo was not pre-eminent, newspapers and media news bulletins led with a great variety of stories. It was also rare for the newspapers to concur in their choice of a major story. Table 5.2 sets out the newspaper front pages throughout the campaign. This phenomenon

Table 5.1 The main themes of the parties' manifestos

	Conservative	Labour	Lib Dems	SNP	Plaid Cymru	Greens	UKIP
The euro	Opposition to entry will be a manifesto commitment at next General Election	Join when the time is right (five tests)	Hold referendum at earliest opportunity	In favour. Would strengthen economy of Independent Scotland	Could bring significant benefits, but Welsh Assembly should decide	UK must not join	Retain sterling, will never adopt euro
Defence	Retain importance of NATO. EU army unnecessary	Not mentioned	Favours common Foreign and Security policy without an EU army	Withdraw from NATO in favour of European defence	Foresees growth of common EU defence policy	Replace NATO with well-resourced OSCE	Common defence force could fall under EU control
EU Reform	Oppose further erosion of veto. Seek greater national decision-making	New structure for Commission	Greater use of QMV to avoid deadlock. EU Constitution.	Additional powers of scrutiny for European Parliament	Strengthen role of European Parliament. Extend QMV	Greater role for Euro Parliament. Restrict role of Commission	Only way to democratise is to withdraw from EU control
EU Budget	Reduce size of EU budget and UK contribution	We secured Britain's rebate at Berlin	Opposed to rise in UK contribution	Expects Independent Scotland to be net receiver of funds	Smaller British rebate, therefore larger grants to regions (including Wales)	No policy	Gain from withdrawal is far in excess of our £9 billion gross contribution
Home Affairs	Oppose Europe-wide criminal justice system. Oppose common immigration policy	Not mentioned	Give Europol more resources. But concerned about civil liberties	Open borders policy. Relax immigration and asylum rules	EU has responsibility for fair asylum policies	Europol not accountable. Must not have a role	Leaving EU will restore border controls
Enlargement	Make enlargement a top priority – expand free trade	Right in itself and good for competitiveness	Pro-enlargement	Pro-enlargement	Supports enlargement	Pro-enlargement	No policy
Fraud	Create a fully independent anti-fraud office. Greater powers for Euro Parliament over Commissioners	Complete overhaul of financial accountability	Strengthen anti-fraud unit. CAP reform	EU Commission reform to target fraud	Key part of campaign. Anti-'gravy-train'	Will continue to highlight instances of fraud	UKIP candidates would not benefit personally as MEPs

Source: Adapted from *The Times*, 21 May 1999 (Pro-Euro Conservatives not included).

Increasing Euro-scepticism characterised the Conservative campaign   Independent (17 May) (Dave Brown)

Table 5.2 Newspaper front-page stories throughout the campaign

	Guardian	Independent	Times	Financial Times	Daily Telegraph
17 May	- Netanyahu faces defeat - Blair flies out to Balkans	- Kosovo - Legal rights for mistresses - Israel election	- Kosovo - Greg Dyke Labour donation	- IMF on conditions for joining single currency - US telecom merger	- Millennium bug - Kosovo - Ulster
18	- Labour victory in Israel - Labour welfare revolt - Asian visa checks	- Labour victory in Israel - Kosovo	- Labour victory in Israel - Visa tests for Asians - Kosovo	- Labour victory in Israel - US interest rates	- Labour victory in Israel - Conservatives encourage benefits revolt - Kosovo
19	- NATO splits - GM food research - Roy Keane's arrest	- Removal of right to jury trial - Blair's Albanian visit - Israeli election	- Kosovo - New Poet Laureate - Jill Dando investigation	- US inflation fears - Brown rejects IMF call for devaluation	- Labour Manifesto Launch 'Blair backs Socialist Europe'
20	- Desertion of Serb soldiers - Glyn Ford story	- GM crops - Desertion of Serb soldiers	- Desertion of Serb soldiers - Discovery of unknown half-brother of John Major	- Desertion of Serb soldiers - Bank of England and possible devaluation	- Desertion of Serb soldiers
21	- Conviction serial rapist and former DJ - Labour backbench revolt on welfare reform	- Tories sign Pro-Euro declaration - 80 MPs defy Blair on welfare reform - Kosovo - GM food	- Conviction serial rapist and former DJ - Labour backbench revolt on welfare reform	- Gloomy economic prospects for Europe - Fines for cartels - poor European air traffic control	- Conviction serial rapist and former DJ - Labour backbench revolt on welfare reform
22	- Jill Dando's funeral - Kosovo - GMOs - Dallaglio - GM food	- Jill Dando's funeral - Kosovo - GMOs - Kosovo - Freedom of Information Bill - BBC DJs	- Jill Dando's funeral - Kosovo - GMOs - Kosovo - Dallaglio	- Bank of Ireland merger - Olivetti takeover of Telecom Italia	- Jill Dando's funeral - Kosovo - GMOs - Kosovo - Dallaglio
24				- Bank of Ireland merger - business wages - Kosovo	

25	- Dallaglio - The 'flat cap robber'	- Dallaglio - Kosovo - Freedom of Information Bill	- Dallaglio - Kosovo	- New York stock exchange - Private Finance Initiative for Post Office scrapped	- Dallaglio - Kosovo
26	- Dallaglio - Govt pledge to reduce drug abuse - Kosovo	- Dallaglio - Govt pledge to reduce drug abuse - Kosovo	- Dallaglio - Cabinet revolt over pay levels - Diana Memorial Fund	- European finance ministers loosen stability pact conditions on Italy - Drinks firm chief executive resigns - 'EU ministers to limit junior doctors' hours'	- Manchester United - Dallaglio
27	- Sophie Rhys-Jones - Milosevic indictment/ Kosovo - Manchester United	- Sophie Rhys-Jones - Milosevic indictment/ Kosovo - Manchester United	- Sophie Rhys-Jones - Milosevic indictment/ Kosovo - Manchester United - 1st MORI poll on euro elections and Riddell analysis	- Milosevic indictment - Euro hits new low - Public access to artwork	- Sophie Rhys-Jones - Milosevic indictment/ Kosovo - Manchester United
28	- GMOs - De Klerk link to killings - Indictment of Milosevic	- Indictment of Milosevic - Manchester Utd - BBC Governorship - EU Tax harmonisation	- Manchester Utd - Kashmir - Eddie George EMU - Sophie Rhys-Jones - MORI poll analysis + Lab analysis	- Russian peace initiative/Kosovo - Brown's tax and benefit reform plans - Joining euro 'act of faith' says Eddie George	- Kashmir - Eddie George and EMU - Sophie Rhys-Jones
29	- Return of bodies of IRA victims - Kashmir conflict	- Serial paedophile's life sentence - Return of bodies of IRA victims - Kashmir conflict	- Serial paedophile's life sentence - Kashmir conflict - 'Dyke' cash to Labour	- Political crisis in Russia - Controversy over Lib Dem logo - Storehouse group	- Serial paedophile's life sentence - Alleged manipulation of national curriculum pass marks - return of bodies of IRA victims

continued

Table 5.2 continued

	Guardian	Independent	Times	Financial Times	Daily Telegraph
31	- Britain out of Cricket World Cup - Resue Plan to halt euro slide - Another NATO blunder	- Britain out of Cricket World Cup - Another NATO blunder	- Britain out of Cricket World Cup - JFK's Dallas coffin dumped in Atlantic - Backlash at IRA over body hunt	- Gatwick Airport capacity - European leaders try to stop euro's fall - Kosovo	- Britain out of Cricket World Cup - 'Children becoming softies as red tape halts adventure' - 'Tories increase pressure over EU tax targets' - IRA 'disappeared' - Kosovo - Glider crash
1 June	- Kosovo - Eurobarometer poll - Resignation of Rangers FC Vice Chairman - Ocalan trial	- Kosovo - 'One black MP for all Europe'	- Kosovo - Benefits fraud crackdown	- Common EU defence policy agreed - Call for end to judges' role in Lords	- Kosovo
2	- Kosovo - Belgium, eggs - Hague's progressive hardening of stance on euro	- Kosovo - Hague and the euro	- GM food and Prince of Wales - BBC job/Greg Dyke - Kosovo - Hague's progressive hardening of stance on euro	- GM food and Prince of Wales - 'Japan fears rise in male jobless makes cultural change' - Hague's progressive hardening of stance on euro	- Kosovo - Hague and the euro - Hague's progressive hardening of stance on euro
3	- Kosovo Peace Plan - Aborted Bank of Scotland/Pat Robertson deal - High winds capsize yachts	- Kosovo Peace Plan - South African elections	- Kosovo Peace Plan - Holocaust money	- ECB on sidelines as euro all-time low	- Kosovo - Boiled vegetables best - Sophie Rhys-Jones
4	- Kosovo Peace Deal - Belgian food crisis	- Kosovo	- Kosovo Peace Deal	- Kosovo Peace Deal - Airtours bid for First Choice	- Kosovo Peace Deal - Bloody Sunday soldiers - Gallup poll results
5	- Kosovo/Milosevic	- Kosovo/Milosevic - Portillo and NATO	- Kosovo/Milosevic - Massive donations to Tories	- Kosovo/Milosevic - EU Leaders fail to project unity over euro policy	- Kosovo/Milosevic - Alan Clark brain surgery - Portillo next NATO chief? - Blair loses battle on Duty Free

7	- Kosovo - GM foods - G7 debt deal - G8/ Kosovo - ICM poll	- Kosovo - Tories in secret talks with Neo-Fascists - G8/ Kosovo	- Kosovo - Brown relaxes rules on spending - G8/ Kosovo - Austrian whitewater rafting accident	- Kosovo & NATO - Flotation of Dixon's Freeserve - G8/ Kosovo - Weak euro	- Kosovo - Pro-Euro Tory 'worked with Labour' - G8/ Kosovo - Austrian whitewater rafting accident
8	- Blair pledge to cut taxes	- Blair pledges tax cuts	- Anglo-German economic reform document		
9	- Kosovo/UN resolution - Aitken imprisonment	- Kosovo/UN resolution - Aitken imprisonment	- Kosovo/UN resolution - Aitken imprisonment	- Schröder–Blair meeting and document - Kosovo/UN resolution	- Aitken imprisonment - Kosovo - Portillo backs Hague over focus on pound in Euro-elections
10	- Kosovo agreement - England draw with Bulgaria - Rebranding of London MET - Voter apathy	- Kosovo agreement - Hague bid for Tory treasurer peerage blocked	- Kosovo agreement - 'Top Tories gun for Hague over euro' - Ffion Hague's pound-shaped diamond necklace - Aitken's forced house sale	- Kosovo - Procter & Gamble job cuts - OFT threat of legal action against airlines	- Kosovo agreement - Bloody Sunday Inquiry - 'Blair expects Labour losses' - Prince backs GM scientist
11	- British troops into Kosovo - Ashdown claims Blair a closet Liberal	- British troops into Kosovo - Interest rates at lowest level since 1977	- British troops into Kosovo - Michael Ashcroft - Low interest rates	- Interest rate cut in response to sterling's strength - Telecom mergers - Kosovo	- British troops into Kosovo - Bloody Sunday soldiers' anonymity
12	- Russians race into Kosovo	- Russians race into Kosovo	- Russians race into Kosovo - Manchester United victory - Dismal euro poll	- Russians race into Kosovo - Virus hits computers - Ferguson knighted	- Russians race into Kosovo
14	- NATO push across Kosovo - Labour inquest after election slump	- NATO push across Kosovo - Tories' big gains in euro election	- NATO push across Kosovo - Blair urged to bring back minister	- NATO push across Kosovo - Voter apathy across EU	- NATO push across Kosovo - Blair faces PR backlash after euro election flop

Table 5.2 continued

	Daily Mail	Express	Sun	Mirror
17 May	- Tom Parker-Bowles and cocaine (Charles lectures sons on drugs)	- Tom Parker-Bowles and cocaine - Manchester United win Premiership	- Manchester United win Premiership - Charles rants at Tom Parker-Bowles	- Tom Parker-Bowles and cocaine
18	- New drug for breast cancer prevention - Dewar announces Scottish Cabinet	- Nurses threaten strike action over New Year period - Arrest of Roy Keane	- Mel B's marriage problems - Arrest of Roy Keane	- Exposé on rape trial DJ, Richard Baker
19	- Jack Straw's intention to restrict trial by jury - Alleged collapse Mick Jagger's marriage	- Series of 'exposures' of MEPs alleged malpractices; Glyn Ford	- Eton pupil takes drugs - Mick Jagger's new son	- Arrest of Roy Keane
20	- Desertion Serb soldiers	- Fraud story: 'sack the fiddling MEPs'	- Anthea Turner and her lover's wife	- The *Mirror*'s 'Pride of Britain' awards
21	- Conviction serial rapist and former DJ - Labour backbench revolt on welfare reform	- Conviction serial rapist and former DJ	- Feature on serial rapist and former DJ	- The *Mirror*'s 'Pride of Britain' awards ceremony
22	- Jill Dando's funeral - Kosovo	- Jill Dando's funeral - Kosovo	- Jill Dando's funeral	- Jill Dando's funeral
24	- New mobile phone fears - Dallaglio	- Smuggled pets	- Lenny Henry adultery	- Dallaglio - Princes Charles and Harry
25	- Dallaglio	- Dallaglio - NHS waiting lists	- Botham's 'secret lover'	- Alleged link between nail bomb suspect and the BNP - Lenny Henry marriage problems - Dallaglio
26	- Pictures of Sophie Rhys-Jones	- Suicide of bullied girl	- Topless photos of Sophie Rhys-Jones	- Sophie Rhys-Jones - Lenny Henry
27	- Sophie Rhys-Jones - Manchester United	- Sophie Rhys-Jones - Manchester United	- Manchester United win European Cup and the treble	- Manchester United win European cup - Sophie Rhys-Jones

Date					
28	- Manchester United - Bloody Sunday inquiry - Sophie Rhys-Jones	- Manchester United - Bloody Sunday Inquiry	- Manchester United	- Manchester United	- Manchester United
29	- Manchester United - Bloody Sunday Inquiry	- Serial paedophile's life sentence	- Manchester United	- Manchester United - Kosovo - Sophie Rhys-Jones	- Jill Dando murder
31	- 'Divorce reforms not working'	- Britain out of Cricket World Cup - Report says Britain spends least on school books	- Manchester United	- 'Harrods slur on East End bride'	- James Major–Emma Noble wedding
1 June	- Prince of Wales anti GM speech - 'Jetski trial Briton' - GM food and Prince of Wales - Sophie Rhys-Jones	- Threat of antibiotic resistant superbug - Low calf prices		- 14-year-old girl abducted	- Jonathan Ross marriage split
2				- Villeneuve's fiancée - 'Ciggies make blokes floppy in bed'	- Jonathan Ross' marriage - Camelot
3	- Blair blast at grammar schools	- GM food and Prince of Wales		- Gazza holiday trip	- Rhys-Jones/*Sun* apology. Chris Tarrant refuses to advertise in the *Sun*
4	- Kosovo Peace Deal - Bloody Sunday Inquiry	- Kosovo Peace Deal - Kosovo/Milosevic		- Kosovo Peace Deal - Jill Dando - Mark Bosnich - Kosovo	- Kosovo - Mark Bosnich
5					- Kosovo
7	- Kosovo	- Kosovo		- Pregnant Patsy Kensit - Nurses win Lotto - Brooklyn Spice	- 'Jetski Mum's joy as she is cleared'
8	- Austrian whitewater rafting accident - Brooklyn Spice	- Austrian whitewater rafting accident			- G8/ Kosovo
9	- Aitken imprisonment	- Aitken imprisonment		- Aitken imprisonment - Whitewater rafting accident	- Aitken imprisonment
10	- Bloody Sunday Inquiry	- Ben Jones deportation case		- Kosovo agreement - '10 wacky things to do with ballot paper' - *Vanessa* show axed	- Kosovo
11	- British troops into Kosovo - Lone mothers hostel plan - NATO push across Kosovo	- British troops into Kosovo - Russians race into Kosovo - NATO push across Kosovo - Driving ban on absent fathers		- Tony Adams' MBE - Russians race into Kosovo - Kosovo - Tory success in Euro elections	- Kosovo
12					- Russians race into Kosovo
14					- Kosovo

Table 5.2 continued

	Observer	Independent on Sunday	Sunday Times	Sunday Telegraph
23 May	- Manchester United Double - Kosovo - Drugs in Britain	- Manchester United Double - GM foods - TV licence for elderly - Kosovo	- Manchester United Double - Kosovo - Royal Family	- Kosovo - New Poet Laureate
30 May	- 'Labour chase late winner with Ferguson'	- 'Snooker beats ban on tobacco sponsorship'	- NHS doctors - Kosovo	- Mandela and Gaddafi - Kosovo - Major–Noble wedding
6 June	- Serbs burning evidence - England in goalless draw against Sweden	- Humiliation of the Serbs - Cherie Blair against GM foods (says Prince) - Animal lobby gives £50,000 to Greens	- British commander to take Serb surrender - BA ditches ethnic tailfin decorations - Mandela to lead South Africa's World Cup bid	- NATO peace plan - Passport delays

	Mail on Sunday	Sunday Express	News of the World	Sunday Mirror
30 May	- Raped heiress	- Labour asks Manchester United Manager for support in Euro-election campaign - Kosovo	- Giggsy in punch-up at Euro Bash	- Jill Dando case
6 June	- 'Minister took top nightclub favour' - Hague and the euro - Tebbit article on support for Hague - Stewart Steven article on obligation to vote	- Kosovo	- Prince Charles bans Tara Palmer-Tomkinson - Low voter turnout expected - Hague article on 'saving the pound' - Prescott article on 'taking a lead in Europe' - Kosovo - Ron Davies MP 'A public menace'	- Sophie Rhys-Jones
13 June	- Dallaglio - Sophie Rhys-Jones–Prince Edward wedding	- Kosovo		- Kosovo

was a far cry from the media's behaviour in a typical election campaign, where electoral coverage would be *de rigeur*, and teams of journalists assigned to the campaign would seek out 'original angles'. Whatever the reasons, from the very beginnings of the campaign, the Euro-elections simply failed to make the headlines.

The single currency and GM foods

A fifth trend related to the two exceptions to the above observation about the absence of policy differences. First, one theme, despite new Labour's wishes, rose inexorably to the fore: the euro. It did so primarily because of Mr Hague's decision to stress the issue, in an attempt to mobilise the Conservatives' core pro-sterling vote. The tactics were helped by the euro's steady decline throughout the campaign, but could not have worked if Mr Hague's emphasis had not been taken up by the Euro-sceptical press, particularly *The Times*, the *Daily Telegraph*, the *Daily Express*, the *Daily Mail* and the *Sun*. As the campaign progressed, these papers repeatedly reported on 'shifts' in the government's and the Prime Minister's stance although, on any objective reading, the government's official pronouncements remained the same throughout the campaign. A vivid early example of this was provided by the *Daily Mail*'s reportage of an interview Margaret Beckett gave to BBC 1's *On the Record* programme (May 24). Mrs Beckett repeated the government's standard position that the economic conditions had to be right for sterling to join the single currency, adding that it was too soon to say when that might be. The *Daily Mail*'s headline the next day was 'LABOUR'S DATE WITH THE EURO NINE YEARS AWAY'.

As Chapters 7 and 8 discuss, these tactics would have been far less effective if the Government and/or the pro-euro movement had actively countered them. Moreover, even among the less Euro-sceptical media there was a sense that the parties' positions on the single currency were, if not the defining issue, certainly the major story of the campaign, and one which had wide-ranging repercussions, domestic and European.

The second exception was the GM foods issue, the dark horse of the 1999 Euro-election campaign. The story of how GM foods would be regulated, and particularly the issue of experimental GM plantations in the UK, seemed unconnected to the Euro-election campaign. The government's position, muscularly espoused by the Prime Minister, was widely portrayed as being pro-GM (and hence pro-industry and pro-US). The national media reported on the story, but not as a campaign issue. However, at the sub-national level, the Greens were able to plug into public apprehension, particularly in those regions where they already enjoyed strong support.

The campaign unfolds

The Labour Party

Until the 27 May *Times*/MORI poll, with its lesson of differential turnout, it was generally believed at Labour headquarters that the party would do much better than governing parties normally did in mid-term elections. The Prime Minister continued to ride extraordinarily high in the popularity ratings and the party's understandable strategy was to plug into this, with the general campaign slogan of '*Leadership in Europe*' and the stress in party election broadcasts (PEBs) on what the government had achieved in Europe and domestically. Millbank recognised that there would be losses, but it was felt these could be partly explained by the change of electoral system. The government was further comforted by an LSE/Adamson Associates forecast (Hix, 1999) of the election results which predicted that Labour would poll well in the UK and that the left would maintain its overall majority within the European Parliament.

At the same time, the shock results of the 6 May elections had left the Labour Party in a protracted period of introspection. There was reported to be much resentment among activists at Millbank's heavy-handedness in imposing candidates. A 25 May NEC decision to review the party's structure to take account of the Scottish Parliament and Welsh Assembly was headlined in the *Independent* as 'MILLBANK TO RELAX "CONTROL FREAK" POLICY', while the *Guardian* reported that Millbank intended to adopt a far more relaxed attitude towards the forthcoming NEC elections. The issue of 'control-freakery' and New Labour's concomitant pursuit of Middle England was a constant sub-theme to the campaign, culminating in a 7 June Peter Hain interview in the *New Statesman* in which the junior minister controversially argued:

> If our traditional supporters feel neglected by the time of the general election they could stay at home again ... I have become convinced we have a big problem with our core vote. At the elections last month they felt ignored as if we, as a government, are not for them. There are real dangers in this relentless pursuit of the *Daily Mail* Middle England voter.

Mr Hain went on to point out that the most alarming features of the 6 May elections were the very low turnout and the lack of activity on the ground: 'There's more to government than dominating the news agenda. We need to mobilise our activists to campaign enthusiastically.' Although Mr Hain became the focus of much criticism from Blairite loyalists, the state of health of Labour's core vote and the Labour heartlands was to become the *leitmotif* of Labour's electoral post-mortem (Chapter 8).

Over and above Mr Blair's absence and the unexpected success of Mr Hague's tactics, Labour's unfolding campaign left a mixed impression. Some genuine campaign innovations suggested that the party was initially well-prepared. At the innovatory level, Millbank made much of its planned 'cold-call' telephone campaigning to traditional Labour supporters, who would each receive a pre-recorded 'personal message' from Tony Blair. But data protection legislation obliged callers first to signal their agreement to receiving Mr Blair's message, and much of the spontaneity was thus removed. When Peter Riddell argued in the *The Times* that Labour had not done enough, Margaret Beckett fired off an angry letter pointing to about '20 ministerial campaigning visits ... and a record 64 million leaflets' (9 June). But while there *was* considerable ministerial involvement, a lot of it went unremarked by the national media and, through a mixture of inefficiency and indifference, many of the leaflets were not delivered.

As Mr Hague's bandwagon gathered momentum, there were increasingly heavy hints from Labour ministers, MPs and, more critically, from Euro-candidates, that Millbank had fielded 'the B team'. In impressionistic terms, there certainly seemed to be an absence of the slick professionalism so obvious in 1997. More profoundly, Labour seemed locked into a pre-determined and inflexible electoral strategy. As Anne McElvoy wrote in the *Independent* (9 June), 'New Labour has got hold of "Hague the loser/Blair the winner" as the central paradigm of British politics.' In view of the Tories' gains on 6 May and the growing success of Mr Hague's anti-euro tactics, this seemed increasingly inappropriate. Similarly, Labour's last campaign poster, unveiled on 9 June, read: 'Speaking with one voice on Europe.' This had clearly been predicated on the assumption of Tory divisions and a fragmented message but, in reality, the Tories were united on a strong and undivided message. Another example was the party's slogan not to 'let the Tories back in'. An 8 June *Independent* article reported that Labour's focus groups had suggested that the warning cut little ice with voters: 'people do not regard the Tories as a threat', said one report. Yet Labour maintained the slogan until the end.

The Prime Minister's role

Whenever Mr Blair intervened in the campaign he generated headlines and was effective in countering the Conservatives' political arguments. The threefold problem was that Mr Blair intervened infrequently, was inevitably quizzed most about Kosovo and, when he spoke about the single currency, seemed reactive rather than proactive. The Prime Minister revealed impatience and exasperation with regard to these phenomena.

At the party's last national press conference (9 June), Mr Blair explained how it was difficult to get a debate on the Euro-elections going: 'I can't not reply if people ask me – as they do all the time – about Kosovo.' The Prime Minister seemed particularly exasperated about the persistent press quizzing on the single currency and the subsequent spin put on his remarks. When, again at the party's last national press conference, Mr Blair agreed that, 'There *is* a vote in anti-Europeanism and a section of the press will support it,' many of the next day's headlines were of the 'BLAIR ADMITS DEFEAT' variety. When he recognised that a majority would vote against a single currency if a referendum were to be held the next day, he seemed surprised that, again, journalists saw this as an acknowledgement of defeat, rather than a simple recognition of fact. When he was accused of avoiding the euro issue, the Prime Minister pointed out that he *had* delivered speeches on the theme (notably in Swansea on 1 June), but that these had gone largely unreported.

Nevertheless, there was a generalised impression that the Prime Minister was absent – from the country and from the campaign. When, for example, Mr Blair attended a 27 May Paris rally of socialist and social democrat parties, his speech was dominated by Kosovo and stressed NATO unity (*Financial Times*, 28 May), and the *Guardian* reported that a similar rally planned for Britain was 'dropped because Mr Blair did not want to be seen endorsing a radical European programme'. Indeed, he was present at a 4 June PvdA rally in Rotterdam, where he urged voters to turn out – 'If you believe in Europe as a way of getting things right then you should turn out and vote.' But he did not attend any similar rally in the UK. On the other hand, Mr Blair was much in evidence at the 3–4 June Cologne summit of European leaders, where he championed the euro's cause. The impression of absence was so strong that the *Daily Express* could headline a 10 June story: 'LABOUR GET READY FOR A BEATING AND STILL BLAIR STAYS AWAY'.

Mr Blair also seemed increasingly tired. At the 9 June Prime Minister's Questions in the House of Commons, Mr Hague pursued the Prime Minister doggedly over the government's position on the euro.

Commentators reckoned Mr Blair had had an 'off day', resorting to generally critical comment about the Tory position rather than advancing any strong argument. Writing in the *Daily Telegraph*, Quentin Letts described how 'The conquering hero had a grotty afternoon, his worst in the chamber for several months', giving the impression that 'When you have elevated yourself to global statesman, domestic politics can be a frightful bore.'

In one sense the Prime Minister was very much present, namely by means of an unprecedented level of journalistic output which reached a new pitch in the last week of the campaign. Mr Blair, the *Independent* reported, had written for every national newspaper since he came to power – roughly 166 articles, compared to 46 by Mr Hague and 33 by Mr Ashdown. There was heavy emphasis on the tabloids (30 pieces for the *Sun*). The 'key to the Government's communication strategy is the targeting of different readers', and there was also a deliberate attempt to go 'over the heads' of the political journalists directly to the people. Thus, on 9 June, Mr Blair wrote an article in the *Sun*, almost alongside a critical editorial about him, stating: 'YOUR VOTE TOMORROW IS VITAL FOR OUR FUTURE' (Mr Hague had written the previous day in the same paper: 'YOUR CHANCE TO CAST A VOTE FOR FREEDOM'). But sometimes the Prime Minister's press policy seemed on auto-pilot. For example, on 14 June, the day the Euro-election results broke, the *Daily Mail* carried an 'exclusive' article by Tony Blair on 'WHY WE SHOULD STOP GIVING TEENAGE MOTHERS COUNCIL HOMES'.

The more Euro-enthusiastic parts of the press were clearly disappointed. Writing in *The Times* (7 June), Peter Riddell argued that: 'There has been no real attempt to follow up Mr Blair's pledge in Aachen last month to end 50 years of half-heartedness and ambivalence in Britain's relations with Europe.' He further argued that Labour had signally failed to exploit the deep flaws in Mr Hague's position on the euro and on a 'mix and match' Europe.

John Prescott

The Deputy Prime Minister was locked into two major campaign tours, the first a train journey and the second a 2,000-mile, three-day cross-country drive on the eve of the poll. Grateful activists and candidates acknowledged that Mr Prescott had had some impact but he must have been disappointed with the level and nature of national coverage his tours received. For example, the *Independent* headlined a story covering the tour: 'SPIN DOCTORS SQUIRM AS PERKY PRESCOTT GOES ON A WALKABOUT' (8 June). In a whistlestop tour of a Reading branch of Sainsbury's, Mr Prescott asked a Labour-supporting teenager, 'What do you think of

Europe?' , then added: 'I know it's a loaded question but I'm praying you get it right!'

Gordon Brown

In the Prime Minister's absence, the government's biggest gun was undoubtedly the Chancellor of the Exchequer. Although he delivered several major speeches in the campaign period, Mr Brown avoided the single currency issue, even when, on 28 May, several papers ran major stories about a statement by Eddie George, Governor of the Bank of England, disclosing 'growing concerns' about the European single currency to the House of Commons Select Committee. Mr George agreed with MPs that it would be 'an act of faith' for sterling to join, and said 'the jury was still out' on how well EMU was working and whether it would suit Britain. The impression given throughout the campaign was that Mr Brown refused to be drawn on the single currency and preferred to concentrate on the government's domestic economic record. Some political commentators speculated that Mr Brown was keen to avoid the euro-issue because he wished to fight the next General Election on the government's domestic economic record. On the other hand, in a 31 July *Spectator* article, 'the real reason why the Chancellor is less keen on the euro' was attributed, not to strategic calculations about the best way to win the next General Election, but to the fact that Mr Brown had gone 'Treasury native', and that the Treasury was naturally Euro-sceptic.

Nevertheless, Mr Brown took the fight to the Conservatives in two important ways. The first was to lead Labour's charge that the Conservatives had been toying with the possibility of an alliance with the Italian neo-fascist *Alleanza Nazionale* (see below) – Labour's only clear 'hit' during the campaign. The second was a 7 June article in the *Daily Telegraph*: 'TO BE A CONSERVATIVE YOU NEED TO BE ANTI-EUROPEAN'. Mr Brown took up the Prime Minister's argument that the logic of Mr Hague's position would lead inexorably to withdrawal from the EU: 'Perhaps it is true that once in every generation the case for Europe has to be restated. Certainly the last few days of the European elections campaign must see all pro-Europeans put the case for Europe. Britain is in Europe – and in Europe to stay.'

The Blair–Schröder initiative

On 8 June Mr Blair hosted the German Chancellor, Gerhard Schröder, at a Downing Street summit. Afterwards, at a Millbank press conference, the two men unveiled an Anglo-German policy document, *The way forward for Europe's Social Democrats*. The document, which had been jointly drafted by Peter Mandelson and Bodo Hombach, was flagged up as the 'ANGLO-GERMAN BLUEPRINT FOR THIRD WAY' (*The Times*, 8 June). Political commentators noted the document's hardline language on public expenditure, but seemed bemused by its sudden appearance at the very end of the campaign. It reportedly prompted a hostile reaction among many party activists and Labour's Continental confrères (see pp. 195–6).

The Conservative Party

As Matthew d'Ancona pointed out in the *Sunday Telegraph* (30 May), by concentrating on a single issue, Mr Hague had learnt from the Greens in 1989. As the campaign progressed, and as Mr Hague was further encouraged by the lack of substantial opposition, so his image was transformed from that of a weak leader and potential loser into that of a playmaker.

Hague transformed

As journalists scrabbled for potential stories, light was occasionally shone on the inner politics of the Conservative Party where there had been a growing expectation that Mr Hague's leadership would founder in May and sink in June. There were, for example, minor, but regular, reports about the 'hardening' language of the Shadow Chancellor, Francis Maude, with regard to the euro. Lobby journalists were convinced that Mr Maude was setting out his Euro-sceptical stall, in the expectation that a leadership crisis might result from a poor result. Whether true or not, the ironic consequence of Mr Maude's hardened vocabulary was to pull Mr Hague's language further towards the Maude position. Perhaps as a result of this, Mr Hague found himself unexpectedly reconciled with the 'dauphin' of the Euro-sceptic right, Michael Portillo. In a 7 June Birmingham rally, Mr Portillo provided the 'warm-up' act to Mr Hague's appearance. Cynics suspected Mr Portillo of being eager not to miss out on Mr Hague's success but, whatever interpretation was put on individual motivations, it was clear that Mr Hague's choice of tactics was paying off.

As the campaign progressed, three stories rocked the Conservatives' campaign boat but, because of this transformation of perceptions, in each case Mr Hague was able either to shrug them off or to turn them to his advantage.

Tory defections

The first was a series of items about Tory 'defections', where Mr Hague and the Party Chairman, Michael Ancram, deftly exploited the situation to impose 'harsh' discipline underlining the party leader's authority. On

4 June the *Daily Telegraph* reported that Dr Adrian Rogers, founder of the Conservative Family Association, who had written to the paper encouraging people to vote UKIP, had received a letter from Mr Ancram which declared: 'you appear to have terminated your membership'. On 5 June the *Daily Telegraph* and *The Times* reported that the Tories were 'SET TO EXPEL EX-MP'. Tim Rathbone, a Conservative MP for 23 years, had written to the *Daily Telegraph* arguing that the real choice was between the Pro-Euro Conservatives and the UKIP.

On 8 June, on BBC Radio 4's *Today* programme, Sir Julian Critchley advised Conservatives to vote for the Pro-Euro Conservatives. *The Times* of the same day carried a letter signed by Sir Julian and a mixture of former Conservative MPs and MEPs (Margaret Daly, Adam Fergusson, Robert Hicks, David Knox, Nicholas Scott, Madron Seligman and Anthony Simpson) expressing concern at 'the present tendency of Conservative policy towards Europe' as set out in Mr Hague's Budapest speech: 'We would have wished that William Hague's party had put forward a manifesto more like that of the Pro-Euro Conservative Party. Like many Conservatives, we shall find it very difficult to know how best to cast our vote on June 10.' In addition to the signatories to the letter, Lord Gilmour informed *The Times* that he would vote for the Pro-Euro Conservatives. Nicholas Scott later 'clarified' his argument by saying that he would be voting Conservative, but some of the other signatories of the letter and Lord Gilmour were informed that they were deemed to have terminated their membership of the party.[1]

When, on 10 June, Lady Nicholson, Hugh Dykes, James Moorhouse and Peter Price (all ex-Conservative MPs or MEPs) urged a vote for the Liberal Democrats, Smith Square simply ignored them. Had Mr Hague's perceived position been as weak as it had been before the 6 May elections, any one of these stories would have been portrayed as injuring his chances of remaining Leader. But because Mr Hague's Euro-sceptical tactics were paying off, he was able to assert his leadership by disciplining and even expelling those guilty of 'infractions' against the party's constitution.

Continental links

The issue of the Conservative Party's links to Continental parties was one of the areas where Labour scored a 'hit' during the campaign. In fact, there were three facets to the issue. The first concerned the Party's previous relationship with the Christian Democratic grouping within the European Parliament, the Group of the European Peoples' Party (EPP).

Would this be continued, given the EPP Group's basically federalist stance and enthusiastic support for the single currency? Mr Blair wrote a letter to Mr Hague over the 30–31 May Bank Holiday weekend demanding to know whether Mr Hague was fully signed up to the EPP manifesto. Mr Hague was able truthfully to counter, as his predecessor had done in 1994, that the Conservatives were not signed up to the EPP manifesto.

The second facet concerned the potential for splits within the group of Conservative MEPs, given the extremely Euro-sceptical stance of some and the extremely Euro-enthusiastic stance of others. On 1 June the *Independent* reported that 'a group of hard-line Thatcherite anti-euro Conservatives', allegedly led by Daniel Hannan, were plotting to form a breakaway group. Mr Hague and Mr McMillan-Scott killed the story by insisting at national press conferences that there was no such plot and that the alleged perpetrators had themselves denied the allegations.

The third aspect concerned alleged 'SECRET ALLIANCE TALKS WITH NEO-FASCISTS' (*Independent*, 7 June). Mr Brown pressed Labour's accusations hard, and press analyses showed that there clearly *had* been talks between *some* Conservative MPs (though nobody in authority) and some representatives of the Italian *Alleanza Nazionale* (see, for example, *Financial Times*, 8 June). There was also some confusion in the Conservative line. Mr McMillan-Scott said: 'This is a neo-fascist party. There is no question of any link with them. We are intending to rejoin the European People's Party.' But although at the national press conferences he denied any links with neo-fascists, a canny Mr Hague refused to confirm a simple renewal of the party's links with the EPP Group.

Michael Ashcroft

On 5 June the press began to publish articles about the Conservative Party's Treasurer, Michael Ashcroft. It was alleged that Mr Ashcroft was effectively bankrolling the party and that, among other things, he was forcing Mr Hague into a Euro-sceptic line. As media interest grew over the next few days, it became plain that Mr Ashcroft was a colourful and potentially controversial figure but, far from disowning him, Mr Hague stood by him, arguing that he had created a far broader basis to the party's finances, as a forthcoming report would show.

Changing perceptions

Even Mr Hague's 'bad' stories turned into good ones. For example, Mr Blair's decision to nominate Chris Patten as the UK's second European Commissioner (thereby delivering a snub to Mr Hague who had nominated Sir Alistair Goodlad), was presented, critically, as another example of the Prime Minister's cynical 'OPERATION HOOVER' (*Daily Express*, 26 May) on the one hand, and as a removal of a potent threat to Mr Hague's leadership (*Independent*, 26 May) on the other. When, on 5 June, *The Times* published a rumour (unfounded, apparently) that Michael Portillo might become the next Secretary-General of NATO, Mr Hague must have looked up to the stars in gratitude.

Wherever he could, Mr Hague tolled the Euro-sceptical bell and stressed Atlantic cooperation. For example, on 4 June, in a Glasgow speech to the British Chamber of Commerce, he floated the idea of British membership of NAFTA as a first step towards global free trade. Hence, despite the apparent strains highlighted by the media, Smith Square remained quietly confident that the Conservative Party remained the only reasonable repositary for the Euro-sceptic vote.

The Liberal Democrats

In 1994, the death of John Smith turned the Euro-elections into a phoney leadership campaign for the Labour Party, with the 'Blair phenomenon' becoming ever more apparent. In 1999, Paddy Ashdown's announcement that he would be stepping down from the leadership after the Euro-elections had a similar effect for the Liberal Democrats, despite an identical ban on leadership campaigning until after the Euro-poll. There was one immediate front-runner, Charles Kennedy, and a growing subtext about the future of the Liberal Democrats' cooperation with the Labour government. After all, PR for the European elections had been one of the first tangible fruits of the cooperation Mr Ashdown had championed.

Phoney leadership campaign

Early reporting indicated that the press was relishing a phoney leadership campaign, primarily because of the implications it would have for the Blairite 'project'. But then, on 27 May, the much-respected Menzies Campbell announced that he would not be standing. He had been regarded as the likeliest contender to run Mr Kennedy close. His move left Don Foster as the most prominent likely candidate to stand on a ticket of maintaining Mr Ashdown's close links with Labour. But Mr Foster's potential candidature failed to fizz, leaving Mr Kennedy to play a balancing act between 'traditional' and 'modernist' party members and to develop a confidently patrician stance.

The leadership race seemed a foregone conclusion before it had even started. However, as the Euro-campaign progressed, an increasing number of Liberal Democrat politicians intimated that they would be throwing their hats into the ring and began to jockey for position. This led a 2 June *Independent* editorial to describe the Euro-campaign as 'A RACE TO STOP THE LIB DEMS FROM LOOKING VERY SILLY', and when seven candidates declared themselves on 11 June, *The Times*' cartoonist swiftly obliged with an image of Paddy Ashdown and the seven dwarfs (see p. 64).

The reverse of this coin was the pre-eminence of Mr Ashdown. Even if there had not been a Kosovo crisis on which he could expertly pronounce, he was always likely to take the lion's share of the Liberal Democrats' media coverage. This was his swansong. On 29 May, for example, the newspapers reported on how Mr Ashdown had lived up to his action-man image by diving into a canal to save a drunk who had apparently been seeking his autograph. The Liberal Democrats' second party political broadcast (PPB) broadcast on 3 June was immediately dubbed 'Paddy, the movie' (an echo of Hugh Hudson's epic 1987 PPB of Neil Kinnock).

But there was a dangerous edge to this attention. Mr Ashdown was standing down, so voters could not vote 'for' him, but virtually all of his successors were obscure. Moreover, as pointed out above, the Liberal Democrats' campaigning message on domestic political issues was swamped by Kosovo. The combination left the traditional Liberal Democrat vote dangerously vulnerable to alternative repositories for the 'protest vote' – most notably the Greens and the UKIP.

Other parties

The United Kingdom Independence Party

With the exception of Dr Alan Sked's pronouncements (below) and a few isolated articles about candidates, the UKIP received virtually no national media coverage. It is a moot point as to whether Mr Hague stole the UKIP's thunder or whether the UKIP was able to free ride on the back of the wave of Euro-scepticism Mr Hague created. On 5 June, *The Times* broke a story about how UKIP leader Michael Holmes had rebuked Nigel Farage, the party's president and the man with the best chance of winning a seat, for being photographed with the BNP's head of research. Mr Farage argued that he had been 'stitched up', but party founder Dr Alan Sked, who quit after clashes with Mr Holmes and Mr Farage, argued: 'There should be a full-scale investigation into UKIP – because it is not the party I founded. Many of us who left did so because we feared it was infiltrated by the far right ... The fact that BNP praises UKIP is a real worry.' The controversy soon subsided and apparently did UKIP little damage.

The Pro-Euro Conservatives

The Pro-Euro Conservatives, on the other hand, received more coverage – though much of it was critical. The general feeling among commentators was that the party blew any chance it had left through its broadcast, shown in England on 24 May. The party's leader, John Stevens, argued that in portraying a Mr Hague lookalike as a tramp, the party had been addressing in a brutal way the basic issue that 'we have to be part of the real world which is interdependent and that the price of denying that could be a heavy one … We are saying that the attitudes that Mr Hague is enunciating are exactly the same as those of someone who has opted out of society' (*Independent*, 22 May). But critics argued that the broadcast and a leaflet showing Mr Hague as 'Bill Duce' sought to 'dumb down' the debate. The party also fell foul of the anti-euro press. An extraordinarily vituperative piece in the *Sun* (28 May) complained about 'the true contempt Euro-fanatics feel for the vast majority of their fellow citizens' and argued that they used 'Goebbels-like techniques'.

The Pro-Euro Conservatives' campaign was grievously weakened by their inability to win over the support of Mr Clarke or Mr Heseltine (see p. 190). A flurry of stories around 30 May described how Mr Clarke and Mr Heseltine had refused the party's advances. Thereafter, the Pro-Euro Conservatives' national campaign became invisible.

The Greens

Apart from brief reportage of the Green Party's 25 May campaign launch and some interest sparked off by the party's highly professional PEB, there was virtually no national coverage of the party's campaign. The party had deliberately chosen to target its strongest regions, and other parties' candidates began to report a steady groundswell of support in the south, yet the radar of the London-based media failed to pick this up.

The British National Party

The BNP generated some, almost entirely negative, coverage during the campaign. Ethnic groups and Operation Black Vote were worried that PR might give the BNP an electoral advantage, particularly on a low turnout, but the polls taken during the campaign showed this fear to be unfounded. (Although according to *Searchlight* in May 1999, 'the only reason the party is fighting this election is to reap the crop of potential new recruits from the television broadcast.') On 25 May, the *Daily Mirror* ran a whole front page on the links between the Soho nail bomber and the BNP. On 29 May, *The Times* reported in detail on the modernising strategy of Nick Griffin, a Cambridge graduate and Welsh borders farmer, who hoped to use the Euro-elections as a springboard to oust John Tyndall as leader of the British National Party. In the event, this courtroom revolution did not occur. Lastly, on 7 June, several papers ran stories alleging that the BNP had fielded 'false' candidates to qualify for its PEB.

The Socialist Labour Party

By fielding 84 candidates the Socialist Labour Party qualified for a PEB, broadcast on 28 May, but its best hopes lay in London, where its leader and highest-profile candidate, Arthur Scargill, was heading the list. The television news bulletins very briefly covered the party's 25 May launch, which was slightly disrupted by a group of protestors from the Communist Party of Great Britain. Thereafter, Mr Scargill and his party were absent from the national stage.

The 'gravy train'

Media coverage of the campaign was peppered with stories about 'GREED AND THE GRAVY TRAIN' (*Sunday Telegraph*, 23 May). For example, on 24 May a *Sun* editorial, 'EURO JACKPOT', argued that 'a ticket to Strasbourg is like getting all six numbers plus the bonus ball'. The next day the same paper ran a critical analysis of MEPs' salaries and allowances. Allegations about individual MEPs' supposed misdoings were later leavened with more general stories about fraud probes and alleged scams (for example, the *Daily Express*, BBC 2's *Newsnight*, 8 June). These stories came on the heels of the events of the Spring, which had culminated in the resignation of the Santer Commission, and many candidates felt that, in a campaign where it was anyway difficult to differentiate between the European institutions, this media coverage created the impression that the European Parliament was itself a tainted institution.

The 'alien' system

The 1999 Euro-elections represented the first occasion in which a nationwide electoral contest was fought in the UK on a PR basis. This triggered some interest about the possible psephological consequences, particularly for the smaller political parties (see, for example, the *Financial Times*, 25 May). Yet to a considerable extent the revolutionary effects of PR had already been experienced in the 6 May regional elections in Scotland and Wales where, coincidentally, the number of probable small party/independent beneficiaries was greatest. By 10 June the issue was not whether Plaid Cymru would win in the Labour strongholds of Islwyn and the Rhondda, for example, but whether Plaid could capitalise on the extraordinary gains it had already made. The sense of anticlimax was exacerbated by the emerging opinion polls, which showed the major political parties maintaining their stranglehold on a much-reduced turnout.

Conscious of its obligations in unprecedented electoral waters, the Home Office took out full-page advertisements in all of the daily newspapers, opened a website, and delivered information leaflets about the new system to all homes in the United Kingdom (see Chapter 2). (However, there is plenty of anecdotal evidence to suggest that deliveries of the leaflet in many areas were patchy at best.) The leaflet began with the basics, explaining first what the European Parliament was and what MEPs did. The voting system, and the method of voting, were briefly described. The general opinion among party activists was that the Home Office's efforts were necessary but insufficient. In particular, it was felt that the government should have done more to reassure voters about the new arrangements and counter the generalised prejudice against a system which removed the British voters' hallowed right to vote for a particular candidate, rather than for the preferred candidate of the party. Ironically, that prejudice was felt most strongly among Labour Party activists. As one put it: 'Why should I bust a gut to get somebody elected who has been imposed on me by party hacks in London through a system which nobody wanted?'

The Euro-sceptic and Conservative press pandered to the anti-PR prejudice. The *Daily Telegraph*, for example, declared that 'PR ROBS VOTERS OF RIGHT TO PICK THEIR LOCAL MEP' (2 June). On the same day, *The Times* pointed out that 'WHICHEVER WAY YOU VOTE, THIS WOMAN WILL WIN', because Pauline Green topped the London list. Indeed, London became the PR-sceptics' *bête noire*. In a 'disturbing dispatch from the front line', Anne Leslie wrote in the *Daily Mail* (10 June) about Pauline Green on the campaign trail under the headline: 'THIRD-RATERS, CLUB CLASS CORRUPTION AND A GRAND FROMAGE WHO JUST CAN'T LOSE'. The ballot paper was 'huge' (77.5 by 17.5 cm); there were no less than 18 lists/candidates; the unfortunate counters had to stand to unfold and count the papers. Everything about the system was, apparently, alien or impracticable. A Truro presiding officer wrote to *The Times* (29 May) to say he had received a 1.3 kg information pack. Every day the letters pages of the major dailies sported complaints about the system. (See pp. 229–31 and 251–3 for further discussion of the system.)

The anti-PR campaign culminated on polling day when, in inimitable *Sun* fashion, the tabloid ran a whole page, together with a model and the help of the British Origami Society, on '10 USES FOR A LOAD OF EURO BALLOTS'. In the face of such an onslaught, it was perhaps not surprising that the vast majority of electors did not consider it worth voting. As one candidate observed: 'After all that, it was a bit rich for the newspapers to turn around – as they all did – and tell people that they ought to turn out and vote.' On 14 June the *Daily Telegraph* argued: 'PR IS UNDEMOCRA-TIC' – 'How pathetic the voting system of the Euro-elections has turned out to be ... PR is unsuited to Britain. Visible proof of this could be found in London, where the traditional booths were too narrow for the new ballot papers ... PR is showing itself to be a malign influence on democracy ... .'

'I think it's the euro – but is it waving or drowning?'

Daily Mail (8 June) (Kenneth Mahood)

Introspection

As it became increasingly apparent that turnout was likely to be very low, the media began to engage in some introspection about British electoral habits. Thus, on 6 June, the *Mail on Sunday* argued that 'people have a moral, democratic obligation to turn out and vote on Thursday'. On 7 June a *New Statesman* editorial contrasted South Africa's General Election queues with the probable low turnout in the Euro-elections: 'Indications are that it will be lower than in 1994, since applications for postal and proxy votes are already known to be 20 per cent down.' Also, 'What, one wonders, would an international observer such as David Steel, currently in South Africa to ensure fair play, say in his election report if he heard that one area (in London, as it happens) has had printed only half as many ballot papers as it has voters on the electoral roll?'

As the elections approached, the broadsheets sought to explain the phenomenon. A 12 June *Guardian* editorial argued that 'New Labour's success in transforming itself into a party of national consensus has had the unhappy side effect of sucking all the energy out of British politics ... .' Contrarily, on 13 June the *Sunday Telegraph* highlighted the difference between a 'feel-good factor and a feel-nothing factor'; 'the truth is that this country, which led the world in the habit of lively political debate, is losing interest in its own institutions. This owes much to Labour's sidelining of Parliament ... .'

Campaign 'hits'

The 1999 Euro-campaign was largely devoid of policy issues, and there were only three discernible campaign 'hits': tax integration, the Conservative Party's links to Continental parties, and the euro.

Tax

The first of these was media-generated. On 24 May, on the eve of an ECOFIN (Economics and Finance) Council meeting in Brussels, the *Daily Mail* reported on a Dutch minister's website which seemed to give the impression that wholesale tax harmonisation was secretly on the EU's agenda. The *Sun* ran this story as an editorial about Britain's firms being 'hammered into recession just like those in Euroland,' whilst the *Independent* reported that Labour had been 'forced on to the defensive' after the Treasury was accused of 'preparing to harmonise nearly 200 different taxes across the EU'. The story was conflated into another, also related to the ECOFIN agenda, about Commission proposals for a tax on interest on savings which, the City of London argued, would destroy its competitive advantage. Perhaps inadvisedly, government spokesmen sought to kill the story by pointing out that taxation was an area where the national veto existed and could be used, if necessary.

In the 25 May ECOFIN Council meeting, Mr Brown negotiated an interim compromise involving the drafting of an exploratory paper. This was classic Council stuff, but it was portrayed in the press as a 'sell-out' and 'cave-in' by Gordon Brown in part because the spin-doctors had talked about threatening the use of 'the veto'.

The story, and the confused perceptions about what might have occurred, ran on for several more days. On 27 May, the *Independent* ran a three-column article on how 'BLAIR INSISTS HE WILL VETO SAVINGS TAX', but a Stephen Pollard column in the *Daily Express*, 'ON LABOUR'S EURO DOUBLE-SPEAK', argued: 'BROWN AND EU READY TO KILL OFF THE CITY'.

The tax issue was an early illustration of the way the government's fabled spin machine seemed not to have its eye entirely on the ball. On the one hand, the 25 May ECOFIN agenda was an obvious quarry for journalists in search of stories. On the other, the threatened use of the veto (when no veto would be necessary) was bound to be seen as either overkill or anti-climactic bravado.

The Conservative Party's links to the EPP Group and the *Alleanza Nazionale*

Labour's one clear hit of the campaign related to the Conservative Party's links to continental parties. In part, the issue was a hoary old chestnut of Euro-election campaigns. The Conservative Party did not belong to any of the major Continental European party political families. In 1979, when the first-past-the-post electoral system had distortedly swollen their numbers, Tory MEPs had managed to sit, virtually alone, as the third largest grouping within the European Parliament. Since then, as their numbers declined, they had had prag-matically to seek out an alliance within the European Parliament which would guarantee them the financial and other benefits of political group membership. The obvious choice was the broad Christian Democrat grouping, the Group of the European Peoples' Party (EPP), but there were some major ideological differences, particularly over the Social Chapter and the single currency. The Conservatives had therefore negotiated a longstanding arrangement whereby individual Conservative MEPs were 'allied' to the EPP Group but not bound by the manifesto commitments of the parallel EPP transnational party. Labour had sought to exploit the contradictions implicit in this alliance in 1994. In anticipation of similar attacks, Mr McMillan-Scott had sought out clear statements from the then EPP Group Chairman, Wilfried Martens, confirming the Conservatives' independence.

Nevertheless, over the Bank Holiday weekend of 29–31 May, Mr Blair sent Mr McMillan-Scott a letter pointing up contradictions between Mr Hague's line and that of the EPP. Smith Square was proud to have been immediately wise to the ruse, despite the holiday period, but was unable to prevent some air play on hard-up news programmes.

Potentially more damaging was a 7 June attack, led by Gordon Brown, on alleged links between the Conservatives and the Italian neo-fascists – an allegation for which there was some factual basis (see above). Mr McMillan-Scott sought to kill the story by simply pointing out the party's intention of maintaining its alliance with the EPP Group. Indeed, at the EPP's 2 June pre-Cologne summit meeting in Bonn, Mr Hague had reached agreement in principle with Wolfgang Schäuble on such a continued alliance. But Mr Hague doubtless sensed that this would give ammunition to his opponents, contradict his Euro-sceptic tactics and weaken his post-election negotiating position. He therefore refused to say more than that the party would review its position after the elections.

The euro

Chapter 7 offers a detailed analysis of this issue. Mr Hague's chosen tactics benefited from a combination of circumstances. Among the most important were the constant decline in value of the euro, a vociferously supportive stance by the Euro-sceptical press, and the absence of any concerted campaign in the single currency's favour. Moreover, as Mr Hague's campaign gathered momentum, his choice of tactics was consolidated and his authority reinforced.

Polls

Opinion polls played a small part in the Euro-elections but it was to some extent a misleading one. None of them put the Conservatives ahead. Polls had been used quite extensively in the Scottish and Welsh contests in May, but they were scarcely headlined after that. There were, for the first time, no publicised eve-of-poll surveys.[2] The routine nationwide polls on Westminster voting intentions by MORI, Gallup and ICM were reported but, because they showed no departure from the picture of the last two years – a 20 per cent Labour lead – they seemed only to confirm the impression that Labour would win.

Table 5.3 Poll findings 1997–99

'How would you vote if there was a General Election tomorrow?'
(Average of nationwide surveys) (%)

	Con	Lab	Lib Dem
Gen Election Vote	31	44	17
Jul–Dec 1997	26	57	13
Jan–Jun 1998	28	53	15
Jul–Dec 1998	28	53	15
Jan–Mar 1999	28	53	14
Apr 1999	27	54	14
May 1999	28	51	15
Jun 1999	27	50	16
Jul 1999	29	50	15

In so far as polls in the run-up to June 10 were helpful, they clearly indicated a low turnout. In May 1994, 36 per cent of the electorate told MORI that they were 'certain to vote' (35 per cent did so); in May 1999, only 30 per cent were 'certain to vote' (23 per cent did so). However, there was a heavy Labour majority in all surveys on Euro-voting intention and even after filtering out those who showed hesitancy about going to the polls, there was still a Labour majority among all those 'certain to vote'.

A MORI survey conducted on 27–28 May found this category divided Labour 45 per cent, Conservative 31 per cent, Liberal Democrat 15 per cent. An ICM poll conducted on 3–4 June found certain voters divided 38 per cent Labour to 31 per cent Conservative. A Gallup poll conducted 26 May–2 June found certain voters divided 41 per cent to 28 per cent, although all voters divided 52 per cent to 24 per cent.

Table 5.4 Opinion polls published during the Euro-elections campaign (%)

Poll	Published		Gen El. Voting Intention			Likely to Vote in Election		
			Con	Lab	Lib Dem	Con	Lab	Lib Dem
MORI	Times 27 May	27–28.05	28	52	14	31	45	15
ICM	Guardian 8 June	03–04.06	29	46	19	31	48	
Gallup	Telegraph 4 June	26.05– 02.06	24	52	16	28	41	

The parties did little private polling and the main lesson from their focus groups was of indifference or scepticism towards Europe and towards voting. However, the minor parties sponsored polls which certainly encouraged them. A private poll by MORI for John Stevens encouraged him to go ahead with a nationwide campaign by the Pro-Euro Conservative Party. Offered a choice between a Conservative Party led by Mr Hague and a pro-Euro alternative, the survey found 20 per cent who would vote for the former and 11 per cent for the latter. This was enough to convince Mr Stevens that his intervention could topple William Hague. It also encouraged the parties and the media to take his intervention more seriously than events ultimately justified.

The Greens sponsored a MORI poll in May 1999. Only 35 per cent were going to vote on 'the parties' policies on Europe', as against 41 per cent who were going to vote on 'the way the Government is running the country'. Only 11 per cent who were going to vote on policies on Europe mentioned agriculture/fishing/food safety and 9 per cent 'protecting the natural environment'.

The UK Independence Party also sponsored a MORI poll in May 1999. The party certainly found encouragement in the answers to a somewhat leading question: 'At the European Elections, the UK Independence party will be campaigning nation-wide for Britain to retain the pound for ever and to leave the European Union. Assuming the UK Independence Party is the only party campaigning for these policies, how would you vote?' Of the respondents, 25 per cent answered 'UKIP' and these included 30 per cent of normally Conservative voters and 18 per cent of normally Labour voters.

As Table 5.6 demonstrates, all polls were showing increasing hostility to any switch to a common currency.

Table 5.5 'If there were a referendum now on whether Britain should stay in or get out of the European Union, how would you vote? (%)

	1990	1992	May 96	Apr 97	Nov 97	Jun 98	Jun 99
Stay in	68	60	53	50	58	54	53
Get out	32	40	47	50	42	46	47

However, there was one question which gave more hope to those who favoured the euro. In a June MORI survey, only 23 per cent said they were unequivocally opposed to British involvement. A further 36 per cent said they were generally opposed but could be persuaded if they thought it would be good for the British economy. By 39 per cent to 34 per cent, respondents thought that the single currency would be a success in the eleven countries which had adopted it. Although the numbers opposed to the single currency went up in a succession of MORI polls for Salomon Smith Barney, among them the number who said they could be persuaded if the government strongly recommended entry also increased significantly.

Table 5.6 'If there were a referendum now on whether Britain should be part of a single European currency, how would you vote?'

	Nov 91	May 96	Apr 97	Nov 97	Jul 98	May 99	Jun 99
Yes	38	28	33	33	40	37	30
No	62	72	67	67	60	63	70

However, the main lesson of all the polls was of public indifference. Europe came well behind all sorts of domestic issues whenever people were asked what issues would matter to them in the next General Election; only 30 per cent mentioned Europe, compared to 61 per cent who mentioned the Health Service, 52 per cent education, 43 per cent 'law and order' and 41 per cent unemployment. It was notable that, among voters who thought Europe was important, 'Europe' was the only issue on which the Conservatives, by a significant margin, were considered to have the best policies.

Ever since the debâcle of 1992, the opinion pollsters have been wary about potential hidden trends. In the 1999 Euro-elections the unknown variable was the effect of turnout. Towards the end of the campaign the polls revealed a growing paradox; Mr Blair and the government remained very popular, but it seemed they would not benefit from this popularity in the Euro-elections. The reverse of this paradox became apparent after the Euro-elections; the Conservatives' 'success' in the elections had no impact on national voting intentions.

The media

After the elections, some party activists were critical of the way in which the media had failed to cover the elections, or failed to take them seriously, or created the impression of an alien system. But it is a moot point as to whether the lack of coverage was causal or a reflection of readers' attitudes. As Box 5.1 shows, most newspaper editorials urged their readers to turn out and vote. Of more potential significance was the pronounced Euro-sceptical stance of a large swathe of the tabloids and broadsheets, which played a large part in the success of Mr Hague's tactics.

The televisual media argued that, if anything, it had improved its coverage. The BBC, for example, was proud to announce more extensive and comprehensive coverage of the Euro-election than ever before, both in the United Kingdom and throughout Europe, culminating in a four-hour television special on BBC 2 on the evening of Sunday 13 June. BBC World, Radio 4 longwave and the World Service also offered frequent coverage, with four European correspondents reporting from Brussels and live reports from other European capitals. Sky television news bulletins similarly covered the campaign. The Euro-elections also received a great deal of coverage through the Internet. In addition to the European Parliament's own sites (both Brussels and the London Office), the BBC gave detailed, in-depth coverage through its site, BBC News Online, and a number of newspapers ran their own pages on the elections, from the *Financial Times* to the *Guardian* (which *inter alia* sported Pauline Green's regularly updated election diary).[3]

Box 5.1 A selection of newspaper and magazine editorials

Financial Times (25 May):	'THE PLACE FOR EU DEMOCRACY' – the EP matters.
The Times (26 May):	'SEND A MESSAGE – A VITAL EUROPEAN ELECTION AWAITS APATHETIC VOTERS' – bemoans apathetic voters, a strong Conservative vote may postpone Mr Blair's euro timetable.
European Voice (27 May):	'KEY TEST OF PARLIAMENT'S CREDIBILITY'
Sunday Times (30 May):	'HARSH EURO LESSONS' – the weakening euro.
Independent (31 May):	'NOW, FINALLY, THE EUROPEAN ELECTIONS ARE WORTH YOUR VOTE' – because of PR and the EP's increasing powers.
Guardian (31 May):	'DON'T YAWN FOR EUROPE – APATHY MUST NOT WIN THE ELECTIONS'
Daily Telegraph (2 June):	'EURO CHOICE IS OURS'
The Times (2 June):	'POUNDING LABOUR'
Independent (2 June):	'A RACE TO STOP THE LIB DEMS FROM LOOKING VERY SILLY'
Tribune (4 June):	'OVERWHELMED BY INDIFFERENCE'
Spectator (5 June):	'APATHY IS NOT ENOUGH' – Conservative voters should turn out and vote against federalism and the euro.
The Economist (5 June):	'THIS TIME IT MATTERS' – a strong Conservative vote would postpone Mr Blair's euro timetable.
The Times (7 June):	'VOTE ON THURSDAY – UNLESS YOU THINK THE EU NEEDS NO IMPROVEMENT'
Independent (7 June):	'MR HAGUE IS QUITE WRONG OVER EUROPE, BUT HE IS NOT DAFT' – 'At least vote on Thursday, whatever you do.'

Daily Telegraph (7 June):	'IN THE NATIONAL INTEREST' – 'A vote for the Tories ... is a vote ... for ... the national interest.'
New Statesman (7 June):	'GIVING UP OUR ELECTORAL ROLE' – shame of impending low turnout.
Financial Times (8 June):	'EURO-POLL' – the PM should take the argument to his opponents.
Sun (8 June):	'EUR BACKING A LOSER, TONY' – 'This week's European election is almost irrelevant.' Blair would lose a single currency referendum.
Sun (9 June):	'TIDE TURNS' – against the euro.
The Times (9 June:	'A SINGLE ISSUE – THE TORIES DESERVE BRITAIN'S BACKING TOMORROW' – a strong Tory vote would postpone Mr Blair's euro timetable.
Guardian (10 June):	'VOTE, IF YOU'RE STILL AWAKE' – political parties failed to engage.
Independent (10 June):	'MR BLAIR MUST TAKE ON THE CRITICS AND FIGHT FOR THE EURO'
The Times (10 June):	'THE REAL CHOICE – BLAIR'S SCARE TACTICS ON EUROPE MERIT A FIRM ELECTORAL REBUKE'
Daily Telegraph (10 June):	'VOTE TORY TODAY'
Daily Mail (10 June):	'A HISTORIC CHANCE TO SAVE THE POUND'
Sun (10 June):	'BLAIR KNOWS HE HAS LOST THE BATTLE'
Daily Express (10 June):	'MAKE YOUR VOTE COUNT' – 'Labour deserves our support ... but more important is the need to vote.'

Election broadcasts

There is no formal legal obligation for British television companies to carry any party political broadcast. But in the absence of paid political advertising in the country, there is a longstanding practice that the broadcasters make time available to political parties at election times so that they may address the electorate directly through the medium of television. The content is a matter for the parties, but PEBs have to conform to rules laid down by the broadcasters. They are quite explicit about observing the law on incitement to racial hatred and violence. In order to qualify for a broadcast, the broadcasters devise a threshold for parties to reach. The threshold for the European elections was the highest it was possible to set, in that parties had to field a full slate of candidates on every regional list. Across the UK as a whole, nine parties qualified for a broadcast. In addition to the three main parties, six other parties reached the threshold. They were: the Green Party, the Pro-Euro Conservative Party, the UKIP, the Natural Law Party, the Socialist Labour

Party and the British National Party. The inclusion of the BNP caused some controversy, though its PEB observed the broadcasters' strictures and was entirely about Europe.

The result, as Box 5.2 shows, was a plethora of party broadcasts. Overall, during the April–May–June period (local elections, National Assembly elections and European elections), the English viewer was treated to 21 PEBs (6 + 15), the Welsh viewer to 33 (16 + 17), and the Scottish viewer to no less than 37 (17 + 20).

The major parties employed notably different techniques in their PEBs. Labour stressed Mr Blair's leadership qualities. Its third broadcast sported a string of supportive 'luvvies', culminating with successful Manchester United football manager, Alex Ferguson. The Conservatives stuck mainly with their Chris and Debbie 'docu-dramas', but switched in their third broadcast to the slogan 'The Pound is only Safe with the Conservatives' in order to counter the UKIP's appeal. The Liberal Democrats switched from a mock news bulletin in their first broadcast to a more personal 'Paddy, the movie' style in their last. The Pro-Euro Conservatives

---

Box 5.2 Party political broadcasts during the Euro-elections campaign

Monday 17 May	Labour Party
Tuesday 18 May	Conservative Party
Wednesday 19 May	Liberal Democrat Party
Thursday 20 May	None
Friday 21 May	British National Party
Monday 24 May	Pro-Euro Conservative Party
Tuesday 25 May	Labour Party
Wednesday 26 May	Conservative Party
Thursday 27 May	Liberal Democrat Party
Friday 28 May	Socialist Labour Party
Monday 31 May	Natural Law Party
Tuesday 1 June	United Kingdom Independence Party
Wednesday 2 June	Green Party
Thursday 3 June	Liberal Democrat Party
Friday 4 June	None
Monday 7 June	Conservative Party
Tuesday 8 June	Labour Party
Wednesday 9 June	None
Thursday 10 June	Polling Day

Note: English schedule. Schedules in Scotland, Wales and Northern Ireland differed.

generated controversy with their depiction of a William Hague lookalike as a tramp. The UKIP portrayed European integration as a black-clad cat-burglar making off with the country's assets. The BNP showed its leader John Tyndall at the Cenotaph. Arthur Scargill's Socialist Labour Party broadcast sported (deliberately?) poor sound and grainy images. The Greens' zany high-tech broadcast was generally thought to have been the most effective.

The BNP received some adverse publicity as the campaign developed. Initially, they had nominated candidates in only three regions but when it became plain that broadcasts would only be allocated to parties fighting all of the 71 English seats, they quickly nominated a full slate. However, enterprising researchers found that several of their candidates had obsolete or bogus addresses. A Commons motion supported by Conservative and Labour MPs drew attention to the abuse and penalties were demanded. The Home Office promised to look into the matter in its post-election review.

Party expenditure

The expenditure of the parties, nationally and regionally, had to be reported to the Home Office by 23 August. Table 5.7 shows the overall totals.

Table 5.7 Total expenditure of parties

Party	Total
Conservative	£1,350,000
Labour	£1,201,000
Liberal Democrat	£1,061,000
UKIP	£358,000
Green	£215,000
Pro-Euro Conservative	£229,000
SNP	£100,000
PC	£66,000
SSP	£16,000
SLP	£16,000
Left Alliance	£10,000
Liberal	£10,000
Humanist	£6,000

For most parties, the outlay by region was fairly proportionate to the electorate. However, Labour spent an exceptionally high amount in Wales, while the Greens spent exceptionally little there.

This was the first occasion when the parties had been required to present detailed national accounts. The figures sent in to the Home Office were, indeed, detailed. Since all parties spent so much less than the permitted maximum there was no reason to inquire in detail about the accounting – but anyone looking at the very diverse accounting could see how, in a close-fought contest, the new procedures left unlimited possibilities for investigation and litigation. The Labour Party prudently included in its returns £20 for each of the 641 Westminster constituencies to cover accidentally unreported expenditures.

The great bulk of the money was spent on printing. It was interesting that the reports of spending on preparing election broadcasts varied from £4,000 for Labour's first broadcast to £65,000 for their third, and from £9,000 for the Greens to £50,000 for the Pro-Euro Conservatives.

All parties that had MEPs elected (that is, Conservative, Labour, Liberal Democrat, SNP, Plaid Cymru, the Greens and the UKIP) retained all of their deposits, with the exception of the UKIP, which lost its deposit in Scotland. The Greens only just retained their deposit in Wales, with 2.6 per cent of the vote. All minor parties that did not return any MEPs (except the Scottish Socialists), and all independents (except Christine Oddy, West Midlands) lost their deposits. The Alternative Labour List in the East Midlands (headed by Ken Coates) only just lost its deposit, polling 2.41 per cent. Thus, 65 party slates lost their deposits which, at £5,000 per deposit, meant that a total of £325,000 in lost deposits was retained by the Treasury.[4]

Conclusion

On the eve of polling there were few signs that an electoral contest was under way. There were no stickers in windows and, indeed, the only public sign the authors noticed all day in Central London was the white van of the European Parliament's London Office in Queen Anne's Gate, which had the date of the elections printed on its sides. An indication of the relaxed campaign was the sight of a senior party official strolling back to Central Office from a leisurely breakfast at 9.30, dabbing his lips with a handkerchief. This was such a far cry, even from 1994, when all hands would have been on deck from 'eight until late'.

'POLL? WHAT POLL?' asked the *Independent*'s front page the next day; it was 'A BIG VOTE FOR APATHY'. A woeful Hugo Young wrote in the *Guardian* about a 'DISMAL CAMPAIGN, DERISORY TURNOUT: EUROPE AS USUAL'. A *Times* editorial described an 'ELECTION WITHOUT VOTERS' (12 June), a case of 'SORRY, CAN'T BE BOTHERED; 'Europe's a bore; so is Leeds Central', it concluded. Writing in the *Mail on Sunday*, Richard Heller described: 'A LANDSLIDE FOR APATHY – BUT WHO CARES?' As Jeremy Paxman put it on BBC's *Newsnight*, the country had been 'seriously underwhelmed'. There was a little consolation in the fact that the UK was not alone. There had, reported the *Independent*, been a 'SWING TO APATHY IN EVERY PART OF EUROPE' (14 June). 'TURNOUT', opined the *Daily Telegraph*, 'REFLECTS EU'S DEMOCRATIC DEFICIT' (14 June).

Notes

1. No such fate befell former party chairman Lord (Norman) Tebbit who wrote in the *Mail on Sunday* (6 June): 'William Hague deserves support for returning the Tories to Euroscepticism. But Labour voters who want Britain to remain self governing can send a clear message to Mr Blair by voting UKIP.'
2. The BBC sponsored an ICM poll on 10 June but prudently refrained from using its figures before or during its 13 June election coverage. The findings, though less misleading than other surveys, would still have put Labour ahead.
3. However, as one (successful) candidate pointed out, 'These were not the media most people read or watch. The World Service and Radio 4 longwave are largely for overseas listeners, BBC World has a fairly small number of viewers in the UK and, as for web-sites, you have to be interested enough to go looking!'
4. *The European Parliamentary Elections Act* provided 2.5 per cent as the threshold for retaining the £5,000 deposit required in each region.

6
Candidates' Views and Activities and the Campaign in the Regions

Candidates' views and activities
Chris Ballinger

The 1999 European Election campaign failed equally to capture the attention of national politicians or the electorate. The euro was far and away the most salient issue amongst those who interested themselves in the election, but many more people, including the Prime Minister, were preoccupied with the war in Kosovo, or with other issues, such as genetically modified organisms, which they did not link to the European Parliament or the June election. Where voters did raise European issues during the campaign, they were generally negative towards the EU: wanting the UK to retreat from involvement in Europe, or complaining about scandals in the European Commission and about 'gravy-train politics'.

Uniquely in the history of twentieth-century elections in Britain, the electoral system was a significant concern for voters throughout the political spectrum. For the first and, if many candidates and voters have their way, the last time, the elections in Britain were fought under a system of closed regional party lists of candidates, rather than the system of single-member constituencies that had operated since 1979. The closed list electoral system impacted upon nearly every aspect of the struggle, except perhaps the parties' national campaigns. To gain an impression of candidates' experiences during the campaign and their opinions of it, we contacted all those candidates who were elected and a number of others who were not elected, and received a high response. The following pages are based largely on what the candidates told us.

Most candidates were not surprised, although many were disappointed, by the low level of turnout. Reasons cited for this included the near absence of positive reporting of the European Parliament and the activities of its members, dislike of the voting system, and the lack of vigour in the national campaign.

The media reporting of the campaign was universally criticised for its negativity. For example, candidates referred to the coverage, in particular coverage by national newspapers, as 'dreadful', 'awful', or 'what media coverage?'. However, several MEPs acknowledged that any change in the public perception of European issues could be achieved only over the five-year lifetime of a Parliament, and not across a five-week election campaign.

A large number of candidates cited the voting system as a reason for the unusually low turnout because of its alleged difficulty and because of a dislike of voting for a list. The media had created the impression in some voters' minds that voting under the closed list proportional representation system would be complex; yet, while there was evidence of some confusion among voters, especially among the elderly, candidates felt that the complexity of the voting system had been overestimated, a fact that was borne out by the low number of spoilt ballot papers. One candidate described voting under the new system as being 'as difficult as turning on a kettle'.

Home Office voter education leaflets explaining the new voting system might have countered fears of complexity, but were apparently not delivered to a large, though unquantifiable, number of homes. Where the leaflets were delivered, they frequently confused supporters of minor parties, minor parties being omitted from the sample ballot papers included on the leaflets. At one stage, 50 per cent of calls made to the Green Party were to ask if it was fielding candidates at all. This exclusion led to a dispute between minor parties and the Home Office and the Public Accounts Committee that continued beyond polling day itself (see Chapters 7 and 8).

The closed list system was widely disliked amongst candidates and the electorate alike. Voters did not like voting for a party; nor did they like voting for a list of candidates rather than for individuals. It seems that much of the electorate is wedded to the traditional notion of representation through single-member constituencies, although some candidates stressed that voters were annoyed by their inability to vote for individual *candidates*, and were not annoyed by the multi-member constituencies *per se*. Voters wanted to know who their MEP would be if they voted for a particular party. Some candidates took to responding, 'If you vote for us, I will be your MEP', to this question, regardless of their position on their party's list.

The lack of vigour in the national campaign, especially on the part of the Labour Party, was the third factor most cited as a reason for the poor turnout in the election. Conservative candidates were much happier with their party's national campaign than the Labour and Liberal Democrat candidates were with theirs. The Tories' slogan – 'In Europe, not run by Europe' – seems to have been effective in striking a responsive chord amongst the electorate and defining the stance of the party as a whole. Some Conservatives regarded the campaign as a 'triumph', 'the best campaign the Conservatives have fought for years', and even those who did not care for William Hague or for his hardened strategy on the single currency conceded that the strategy was effective and the party 'did not wobble too far to the right'.

Labour candidates were less enthusiastic about their party's national campaign. The campaign was described variously as 'lacklustre', 'pathetic' and 'lacking in direction'. Candidates felt that control of the campaign had been lost to the Conservatives: Tony Blair was preoccupied with Kosovo, while 'Hague played a "blinder"'. Some Labour candidates forgave Blair for being too busy to involve himself heavily in the campaign; others accused him of being disinterested in the election, having spoken on Europe in Cologne, Amsterdam, Paris and Bonn among other places, but not in the UK. The Labour message of 'Leading in Europe' clearly lost out to the Euro-sceptic Conservative 'In Europe, not run by Europe'. As one Labour candidate commented: 'My wife summed it up beautifully: "I can tell you the Tory slogan but I'm blowed if I can tell you ours."'

Opinions of the Liberal Democrats' campaign amongst their candidates varied from 'poor' to 'better than before'. The campaign was thought to focus too much on domestic issues and not enough on Europe, and some considered that there was too little pro-European content in the campaign, although others reported a lack of support amongst voters for the party's pro-European stance. The impending resignation of Paddy Ashdown as the party's leader was a distraction for the media that inhibited attempts by candidates to gain media coverage for their policies. Opinion on the personal impact of Mr Ashdown on the campaign divided equally between good and poor.

Conservative candidates were more satisfied with the support that they received from head office than their counterparts in the other main parties. On the whole, Conservatives were appreciative, whereas Labour candidates' opinions of support from Millbank ranged from 'very good' to 'what support?', with particular dissatisfaction about the content of campaign literature.

Campaign tactics on the ground were similar for all main parties. Voter contact was mostly by leafleting at street stalls and through town-centre walkabouts. These were supplemented by visits to factories, and also by meetings with farmers in rural areas. Other open, multi-party meetings were not common, and those that were staged were not well attended: only one member of the public turned up to one of the London meetings, everyone else in the room being either one of the five candidates present, an assistant to a candidate or the meeting's organiser.

Most parties targeted only known supporters. Rather than trying to sway floating voters, the candidates sought to mobilise their own core supporters. Little canvassing was evident, and records from recent local elections and the elections to the Scottish Parliament and the Welsh Assembly were used where available.

For numerous candidates, a key campaign activity was to enthuse activists and to stir them into action. The success of these attemps varied to a high degree. Conservative candidates noted higher constituency party activism than their counterparts, but overall levels differed considerably. Activists, especially those in Scotland and Wales, were tired after their efforts for the May elections. Moreover, the willingness of Labour Party members to give time to the campaign was decreased by their disillusionment with the candidate selection process. The activity of MPs was as variable as that of constituency parties. A few were very helpful; others had reportedly gone on holiday for the duration of the campaign.

The Labour Party's candidate selection process left some candidates and activists with deep scars. Even though all Constituency Labour Parties had endorsed the candidate selection process, many Labour activists felt disenfranchised by the system and therefore decided to take no part in the campaign. Labour suffered further through the knowledge that several sitting MEPs would lose their seats under the new electoral system. The Liberal Democrats involved members through 'one member, one vote' ballots, and experienced fewer problems as a result. A little resentment of 'zipping' (alternating female and male candidates on the list) was evident. Conservatives reported the fewest scars as a result of the candidate selection process. Apart from one or two notable deselections, Conservative morale remained high, especially since, in the event, some candidates who had been placed lower down the list were elected.

The closed list voting system which had forced the parties to alter their candidate selection mechanisms also caused the candidates to adopt new campaigning methods. Because of the large size of the regional constituencies, the division of regions between candidates of the same party became a common campaign tactic, subject to some regional variations. There was also a need to ensure that the candidates worked as a team: if the candidates themselves were not committed to the campaign, it was difficult to see how activists could be so committed; yet most candidates had no prospect of being elected themselves.

Geographical division of the regions was common, with subject areas being divided less frequently. Even where subject portfolios were divided, candidates ended up answering questions on most topics. The Conservatives divided regions into four, with two candidates – one from the bottom of the list and one from the top of the list – sharing each division. This procedure appeared to work well, especially as the candidates at the bottom of the lists were often young activists who had much to gain in the future by working hard in this election. Most Labour candidates played a full part in the campaign, with some exceptions (two candidates in Scotland were reportedly never seen by their colleagues). Existing Labour MEPs did more work in their old constituencies than elsewhere, although Labour used geographical division of the regions less than the Conservatives. Labour's approach in some areas of 'everyone going everywhere' proved difficult to make a success. The Liberal Democrats seemed to have the least depth to their lists of candidates. A good team effort was evident in strong areas, but elsewhere the top few candidates did most of the campaigning, although others were supportive.

Even where candidates did successfully adapt to the challenge of working in teams within the new regions, they were faced with a lack of regional identity and therefore a lack, amongst voters, of identity with the constituency. This was especially the case in the South-East, where the constituency included both Dover and Oxford. Contrariwise, in London, which does have a regional identity, candidates found it difficult to make an impact in such a large constituency. Scotland and Wales were two regions that had existed independently of the European elections, yet these identities posed different problems for the parties. In Scotland, the parties' national campaigns from London had only marginal relevance to many, and the Scottish Nationalist Party promoted its manifesto, which raised the issue of 'Scotland in Europe' as being 'actually produced in Scotland'. As one party activist pointed out, had Labour produced its Scottish leaflets in a similar manner, it might have avoided sending 60,000 of them to Wales in error. Conservative activists had been rallied by having 18 MSPs elected at the beginning of May. There was potential for confusion in the election in Scotland – in addition to the two Conservative parties that were fielding candidates, there were Scottish Socialist, Socialist Labour, and Labour parties – but there was no evidence of widespread confusion among voters.

The 1999 elections to the European Parliament were shaped by two factors. First, there was a surfeit of newsworthy stories apart from the election campaign, including the Kosovo war and genetically modified organisms. Second, there were changes to campaigning techniques and internal party organisation that were posed by the change from a single-member plurality vote to the multi-member closed list system of proportional representation. The other issues seem to have easily distracted the attention of an already disinterested public. The electoral system caused the voters less problems than had been predicted by the media, but it did cause a number of concerns for the parties, concerns which were reflected in lessened enthusiasm among activists for campaigning, rifts between the parties and longstanding members, and problems in campaigning techniques. These effects of the change in the electoral system, noted by candidates during their election campaigning, are, however, secondary effects of the change in the electoral system, arising from the parties' reactions to the electoral changes, and not directly from those changes themselves.

The response from candidates revealed three major underlying themes. The first was that the new electoral system represented a genuine shock to the 'electoral establishment', the ramifications of which were far from assimilated by the time of the Euro-election. The second was a generalised impression of how far 'parliamentary politics' had become detached from economic and social Britain. The third was a distinct impression that the regional press and television failed to make the effort to cover the Euro-elections in the way that Euro-candidates felt they deserved. Paradoxically, although individual votes counted more than they ever had before, many candidates concurred that the 1999 Euro-election was the least exciting of the five contests.

The South-West
John Fitzmaurice

The South-West, with only seven seats at stake, was one of the smaller, but also one of the potentially more interesting regions. Here some of the key questions surrounding the election – such as the effect of PR (especially in regard to tactical voting), the solidity of the Liberal

Democrat vote, and the perspectives for smaller parties to do well – were posed with acuity.

The campaigns

The nature of the electoral system and the electoral mechanics – the need, for example, to appoint one agent for all seven candidates on each list – militated strongly in favour of a centralised approach, with coordination of each candidate team and of a major part of the campaign resources available to each party in terms of funds, literature, the free post communication, campaign buses and key campaigners from a regional centre. There was little or no localised literature. Traditional canvassing was limited to core support areas and was often done by telephone, again from a central point. Voters tended to receive one single, centrally produced team leaflet by the free post and some form of party newspaper (Labour's *Rose*, for example, or the Liberal Democrats' *Focus*) and leaflets were used in street and door-to-door activities. This literature was often only very slightly adapted from regional to region. Literature with no sub-regional or local content gave the campaign a distant, disembodied feel.

Inevitably, too, there was a centrally planned use of campaign buses, candidate teams' diaries and key campaigners, such as ministers, Shadow ministers and MPs. In general, candidates tended to divide into those who remained localised in one area and 'sweepers' who campaigned across the region. Campaigning was largely confined to 'blitzing' and whistlestops and sought to tease out limited media opportunities in a very low-key campaign. There were, for example, almost none of the usual physical manifestations of an election campaign to be seen.

At the outset of the campaign, Labour's aim was to win three seats, overtake the Liberal Democrats and, perhaps, the Conservatives as well. The party's campaign emphasised three concepts: first, 'team Labour'; second, making every vote count under the new PR system (in other words, explaining to people that under the new system they did not need to vote tactically and could 'come home to Labour'); and, third, 'making Europe work for Britain'. That, the party argued, could best be achieved by giving the South-West a voice in government at all levels: 'Labour's team is working on all local, national and European levels to bring home the benefits of that (EU) membership.' The key picture used on all campaign literature showed the seven-person team of candidates sitting and standing around Tony Blair. The Prime Minister appeared no less than three times in a recto–verso broadsheet campaign newspaper. It emphasised that 'Labour has a strong team in the South-West that is working with the Labour government to get Europe working for Britain.' There were no specific policy commitments and, above all, no mention of the single currency. The most prominent key campaigners were the Deputy Prime Minister, John Prescott, who campaigned by train in the region, and European Commissioner Neil Kinnock. The campaign had difficulty cutting through the Tory barrage on the single currency and getting over a more sophisticated message on the benefits of Europe. There was undoubtedly some demotivation of activists and backwash from the candidate selection procedure.

The Conservatives put the single currency at the cutting edge of their campaign. Without ever entirely ruling out membership at some distant time, the party managed to present itself as anti-single currency and sought to canalise the strongly Euro-sceptical tendencies that have long characterised the region. Interference by 'Brussels' and sleaze in Europe allegations were useful and effective subsidiary themes. However, the campaign was generally perceived as a single issue, anti-single currency campaign. As the Pro-Euro Conservatives were unable to mount a serious challenge, the Conservatives could concentrate on shoring up their Euro-sceptical flank, which they did effectively. Indeed, their campaign succeeded because it provided a focus for a new unity and a new sense of purpose for what was potentially a somewhat divided list in the South-West. Above all, they offered a clear message, but one which was not so radical as to frighten more moderate voters away. For the South-West Conservatives, therefore, it was very much 'mission accomplished'.

Liberal Democrat strategists habitually discount their vote by some 5 per cent in European elections. The Liberal Democrats' campaign was ambiguous and unspecific. It sought to take a critical distance from Euro-enthusiasm. This was the strategy followed nationally, but there were clear divisions among the candidates as to what they regarded as the best strategy. Some wanted to follow the nationally dictated approach. Others wanted a more openly European and less defensive approach, tackling head-on the ambient Euro-sceptical tendency in much of the media, especially the *Western Mail* in Devon and Cornwall. Here, more than anywhere else, the Lib Dems were, with 33.1 per cent of the vote in 1994 and two incumbent MEPs, on the defensive, especially taking into account the fact that close to half of Liberal Democrat voters rejected the party's stance on Europe. Accordingly, they used much space in their campaign literature in attacking the Conservatives' divisions on Europe, Labour's failure to deliver on its domestic campaign promises and the Greens for the Green Group's votes in the European Parliament. Their literature declared that 'The Lib Dems are not pro-Europe at any price.'

It did not mention the single currency and certainly did not mention the party's support for it. Rather, the party concentrated on domestic issues and attacked Labour on these. The key picture in their literature and advertisements showed their two MEPs at an old peoples home, attacking NHS waiting lists – hardly a European issue. The message from Paddy Ashdown reproduced in their literature also concentrated mainly on domestic issues, complaining that there had been a reduction in the number of policemen on the beat. The Liberal Democrat campaign was also quite centralised, but with County Committees, though this structure was reportedly variable in quality.

The UK Independence Party (UKIP) built upon the basis that had been laid by it and the Referendum Party during the 1997 General Election. The South-West has always been fertile Euro-sceptical terrain. The reported splits and the media coverage about the UKIP moving to the right did not hurt it in the region. On the contrary, it benefited from being the most Euro-sceptical party on offer that was not openly on the extreme right.

The Greens mounted a low-key but effective campaign, combining a centrally produced communication with some limited but visible street campaigning in urban areas. They were helped by the electoral system, promising fewer wasted votes, together with the timely intervention of a number of issues which they could capitalise on, such as BSE, GM crops and the Belgian dioxin scandal.

The Pro-Euro Conservatives were unable to mount a visible campaign.

The Results

The turnout in the South-West Region, at 27.8 per cent, was the highest in England. The Conservatives increased their share of the vote to 41.7 per cent, well above their 32.9 per cent in 1994 and 36.5 per cent in 1997, and returned four MEPs as in 1994.

Labour saw its share of the vote drop to 18.1 per cent, well below its 1994 and 1997 results in the region. It did achieve its key campaign objective of overtaking the Liberal Democrats as the second party in the region, reflecting some reduction in the tactical voting for the Liberal Democrats that characterises first-past-the-post elections. Labour's vote held up better than in any other region, falling only 8.3 per cent. But its hopes of increasing its number of MEPs were dashed.

The Liberal Democrats had a disastrous election in the region. Their vote fell to half what it had been at the 1994 and 1997 elections, and they lost one of their two MEPs. The party could no longer benefit from tactical voting by Labour supporters and lost votes to the Greens, but above all to the UKIP, as many Liberal Democrats voters are strongly Euro-sceptical in this region – especially in Cornwall, where farming and fishing are important. This is evidenced, for example, by the dramatic fact that despite Labour's poor result, the Liberal Democrats actually came behind Labour in Dorset.

The Greens achieved their best regional result in the whole country in the South-West – 8.3 per cent (3.4 per cent in 1994) – and in a larger region would have won a seat with such a score. The UKIP also won its best score and only double figure share of the vote (10.3 per cent) throughout the United Kingdom, earning it one seat. The Pro-Euro Conservatives hardly registered anywhere in the country but, as poor results go, their vote in the South-West was among the worst, at just 1.1 per cent.

London and the South-East
George Parker

Max Caller, the returning officer for the London region, had a problem. A total of 120 candidates were contesting the capital's ten seats, including representatives of no fewer than twelve parties. 'It's been very difficult to find a printer who can cope with the size of the ballot paper', he admitted. Come polling day, some scrutineers were using special prodders to compress the mammoth papers in the ballot boxes. Not that things were much easier in the South-East, the UK's largest Euro-region, where 101 candidates appeared on the ballot papers to fill the eleven available seats, representing nine parties.

As with elsewhere in Britain, the politicians were more enthusiastic about the elections than the voters. True, turnout figures in London and the South-East were higher than in most other regions, but in some working-class constituencies fewer than one in seven bothered to vote.

The low turnout contributed to a nightmare result for Labour, particularly in London, where the party had two years earlier soundly beaten the Conservatives. Labour's vote went down by 14.5 per cent in London and 9.5 per cent in the South-East compared to 1997.

Robert Evans, one of the four Labour candidates elected in the capital, said the writing was on the wall during the campaign, when it became obvious that party activists were refusing to get involved. 'There weren't sufficient numbers on the ground, and we needed those people out working to mobilise our core vote', he said. 'It was very disappointing for the candidates.' Labour's inactivity was obvious to other parties too. John Hayball, London regional agent for Arthur Scargill's Socialist Labour Party, said: 'Labour didn't do anything at all – they weren't putting the effort in, and they weren't even manning the polling stations.' According to Labour campaigners, in some parliamentary constituencies only a handful of activists bothered to do anything at all. Tony Blair's campaign had not only failed to enthuse Labour's core vote, it had not even enthused the party's membership. The one bright spot for Labour was North-West London – the scene of some of its greatest triumphs in the 1997 General Election – where keen new MPs and bushy-tailed activists actually fought a campaign.

Robert Evans said he found voters were aware that an election was going on, but that they were largely unaware of why it mattered. Like other Euro-candidates, he was dismayed by the lack of coverage given to the campaign by the London *Evening Standard*, which circulates throughout much of the South-East. The lethargy among Labour members and voters sent warning signals about the party's prospects in the London mayoral elections eleven months later, in May 2000.

If it was a bad night for Labour, the Conservatives were cock-a-hoop. With four candidates elected in London and five in the South-East, and an average vote across the two regions of 33.6 per cent (up 5 per cent on 1994), the party not only saw off its usual rivals but also withstood challenges from the breakaway Pro-Euro Conservatives and the resurgent UK Independence Party. Daniel Hannan, one of those elected in the South-East, said there was a unity of purpose among the Tory candidates, in spite of divergent views on the future development of Europe. He ascribed this to the fact that the most fervent pro-Europeans had already broken away to form the Pro-Euro Conservative Party.

In contrast to the shambolic nature of the Labour campaign, the Tories had an anti-single currency message which galvanised its members, and a strategy for maximising votes. For instance, in the South-East, the Tories broke the huge region into five sectors – broadly along county lines – and assigned two candidates to each: one candidate was in the top half of the list, the other was one of those unlikely to get elected. Mr Hannan said that even the 'no-hopers' worked hard. 'When your volunteers are working hard, all the candidates have to get stuck in too', he said. Mr Hannan, who campaigned in Kent – the nearest county to the EU's heartland – said the Tories were picking up opposition to the idea of a common European immigration policy and reduced border checks at Dover.

Like most parties in the huge regions, the Tory effort was concentrated on mailshots and very targeted canvassing. For instance, Mr Hannan focused his effort on natural Tory voters, such as parents of grammar school pupils, or farmers. However, perhaps a prize for energetic campaigning should be awarded to Nirj Deva, the former Tory MP for Isleworth, who was the fifth Tory to be elected in the South-East. He set out to shake 100,000 hands during the campaign, and was to be seen every morning canvassing on railway platforms or talking to mums on the school run.

The Liberal Democrats probably devoted more effort to campaigning in the South-East than in any other region, and reached their objective of securing two MEPs, Chris Huhne and Lady (Emma) Nicholson, the former Tory MP. However it was a difficult campaign, and in London, the party saw the election of only one candidate. George Dunk, the party's logistics chief in the South-East, admitted the party's relentless enthusiasm for the EU did not go down well with the voters. 'I think the electorate decided it didn't particularly want pro-European candidates to be elected', he said. Reflecting this, the party's election literature in both regions hardly mentioned Europe at all.

It was not a particularly memorable farewell for Paddy Ashdown, the outgoing Liberal Democrat leader, although he did provide the funniest moment of an otherwise lacklustre campaign. While touring North London on a canal, an overweight tramp attempted to board Mr Ashdown's narrow boat. The tramp fell into the water, prompting the former Royal Marine to launch a rescue mission to haul the sodden man out of the water. The fact that he claimed to be a Liberal Democrat probably made it worth while.

There were other hiccups. A flash flood in a South London print warehouse ruined some of the Liberal Democrats' 5–6 million personal leaflets, while the London literature featured Mr Ashdown visiting a Richmond school which the local (Liberal Democrat) council had subsequently closed down.

The Tories aside, the UK Independence Party and the Greens were the undoubted success stories of the European elections in London and the South-East. The Greens won a seat in both regions, with 7.7 per cent of the vote in London (an increase of 7.3 per cent on the 1997 General Election) and 7.4 per cent in the South-East (up 7.1 per cent on 1997). The UKIP surprised almost everyone by winning a seat in the South-East, gaining 9.7 per cent of the vote.

Perhaps the only people who were not surprised were the UKIP themselves. Christopher Skeate, the party's press officer, said 750 new members signed up to the fledgling party in the South-East in the month leading up to polling day, and thousands of pounds in donations were flooding in. The party's biggest concern during the campaign was the Home Office literature explaining the huge ballot papers, which made no mention of genuine (as opposed to fictitious) minor parties. 'We received over 450 calls in the South-East in one week from people who thought we were not standing', said Mr Skeate.

The Greens were boosted significantly by their stylish election broadcast, made in the style of a pop video, which was particularly well received in London and the South-East. The metropolitan target audience was also receptive to the party's message on genetically modified foods, and to its railway station canvassing on the issue of public transport. Green candidates further argued that Kosovo had been an important doorstep issue in London.

As for the Pro-Euro Conservatives, who won less than 2 per cent of the vote in both regions, there were painful lessons to be learned.

The Midlands
Zig Layton-Henry

Middle England as represented by the English Midlands and Eastern England was neither shaken nor stirred by the 1999 elections to the European Parliament. Parties and candidates found it hard to distract the electorate from their daily routines and the media from events in Kosovo. The new electoral system, uncertainty over the euro, and lack of interest in the European Parliament all added to the difficulties of generating enthusiasm in the campaign.

Conservative strategy was to use the local elections in May 1999 as a basis for the European campaign. The canvassing returns from the local elections enabled the party to target Conservative voters and encourage them to turn out. Canvassing seemed inappropriate, given the large scale of the electoral constituencies and the fact that a fair amount had recently been done in the local elections. Conservative candidates worked the region in pairs, leafleting, attending meetings and visiting meetings of sympathetic organisations such as the National Farmers' Union. In the East Midlands, market towns were targeted by the Conservative candidates. However, the priority was to meet and enthuse party workers and to encourage them to help to mobilise the Conservative vote. In some areas the success of the Conservatives in the local elections had increased the morale and enthusiasm of local volunteers.

The national Conservative campaign slogan, 'In Europe, not run by Europe', was considered both memorable and successful. It united the whole party and William Hague was given considerable credit for choosing it. In the East Midlands region the extremely Euro-sceptical Roger Helmer and the pro-European Bill Newton Dunn both campaigned behind it. Conservative organisers also felt that they benefited from widespread disillusionment with the Prime Minister and his administration among Labour party supporters. Many Labour voters were considered to be very dissatisfied with the conservative policies of the government, especially their tight fiscal controls, which meant that they were seen as failing to deliver improvements in the health service, education and social welfare. Moreover, the Labour government was seen as targeting vulnerable groups such as asylum seekers, single mothers and students. In rural areas the Conservatives felt they benefited from strong feelings that the government favoured urban areas and was deaf to rural concerns. Dissatisfaction was high in rural areas over high petrol prices and the failure to help farming in a period of intense crisis.

The Labour campaign in the West Midlands got off to a disastrous start with controversies over the selection and position of Labour candidates on the list. Two popular and active MEPs, David Hallam and Christine Oddy, were given such low positions – fifth and seventh respectively – that they had no chance of re-election. Christine Oddy resigned from the Labour party and stood as an independent. The controversy over the selection of candidates had a damaging effect on the morale of Labour party activists and added fuel to the suspicion of excessive central party control, which had already been generated by the selection of the Labour leader in Wales and the overt battle over who should be the Labour candidate for Mayor of London.

Labour strategy in the Midlands region seemed to be to rely on the national popularity of the Prime Minister and the government. A series of Labour ministers visited the region, including John Prescott, Gordon Brown, Mo Mowlam and Alan Milburn, but party organisers found it hard to gain regional television coverage or even to generate local press interest in the campaign. In the West Midlands, the Labour party used the selection of Michael Cashman, the former star of *EastEnders*, as number two on the list, to generate publicity, while in the East Midlands the Conservatives similarly used the football refereeing connections of Chris Heaton-Harris. However, neither of the major parties managed to generate substantial media or public interest, despite ministerial and Shadow Cabinet visits, photo calls and whistlestop tours of the region. Among Labour supporters in particular there was the feeling that the national Labour campaign was too low-key and that the Labour leadership was afraid to take on the growing support for Euro-scepticism. As a result, some felt that the Labour party had no European strategy and that it was pointless to vote in the European elections. David Hallam, who lost his seat as a Labour MEP in the West Midlands, bitterly condemned the arrogance of the Labour campaign which failed to address the issue of the euro. People, he said, were genuinely worried about the impact of the euro on their money and he argued that the Labour campaign ignored their concerns (*The Times*, 15 June 1999).

The Liberal Democrats confidently expected to benefit from the new electoral system, but the large size of the electoral areas stretched their resources and made local issues more difficult to exploit. Attempts were made to generate local interest; for example, the 'send a Brummie to Brussels' campaign in Birmingham. In the West Midlands they also benefited from having Liz Lynne, the former MP for Rochdale, at the head of their list. Generally, though, the Liberal Democrats found it hard to motivate their supporters and to retain their loyalty.

The surprise of the election was the relatively high vote for the UK Independence Party. This suggested that Euro-scepticism was growing among the electorate and that Hague had accurately judged their mood. Members of the UK Independence Party took this view and felt strongly that Hague and the Conservatives had stolen many of their policies, thereby undermining their support. However, they easily saved their deposits and had the pleasure of seeing Jeffrey Titford returned as an MEP for the Eastern region constituency.

The Greens consistently achieved around 5–6 per cent of the vote and, despite a vigorous campaign in some areas such as Herefordshire, were unable to repeat the dramatic vote they achieved in the European elections of 1989.

There was considerable interest in the West Midlands in the campaign of Christine Oddy, the former Labour MEP, who had resigned from the party and stood as an Independent. Oddy was an extremely active MEP whose political base was in Coventry. She was a lawyer and economist and was fluent in a number of European languages. She produced an extremely effective leaflet attacking Labour for dropping her in favour of two 'London luvvies' and emphasising her own local roots. She also published a league table of the activity of West Midlands MEPs which showed that she was by far the most active (Table 6.1).

Christine Oddy was expected to gain support from disillusioned Labour supporters and in the event she achieved a very creditable vote of 36,849, which was 4.34 per cent of the poll, easily more than enough to save her deposit.

The Pro-Euro Conservatives made no impact on the campaign and did badly across the whole region. The Socialist Alliance also had a disappointing result in the West Midlands, despite having Dave Nellist, a former Labour MP for Coventry South-East, as the first candidate on their list. They gained only 7,203 votes, or 0.85 per cent of the poll. Alternative

Labour did slightly better in the East Midlands, where the veteran left-winger, Ken Coates, headed the list. They achieved 17,409 votes, or 2.41 per cent of the poll.

Table 6.1 West Midlands MEP activity levels

	Speeches	Reports	Written questions	Question time
John Corrie	17	10	9	10
David Hallam	48	15	49	1
Simon Murphy	22	22	7	12
Christine Oddy	108	61	357	111
Mike Tappin	30	53	2	7

Source: European election leaflet produced by Christine Oddy, published by Veronica Lane.

Two ethnic minority MEPs were elected from the Midlands, namely Neena Gill, who was third on the Labour list in the West Midlands, and Bashir Khanbhai, who was similarly placed for the Conservatives in the Eastern area.

As in the country as a whole, the European election campaign was a non-event in Middle England. Apart from leaflets delivered via the free post, few electors were reached by the campaign. The new electoral system failed to generate public interest or to persuade voters that every vote counted. It helped minor parties only slightly, apart from the Liberal Democrats who substantially increased their representation. However, despite the low poll, the main impact was to provide a substantial boost to Conservative party morale and to warn the Labour party that their electoral support could not be taken for granted.

The North of England
Philip Norton

The campaign in the North was largely a non-campaign. Though the candidates from the main parties made some effort to campaign, there was little interest in what they were doing. The fact that an election was taking place failed to excite interest among the regional media and the electors.

In attempting to have some impact on the outcome, candidates faced three problems. The first was the lack of interest on the part of the media. Reporting of the campaign was limited and, in so far as it was covered, it was treated as a national campaign. The limited extent of the reporting was shown in the two regional television news programmes for the

Yorkshire region, *Calendar* (broadcast by Yorkshire Television) and *Look North* (broadcast by BBC North). In the three days prior to polling day, the election was never a lead item on either programme and, on one day, was not even at item at all on *Look North*. *Calendar* devoted a total of twelve minutes to the election – a four-minute report each evening, focusing on structures (What's the Parliament?), policy (What are the policies?) and procedures (How do we vote?). On polling day itself, it devoted two minutes to the election, with the views of foreign tourists in York being solicited about the 'British attitude' to 'Europe'. During the three days prior to voting, *Look North* devoted only seven minutes to the election: a three-minute item on farming and a four-minute report looking at the use to which investment had been put. On the Tuesday, as well as on polling day, there was no coverage of the election.

Local and regional newspapers were more inclined to cover the regional campaign, but even here much of the emphasis was on the national level. There was little coverage of the candidates' activity and what was there was tucked away on the inside pages. The *Hull Daily Mail* did highlight, complete with photograph, the Euro-friendly underwear designed by Pro-Euro Conservative candidate, Julia Gash (underwear with 'don't lie back and think of England' printed on the front) but this was included in an article detailing the complexities of the new voting system (Angus Young, 'All Change at the Euro Ballot Box', *Hull Daily Mail*, 9 June 1999). Alongside a picture of Ms Gash and her underwear was a picture of a city official holding a ballot paper. On election day, the focus was on the low turnout. One local newspaper sent a reporter to a polling station and in the course of one hour reported the arrival of two people: a police officer who had come to check that there were no problems, and a lone voter.

The second problem was a lack of interest on the part of those on the electoral register. There was a notable absence of the normal physical manifestations of an election campaign: posters in windows and on trees. When candidates went on to the streets they encountered little interest. As the *Yorkshire Post* reported, when six of the seven Labour candidates for Yorkshire and the Humber descended on the market town of Brigg, 'Never in the history of the town can so many candidates from one party ... have descended on so many streets, with so much election material, and met so few voters displaying so little enthusiasm' (John Woodcock, 'And the winner is ... apathy', *Yorkshire Post*, 10 June 1999, p. 13). The candidates encountered few comments on policies or mis-management in Brussels: 'No hostility, just apathy and blank expressions.' The occasional news item and the party election leaflets that dropped through the letterbox were not sufficient to overcome a pervasive sense of indifference.

The third problem was the new voting system. In addition to the official leaflet delivered to every household, the media variously made some effort to explain how the new system worked. In so doing, there was a tendency to explain how complicated it was. The voting system may also have served to discourage intense activity by some of the candidates. Why should those Labour and Conservative candidates on the bottom of the party list bother to campaign, given that their chances of winning were slim? The complicated nature of the system was exacerbated by some of the campaign literature. The Labour election leaflet declared 'There's no need for tactical voting – you simply vote for what you believe in.' This was preceded by a section that, in Yorkshire and the Humber, read: 'This June in the European elections, there is a new voting system. And with the level of Lib Dem support in Yorkshire and the Humber, it's clear that the Lib Dems can't come top of the poll. A vote for the Lib Dems could mean more Tories being elected.' The Liberal Democrats, by contrast, demonstrated not so much a lack of understanding of the new system but rather a willingness to exploit the fact that it was not totally proportional: 'The Greens and others cannot win in this region, even with the new voting system. They simply cannot get enough votes to win here' (Yorkshire and the Humber *Focus*, June 1999, p. 2).

The new voting system appears to have contributed to the unwillingness to vote, though by itself cannot explain the fact that the turnout in the three northern regions was lower than in the rest of the country. Here the explanation appears to lie in the concentration of Labour support in the north. The greater the safeness of the Westminster seat for Labour, the lower the turnout in the election. The lowest turnouts in the North were in Liverpool, central Manchester, Hull and Barnsley. Turnout in Hull East, the constituency of Deputy Prime Minister, John Prescott, was 12.7 per cent. The highest turnouts were in safe Conservative seats, notably Richmond (William Hague's seat), Hexham, and Westmoreland and Lonsdale. These were the only three seats in the North to register a turnout in excess of 30 per cent.

The new voting system appears to have had a deflating effect on turnout. It also had a devastating effect on the careers of some candidates who had previously served in the European Parliament. In Yorkshire and the Humber, six of the seven Labour candidates were MEPs. With a proportional system, there was little chance of all six being elected. In the event, only three made it back to the Parliament. The three casualties included Barry Seal, an MEP since 1979. Similarly, in the North-West, six out of the ten Labour candidates were MEPs: only four survived. Conversely, the success of the Conservatives served to resuscitate some parliamentary careers. In the North-West, four of the five successful Conservative candidates had previously served either in the European Parliament (Lord Inglewood) or the House of Commons (Sir Robert Atkins, David Sumberg and Den Dover). In Yorkshire and the Humber, another casualty of the 1997 General Election, Timothy Kirkhope, was elected. The successful Liberal Democrat in the North-West, Chris Davies, was also a former MP.

The Labour and Conservative parties (averaging 36.0 per cent and 33.1 per cent respectively over the three northern regions) dominated in the North. In the three regions combined, ten Labour and nine Conservative candidates were elected. The two remaining places were taken by the Liberal Democrats (on 11.7 per cent of the vote in the North-West and 14.4 per cent in Yorkshire and the Humber). The UK Independence Party came fourth in each region and the Green Party fifth. Both produced short but glossy and pithy election leaflets. (The UK Independence Party leaflet proclaimed 'Keep the Pound, Leave the European Union'. Contrast this with the less than engrossing Alternative Labour List in Yorkshire and the Humber: 'Alternative Labour List supporting Left Alliance'.) The Pro-Euro Conservative Party failed to make an impact: apart from Ms Gash and her underwear, it was almost invisible during the campaign. In each region, it was out-polled by the British National Party. The best result for the Pro-Euro Conservative Party was in Yorkshire and the Humber, where it managed – though only just – to achieve over 1 per cent of the vote. In terms of the absolute number of votes cast, the worst result was achieved by the Natural Law Party (826 votes – 0.21 per cent of the poll – in the North-East). In terms of the percentage share of the poll, the worst performance was by the Weekly Worker in the North-West (0.09 per cent). The real winner in the North was apathy.

Wales
Dafydd Trystan

The first phase of Labour's European election campaign in Wales could not have begun under more difficult circumstances. The electoral musical chairs of Labour's selection procedure provoked widespread discontent among Labour's grassroots following the choice of Lyndon Harrison (formerly MEP for Cheshire West) as number three on Labour's list above both Joe Wilson and David Morris (the then MEPs for North Wales and South Wales West, respectively). Wayne David was the only one of Wales' sitting MEPs not to seek re-election, opting instead for the 'safer' territory of the National Assembly elections. It is illustrative of the remarkable nature of the elections of 1999 in Wales that, rather than being crowned the next Labour representative for the Rhondda with little more than a murmur from the other political parties, David went on to earn the unenviable position in the footnotes of Welsh electoral history of being the man who lost the Rhondda for Labour.

In Wales, 1999 was the year of the first elections to the National Assembly, with the European campaign providing little more than a sideshow to the main event. Thus it was the campaigning themes and events surrounding the Assembly which set the context and tone for the European election campaign.

Few would dissent if the Labour party in Wales were to describe the year leading to the European elections as its *annus horribilis*. From Ron Davies' now infamous 'moment of madness' on Clapham Common to the twists and turns of the subsequent Welsh Labour leadership election and Alun Michael's eventual victory due to the contrived variant of the voting system used to elect Tony Blair as Leader, Labour in Wales lurched from one public relations disaster to another. This culminated at the European elections with the party's worst performance in Wales since 1910.

There was, however, one consolation for Labour in that they succeeded in maintaining their position as the largest party in Wales, despite the expected strong challenge from Plaid Cymru (now officially renamed Plaid Cymru – The Party of Wales). For much of the campaign, the election gave the appearance of being two distinct contests, Labour against Plaid for the honour of being the largest party in Wales, and the Conservatives versus the Liberal Democrats for third place and the one seat which would almost certainly come in its wake.

On the ground in Wales the campaign was very low-key indeed with all parties complaining of 'activist exhaustion' following the exertions of both the Assembly and local council campaigns, only five weeks before the European poll. Thus the campaign in Wales was largely fought in the media. While the euro may have been the defining issue in other parts of the UK, it was not as prominent in the Welsh campaign. Following the attention it received during the Assembly election campaign, match-funding for Objective One projects became an important issue. West Wales and the South Wales Valleys had qualified for European Objective One funding during early 1999 and questions regarding the Treasury's willingness to provide match-funding in addition to the Welsh block grant had come to the fore. It had been assumed that the Prime Minister would make an announcement regarding match-funding at some time during the Assembly election campaign, but such a definite announcement never came, the Prime Minster going no further than asserting that the people of Wales could trust the government to look after their interests. Thus, by the time of the European election, the Labour Party found themselves most definitely on the back foot. Indeed, Glenys Kinnock's last news conference of the campaign specifically addressed this issue, accusing Plaid Cymru of making false claims in relation to Objective One funding.

While Objective One match-funding was the major bone of contention between Labour and Plaid Cymru, the Conservatives and the Liberal Democrats focused more of their attention on the single currency. The Conservatives took their cue from the Conservative UK-wide approach with a vigorous campaign against the euro; the Liberal Democrats took the pro-euro message to every household. Roger Roberts, a longstanding pro European and number one candidate on the Liberal Democrat list was pictured in their election leaflets with a £3,000 cheque purporting the financial benefit to each family of UK membership of the single currency.

The contrast on the night of the count between these two parties was significant indeed. While the Conservatives succeeded in increasing their Assembly percentage, the Liberal Democrats fell away dramatically, failing to secure first place in any individual parliamentary constituency, even in the safe Liberal Democrat territory of rural Montgomeryshire. The Conservatives, on the other hand, saw individual constituencies which had previously seen Conservative majorities only in 1983 return to the Conservative fold.

In Wales, unlike many other parts of the United Kingdom, the smaller parties failed to make any real impact. There appeared to be little active campaigning on behalf of the Greens or the UKIP and in the event neither remotely threatened the larger parties.

While Labour can take some comfort from the fact that they maintained their position as the largest party, the European election results seemed to confirm important changes in Welsh electoral politics already suggested by the Assembly results. It had been assumed by many that while Plaid might gain a few percentage points in the context of an Assembly election, 'normal' service would be resumed at any subsequent 'national' elections. The European election results suggest that this may not be the case, and that 1999 may indeed be seen as a turning point. From being the land of safe Labour industrial seats, where elections bore more resemblance to coronation rituals than any closely fought campaign, Wales would appear to be teetering on the brink of a more pluralist pattern of voting behaviour. Plaid Cymru may not be the only party to benefit from these changes. The Conservatives, following their particularly poor performance in the Assembly elections, have shown in the context of a strong campaign on the single currency that they can command the support of a significant minority of the Welsh electorate. The Labour Party remains the largest party in Wales, but maintaining this position will be a significant challenge in the years ahead.

Table 6.2 Party votes and percentages in Wales 1997–99

	General Election 1997	National Assembly (Constituencies) 1999	National Assembly (Regions) 1999	European Elections 1999
Votes				
Lab	886,935	384,671	361,657	199,690
PC	161,030	290,565	312,048	185,235
Con	317,127	162,133	168,206	142,631
Lib Dem	200,020	137,657	128,008	51,283
Others	54,932	47,992	51,837	47,586
Percentages				
Lab	54.7	37.6	35.4	31.9
PC	9.9	28.4	30.5	29.6
Con	19.6	15.8	16.5	22.8
Lib Dem	12.4	13.5	12.5	8.2
Others	3.4	4.7	5.1	7.6

In a broader context, the European elections in Wales point to an emerging phenomenon of voting behaviour in Wales. Detailed analysis of the results suggests that not only were voters voicing their opinions on the government of the day and on European issues (primarily the single currency) but that specifically Welsh factors also seem to have had a significant impact on voting behaviour for the first time. Thus it may be suggested that a more complex pattern of voting behaviour for different levels of governance based on perceptions of performance at all three levels (European, UK and Welsh) appears to be developing in Wales. For future elections, perceptions of the parties at each level and the relative importance accorded to the various levels may well be the key determinants of electoral trends, and thus crucial to Labour's chances of reasserting its dominance of Welsh electoral politics.

Scotland
James Kellas

The shape of Scottish politics was profoundly changed on 6 May 1999. A Scottish Parliament was elected for the first time since 1707, and a Scottish Executive headed by a 'First Minister' followed soon afterwards. During May and June the focus in Scottish politics was on the activities of these new bodies, which reached a climax when the Queen formally opened the Scottish Parliament on 1 July.

Sandwiched in between these events came the European elections on 10 June, but the only novelty here was the voting system: a Scotland-wide constituency with 8 MEPs elected by proportional representation in place of the eight MEPs elected in separate regions on a first-past-the-post basis. Curiously, the Scottish electorate had become even more familiar with the old European regional constituencies on 6 May, when the 56 'Additional Members' for the Scottish Parliament, out of a total of 129, were elected from these regions, 7 each.

But now Europe had turned its back on such an arrangement. Voters in Scotland on 10 June were faced with a ballot paper which showed the same candidates in Shetland as in Galloway. Most of the names were unfamiliar. Of the previous eight MEPs, only four were standing, three Labour and one SNP. One of the Labour MEPs, Hugh McMahon, was placed fifth on the Labour list, and so would most likely not be elected. Another Labour MEP, Alex Smith (Scotland South) pulled out in January 1999 on the instructions of his constituency party after being placed so low on the list that he too had no chance of being elected.

Meanwhile, Hugh Kerr, a Labour MEP for an English seat, having been rejected for the party, stood for the Scottish Socialist Party and was placed top of their list (this party had secured one seat in the Scottish Parliament, in the person of Tommy Sheridan, a well known Glasgow Councillor). The Scottish Socialist Party obtained 39,720 votes (4.02 per cent) in the whole of Scotland, so Kerr was not elected. (Tommy Sheridan had secured 5,611 votes in Glasgow Pollok alone in the May Scottish Parliament elections, and was elected on his party's Glasgow regional list with 18,581 votes (7.3 per cent).)

Similarly, the Greens obtained one MSP in May, but could not win a European seat, even with 57,142 votes (5.8 per cent). Probably the only really well known MEP from Scotland was Winnie Ewing (SNP), known as '*Madame Ecosse*'. But she did not stand, as she had decided to stand for the Scottish Parliament instead. She was elected to that, and actually opened the Parliament as its oldest member.

The SNP was the only major party to see the European elections as a Scottish election. This is despite the fact that all the main parties campaigned with 'Scottish' in their titles. But this was nothing like the Scottish devolution elections held the previous month. The media was hard-pressed to find news to report, and the party election broadcasts were not Scottish-produced (except for those of the SNP and the Scottish Socialists), but were the same London-produced broadcasts as seen in the rest of Britain.

Party leaflets were notable for their absence. One leaflet that was distributed to all voters was actually produced by the Home Office, a department that hardly functions in Scotland, except for immigration and broadcasting. The Scottish newspapers carried a two-page public information supplement, *EP News*, 'Sponsored by the European Parliament', of which one page was devoted to the parties standing in Scotland. This also had a message in Gaelic from José Maria Gill Robles, President of the European Parliament (*Scotsman*, 3 June 1999). The Glasgow *Herald* produced a 16-page *European Elections Guide* on 8 June. Financing this was the pervasive Scottish Media Group, which owns Scottish Television and Grampian Television, as well as the Glasgow newspapers the *Herald*, *Sunday Herald* and *Evening Times*. The papers generally had little news to report on the European elections (there were no meetings or scandals), and did not usually exhort a party vote. For example, the *Scotsman* editorial on 9 June, 'Voting options on Europe', prescribed only that voters turn out to vote on the basis of their opinions on the euro and European integration. If they were to do that, the poll reported by the paper on 7 June, headlined 'SUPPORT FOR EURO AMONG SCOTS VOTERS TAKES A DIVE', might have been considered a pointer for a Conservative vote. The Editor-in-Chief on the *Scotsman*, Andrew Neil, is a well known Conservative Euro-sceptic.

As it turned out, the Conservatives in Scotland did move forward, with two MEPs elected on 19.7 per cent of the vote. This made the SNP furious, as they too got two MEPs, but with 27.1 per cent of the vote. Indeed, Labour's three seats out of the eight in Scotland were elected on just 28.6 per cent of the vote: only 14,962 ahead of the SNP. The Liberal Democrats got one seat for their 96,971 votes (9.8 per cent), but the Greens got nothing for their 57,142 votes. With only eight Scottish seats to share out, the system could not provide fully proportional representation. If Scotland had the same number of seats as Denmark (16), as it has a similar population size, then that would be possible. But such a scale of representation would require independence.

The SNP used to attack the European connection, as in the 1975 Referendum, when they recommended a No vote, but it is now the most

European of the parties, especially at the leadership level. In the poll on the euro quoted earlier, 39 per cent of SNP respondents were prepared to vote No in a referendum on joining the European single currency, 44 per cent said Yes, and 18 per cent did not know (the other Yes responses were: Labour 39 per cent, Conservative 14 per cent, Lib Dem 25 per cent, and Other 26 per cent; the total for Scotland was: Yes, 30 per cent; No, 48 per cent; Don't Know, 22 per cent) (*Scotsman*, 7 June 1999).

The turnout in Scotland (24.6 per cent) was similar to that elsewhere in Britain, and much less than in the Scottish parliamentary elections (58 per cent). Compared to that election, Labour did worse (28.6 per cent compared with 33.6 per cent), as did the SNP (27.1 per cent compared with 27.3 per cent), and much worse than their previous European elections vote in 1994 (33 per cent). But the SNP claimed that the distribution of votes by constituency would have won them 15 Westminster seats instead of the 6 they currently hold. The Conservatives, with 19.7 per cent, were considerably up on their May 15.4 per cent, but the Lib Dems were well down with 9.0 per cent compared with 12.4 per cent. This would have lost them seats at Edinburgh and Westminster, where in the latter they hold ten seats; but under PR they gained a seat for Europe. (All Scottish Parliament election votes quoted are the second ballot, party list votes.)

It appears that the parties targeted their own supporters, and were therefore not concerned to put up posters, to canvas, or to hold meetings. The low turnout hit Labour especially badly, and the constituency breakdown of the turnouts shows that the two highest Scottish turnouts were in seats where the SNP was strong (32.3 per cent in Galloway and Upper Nithsdale, and 32.0 per cent in North Tayside; both SNP seats). The two worst turnouts were inevitably in Glasgow Labour seats (15.7 per cent in Shettleston, and 16.0 per cent in Maryhill). Labour's European Parliament seats were cut from six to three, which was nevertheless a gross over-representation for its 29 per cent vote. No party other than the big Scottish four was represented.

Northern Ireland
Paul Hainsworth

Context

European elections in Northern Ireland are predictable affairs. First, the same three parties (and, for the most part, the very same individuals) have always monopolised the three Euro-seats allocated to the territory:

the Revd Ian Paisley, leader of the strongly Ulster loyalist Democratic Unionist Party (DUP) has topped the poll at every single Euro-election, followed by John Hume, leader of the constitutional (Irish) nationalist Social Democratic and Labour Party (SDLP), and then by an Ulster Unionist Party (UUP) candidate – first John Taylor (1979–89) and then James Nicholson (1989–99). Second, the Euro-election campaigns tend uniquely to be characterised by a strong emphasis on local/regional/ national political issues relating to Northern Ireland's constitutional status and bound up with polarised-cum-sectarian argument about this fundamental question. In May–June 1999, political commentators were expecting little change in these respects. Significantly, the DUP leader wanted to make the election a *de facto* referendum on the historic Good Friday, or Belfast, Agreement (GFA), negotiated by the British and Irish governments and political parties in Northern Ireland in 1998 and subsequently ratified in referendums (held in Northern Ireland and the Irish Republic simultaneously the same year). Largely, then, this was the context for the staging of Northern Ireland's fifth European election.

Campaign

However, notwithstanding the above-mentioned pattern, there were some specific circumstances relating to the latest European election in Northern Ireland and these generated a fair degree of interest and speculation, which made the occasion and outcome intriguing and, no doubt, helped to make the turnout more impressive than elsewhere. They also meant that the outcome was less certain. Most notably, the pro-Agreement and Euro-enthusiastic Hume looked forward – not without reason – to topping the poll this time (aspiring to benefit from his major role in helping to secure the GFA and his very recent Nobel Peace Prize). Consequently, there was much campaign attention focused on whether the strongly anti-Agreement and Euro-sceptic Paisley would maintain his prime position. It was clear though that the Agreement would figure prominently in voters' minds, despite Hume's hopes and assertions that the election should be fought on European issues. This focus was inevitable not only because of Paisley's campaign thrust and influence, but also because the Agreement incorporated highly tangible, hotly debated, key issues – such as the early release of political prisoners, the decommissioning of paramilitary-held arms and the setting up of a cross-party power-sharing executive and devolved government in Northern Ireland. The debate here also had important ramifications for the UUP candidate, Nicholson, and the way he should pitch his campaign.

As a pro-Agreement Unionist, loyal to his party leader, David Trimble – himself pro-Agreement, also a co-Nobel Laureate and Northern Ireland's First Minister, via the GFA mechanisms – Mr Nicholson was acutely aware of the growing reservations within mainstream unionism (including the UUP) about the Agreement, particularly over prisoner releases and the prospect of sharing power with the republican movement (notably Sinn Féin), prior to decommissioning by (especially) the Irish Republican Army (IRA). He was careful not to sound *too* positive about the GFA and to recruit the leading UUP anti-Agreement voice (Jeffrey Donaldson) to his Euro-election backing team and feature him conspicuously in campaign literature. However, Mr Nicholson's Euro-seat retention prospects still looked vulnerable to the disaffected elements within unionism. At the same time, James Nicholson's personal life had recently attracted a lot of front-page attention: an extramarital relationship had led to calls (including from the party's Deputy Leader, John Taylor) for him to stand down, for fear of alienating disapproving, moralising supporters. But, crucially, Mr Nicholson enjoyed his Leader's backing

Furthermore, the UUP third place was also threatened by a strong Sinn Féin challenge. Undoubtedly, in the Sinn Féin chairperson, Mitchell McLaughlin, the party was fielding its strongest Euro-candidate to date: a high profile, leading party figure, described interestingly by one leading commentator as able to reach the parts other Sinn Féin potential candidates were unable to reach. McLaughlin's campaign broadcast, manifesto and advertisements played up the fact that, in the recent (1998) Northern Ireland Assembly election, Sinn Féin had won more votes than Nicholson had been able to muster on the first ballot in the previous European election (1994). A similar re-run in 1999 would, therefore, seriously discomfit the UUP – in effect, Northern Ireland's largest party at other (non-European) elections – and leave the DUP leader able to claim even more so that the UUP was not up to defending the Union against its bitterest enemies. However, the Sinn Féin challenge was also a challenge to Mr Hume; a good share of the nationalist vote for Mitchell McLaughlin would obviously impede the SDLP Leader's chances of overtaking Ian Paisley. It was these contests within the overall election – nationalist versus unionist, unionist versus unionist, nationalist versus nationalist, and pro-Agreement versus anti-Agreement voices – that made the European campaign and result intriguing.

The battle within unionism was further stretched by the candidacies of two smaller parties: the strongly anti-Agreement Robert McCartney MP, leader of the United Kingdom Unionist Party (UKUP) and the very pro-Agreement David Ervine, representing the Progressive Unionist Party

(PUP), the latter known to have close links to loyalist paramilitarism. The final two candidates were Sean Neeson, the new leader of the centrist Alliance Party (AP) and James Anderson, leader of the Natural Law Party (NL) in Northern Ireland. Compared to previous years, this was a small number of candidates and, strikingly, there were no women contesting the election. Conspicuous absentees and non-runners were the Women's Coalition, the Greens, the Conservative Party and the small left-wing and/or labour candidates/parties that have previously contested these elections.

Despite the preoccupation with local politics, there was evidence of linkage to broader concerns. John Hume, for instance, travelled to Paris for a big rally of European Socialist leaders and he shared many of the visions (for example, of a social, democratic and inclusive Europe) and criticisms of his sister parties over European integration. His manifesto (*Putting People First)* and campaign certainly drew upon 'his membership of the largest and most influential group in the European Parliament'. James Nicholson (a member of the late James Goldsmith's Europe of Nations Group at Strasbourg), in turn, stressed that – unlike Hume and Paisley, both MPs at Westminster – he would again be a 'full-time' MEP, defending Ulster's interests and the powers of the nation state (against Brussels). His *Agenda for the European Elections* called for the setting up of a Northern Ireland Bureau, or Office, in Brussels 'to influence decisions that affect local people'. Ian Paisley's campaign literature (*First in Europe*) promised a 'free and unfettered voice' in Europe, not answerable to 'the Euro-centred bureaucracy or to a political grouping'. As with all the other candidates, he promised to secure European funds for Northern Ireland. The main emphasis of his campaigning, though, was upon the localised dimension: 'One year after the signing of the Belfast Agreement the people of Northern Ireland have a unique opportunity to give their verdict on its outcome. This is Ulster's only chance to reverse the treachery of the past year … John Hume and Jim Nicholson have supported the Agreement which opens the doors for IRA/Sinn Féin's place in government' (*DUP European Election '99 Manifesto*). Sinn Féin, for its part, called in its manifesto (*Peace and Independence in Europe*) for 'a European Union which is representative of its people' and not 'dominated by the larger states and [acting] in the interests of interna-tional finance'. Contesting the election on an all-Ireland basis, Sinn Féin placed emphasis on issues such as sovereignty, neutrality, equality and accountability. The overall party view on the European Union was summed up at the start of the manifesto: 'Sinn Féin recognises the European Union as a key terrain for political struggle and one which we can use to advance our republican aims of national independence and economic and social justice.'

Results

The mode of election in Northern Ireland European elections is proportional representation by single transferable vote (STV), with the whole of the territory constituting a single Euro-constituency. Candidates who reach the quota (number of valid votes ÷ number of seats + 1, then + 1 = the quota) are duly elected and their surplus votes redistributed according to voters' declared preferences. Candidates securing the lesser number of votes on the first count (and then subsequent counts) are progressively eliminated from the contest and their preference votes are redistributed via STV.

The 1999 European election in Northern Ireland followed a familiar pattern. On a relatively respectable turnout (58 per cent, compared to 49 per cent in 1994), Ian Paisley won his bid to become elected first, followed by John Hume and Jim Nicholson. In fact, the Revd Paisley surpassed Mr Hume, and Mr Nicholson beat Sinn Féin by almost identical proportions (around 2000 votes). Both Paisley and Hume enjoyed election on the first count. Nicholson was elected on the third count, benefiting from the transfers of elected or eliminated (pro-Agreement *and*, significantly, anti-Agreement) unionist candidates. While both Paisley's (28.4 per cent) and Hume's (28.1 per cent) share of the poll was similar to their 1994 shares (29.0 and 28.9 per cent, respectively), they both added almost 30,000 votes each to their tallies, on a higher turnout. Hume's 190,731 vote was, in fact, the largest vote ever won by the SDLP. Nicholson, on the other hand, was relieved to settle for a loss of 13,000 voters since 1994, despite the higher overall turnout. Unionist reservations about the GFA, internal party differences, personal/private revelations (see above) and the varying success of rival unionist candidates had all cut into the UUP's share of the poll (17.6 per cent, compared to 23.3 per cent in 1994).

For Sinn Féin, there was consolation in coming runner-up: Mitchell McLaughlin considerably increased his party's share of the poll (17.3 per cent in 1999; 9.9 per cent in 1994) and voters (117,643 in 1999; 55,215 in 1994). What the post-electoral statistics did not reveal was the level of transfers within the nationalist electorate: as explained, Hume reached the quota unaided by transfers, but Nicholson was elected before Hume's own transfers could be redistributed. Theoretically, some of these would probably have gone to McLaughlin, although, significantly, Hume had, on television, not endorsed this practice, protesting that he could not support an anti-EU candidate. At the other end of the scale, there were poor showings for McCartney and Neeson, both squeezed by the winning candidates, but also by the relatively successful first-time performance by the PUP's candidate, who surpassed them.

Unsurprisingly, Paisley interpreted his impressive victory as a defeat for the Agreement and called upon the UK Prime Minister, Tony Blair, to fundamentally reconsider the GFA and even schedule another referendum on it. Paisley claimed that 60 per cent of the unionist electorate had voted for anti-Agreement candidates. In turn, Hume and others suggested that the poll showed that 70 per cent of the voters were still backing the Agreement. These factors would need to be taken into account in the days and weeks ahead. However, the Prime Minister showed no immediate signs of being distracted from implementing the GFA because of the electoral showing of Paisley (and McCartney). On the contrary, and not for the first time, European elections in Northern Ireland were not seen as a definitive or reliable indicator to future political developments. Nevertheless, the repercussions of the anti-Agreement vote and the lingering doubts within Ulster unionism about the GFA's implementation would feed into and impact upon the political process, as indeed would Sinn Féin confidence derived from its good electoral showing. Agreement about the Agreement was certainly not enhanced by the 1999 European election in Northern Ireland.

The Successful Candidates
Chris Ballinger

Conservative MEPs arrived in Strasbourg under clear instructions from William Hague not to 'go native'; to stay loyal to the Westminster party rather than promoting the interests of Europe too freely. But this made a number of assumptions about the people who stand for election, and are elected as MEPs. Are MEPs interested in European politics in particular, or is election as an MEP simply an alternative political option for those unsuccessful at Westminster? Are MEPs unusually interested in matters that are specific to Europe? If so, do they want to represent the British people to the European Parliament, or represent Strasbourg to the British people?

On the whole, most MEPs (excepting members of the UKIP) were well disposed to matters European and entered the Strasbourg Parliament with the intention of participating fully in the European political process and promoting the good work of the Parliament to their constituents back at home. The Conservative MEPs were, however, the least likely of the three major parties' representatives to 'go native' in the European Parliament. Not only did fewer Conservative MEPs have specific career-related interests that favour the European Union than their colleagues in other parties, but one-quarter of the new intake of Conservative MEPs had been, until 1997, colleagues of Mr Hague in the parliamentary Conservative Party. They were therefore fully sensitised to the views of the party at Westminster. Moreover, four Conservative MEPs (including two new MEPs) had business interests in farming (a sector not known for a favourable predisposition to the EU), and the youngest Conservative, Daniel Hannan, is an avowed Euro-sceptic.

Those Labour MEPs who were susceptible to 'going native' to Europe were likely already to have done so: all but five of the 29 Labour MEPs elected in June 1999 were returning to Strasbourg. The new Labour MEPs include Neena Gill, an expert on Europe-wide finance, and Claude Moraes, an immigration consultant, both of whom had a considerable professional interest in European Union issues.

The Liberal Democrats saw three former MPs return to elected office: Chris Davies and Liz Lynne (who both lost their Westminster seats in 1997), and Emma Nicholson, who was a Conservative MP before crossing the floor to become a Liberal Democrat. Baroness Nicholson was one of four Peers taking up seats in Strasbourg, the other three being all Conservatives – the Earl of Stockton, Lord Bethell and Lord Inglewood – of whom the latter two were MEPs until 1994.

The 1999 intake were, on the whole, highly educated, with most having undertaken some higher or further education, and a number having higher degrees and university teaching posts. The professions were well represented among the MEPs: five were former schoolteachers, six were lawyers, and eight were university academics, of which one (Neil MacCormick, SNP) is Professor of Law at Edinburgh University and a specialist in European Union law.

The June election delivered 16 MEPs under the age of 40, two of whom – Catherine Taylor (b. July 1973) and Daniel Hannan (b. September 1971) – were in their twenties. Catherine Taylor, elected third for Labour in Scotland, was almost exactly a year younger than the 'Baby of the House' at Westminster, Christopher Leslie (Labour, Shipley). Ian Paisley (b. May 1926) remained the oldest United Kingdom MEP.

The Liberal Democrats, just as in the 1997 General Election, elected no one under 30, and while they did field four candidates in their late twenties, none had a hope of being elected: the only one that was placed above seventh on his list was Tim Farron (third, North-West). The only

Liberal Democrat MEP to be re-elected (Graham Watson) was, at 43, the equal second youngest among his immediate colleagues.

Table 6.3 Ages of elected MEPs (as at 10 June 1999)

	Age on 10 June 1999						Median age
	20–29	30–39	40–49	50–59	60–69	70–79	
Conservative	1	3	9	18	5	–	52
Labour	1	8	13	5	2	–	44
Lib Dem	–	1	6	3	–	–	46
Other	–	2	3	3	3	1	54
New MEPs	2	8	16	19	5	–	49
All MEPs	2	14	31	29	10	1	49

Table 6.4 Women MEPs across Europe, June 1999

Country	No. Women MEPs	Total No. MEPs	Women as a % of MEPs	Rank ordering (1 = highest % of women)
Austria	8	21	38.1	4
Belgium	7	25	28.0	11
Denmark	6	16	37.5	5
Finland	7	16	43.8	1
France	35	87	40.2	3
Germany	37	99	37.4	6
Greece	4	25	16.0	14
Ireland	5	15	33.3	8 =
Italy	10	87	11.5	15
Luxembourg	2	6	33.3	8 =
Netherlands	11	31	35.5	7
Portugal	5	25	20.0	13
Spain	21	63	33.3	8 =
Sweden	9	22	40.9	2
United Kingdom	20	87	23.0	12
Total	187	600	31.2	–

The Conservatives MEPs' older age-profile reflects the number of older candidates in winning positions. The median age of unsuccessful Conservative candidates was 46 – six years younger than the elected Conservatives – and this may have been a useful electoral strategy: several successful candidates commented on the campaigning energy of the younger candidates, who had no hope of being elected, but who were 'earning their electoral spurs'.

Representation of women and ethnic minorities among the United Kingdom MEPs was added to. The number of British women MEPs increased by a quarter at the 1999 European elections. Of the 87 United Kingdom MEPs, 20 (23 per cent) are women – a figure that compared favourably with Westminster, where at the 1997 General Election 18 per cent of the MPs elected were women. Both Green MEPs are women, and women accounted for half of the Liberal Democrat and Plaid Cymru MEPs (five and one, respectively). Nine of the Labour MEPs were women, a fall in number by three, but a rise in the proportion of all Labour MEPs from 19 per cent to 31 per cent. Three Conservative MEPs were women, but the increase of one on 1994 did not keep pace with the twofold increase in the total number of Conservative MEPs. Table 6.4 illustrates, however, that despite the increase in the number of women MEPs in 1999, the UK still lagged behind other EU members in terms of the proportion of MEPs that are women.

Four of the 87 MEPs now came from ethnic minorities, as against one in 1994: Neena Gill (Labour) in the West Midlands; Bashir Khanbhai (Conservative) in the Eastern region; Nirj Deva (Conservative) in the South-East; and Claude Moraes (Labour) in London.

7
Outcome and Consequences

Thursday, 10 June 1999 was a dry, if overcast, day. To the observer there was little to indicate that a nationwide election was under way. The polling stations echoed emptily, while the politicians had already turned their minds to other matters – notably the impending movement of troops into Kosovo following the Serb withdrawal. Most news bulletins mentioned that this was an election day, but the coverage was brief and anodyne. By the time the polling booths closed at 10.00 p.m. there was a distinct sense of anticlimax and an uneasy silence. But this was, to borrow from Dorothy Parker, a silence in which 'lots of things were happening'.

The count would not begin until Sunday evening, and there were no exit polls. Nevertheless, rumours were soon circulating about unprecedentedly low levels of turnout. Two further indicators pointed to this result. The first was the Leeds Central by-election, occasioned by the death of Foreign Office minister Derek Fatchett, the result of which was announced in the early hours of Friday morning. Hilary Benn was elected on a reduced Labour majority of 2,293 (compared to 20,689 in 1997), and the Liberal Democrats succeeded in beating the Conservatives for second place, but the most eye-catching aspect of the result was the extraordinary low turnout – 19.6 per cent. The longest period without a by-election had culminated in by far the lowest by-election turnout since the war.

A second indicator was the outcome in the Netherlands and Denmark, which had also gone to the polls on Thursday, and where exit polls had been taken. In Denmark, turnout was estimated at about 50 per cent (compared with 52.9 per cent in 1994) and in the Netherlands it was estimated to be at a historic low of about 30 per cent (compared with 35.6 per cent in 1994). Once again, these findings confirmed the expectation of very low turnout levels in the UK, but they also suggested that the low level of involvement was a broader phenomenon and not simply restricted to Britain.

The third, and strongest, indicator was the verification of votes by Westminster constituency on the Thursday night. Although the results could not be announced until the Sunday evening, the verification counts gave a strong factual indicator of low turnout. (It was also possible to get a rough idea of how the parties were doing, although votes were counted face down simply to verify that the numbers recorded as having been cast were the same as the numbers actually coming out of the ballot boxes.)

In June 1994, the European Parliament had organised an electoral evening in its Brussels headquarters, designed to give journalists easy access to the incoming results, while creating some of the traditional excitement of the end of an electoral campaign. The exercise was considered a success and was repeated on 13 June 1999. But, in contrast to 1994, there was an almost total dearth of 'celebrities' – political or otherwise – and only a low buzz of anticipation which soon petered out. Dennis McShane was the only British government representative to put in an appearance. In 1994, the building was still humming with activity and political gossip at 4.00 a.m. But this time, by 3.00 a.m., it had largely emptied out. Throughout the European Union the campaign had failed to ignite.

Back in London, meanwhile, BBC 2 broadcast a full-scale Euro-elections programme, chaired by David Dimbleby, until 3.00 a.m., by which time the UK results were largely clear. There were two main themes to the evening: the low turnout, and the Conservatives' much-better-than-expected performance (and Labour's correspondingly disastrous showing).

Candidates and activists commented on the strangeness of the actual mechanics of the count, with its combination of Westminster single-member constituency counting and PR totalling up. Each result arriving from Westminster constituencies had its own significance as well as bringing its part to the overall regional result.

By the time of the 14 June midday news bulletins, the last results were in (see Table 7.1). William Hague could be pleased with the result. Unexpectedly, his leadership and authority had been consolidated, giving him a clear run through to the next General Election. Tony Blair gave a subdued and reflective press conference in the Downing Street rose garden. There were, he admitted, lessons to be learnt and Labour had to listen to the electorate. Paddy Ashdown's swansong was not quite as victorious as he had hoped. The party had gained nine seats but had lost one and had fallen two short of the twelve seats which bullish party officials had expected at the beginning of the campaign. Moreover, a worrying trend became clear. The party had been depleted in all of its Westminster constituencies bar one, Orkney and Shetland, and its two notional gains from Labour – Birmingham Yardley and Oldham East and Saddleworth – were little consolation. This, pundits argued, was the 'price' the party had paid for its closeness to the Labour Party.

Table 7.1 The overall results (and change over 1994)

Party	Results
Conservatives	36 (+ 18)
Labour	29 (– 33)
Liberal Democrats	10 (+ 8)
United Kingdom Independence Party	3 (+ 3)
Green Party	2 (+ 2)
Plaid Cymru	2 (+ 2)
Scottish National Party	2
Democratic Unionists	1
Social Democratic and Labour Party	1
Ulster Unionist Party	1

In Scotland, the SNP, which had won only 20,000 votes less than Labour (taking three seats), was disappointed to win two seats rather than an expected three, while the Conservatives, with 70,000 fewer votes than the SNP, also won two seats. The Greens (with almost 60,000 votes) were unable to climb over the threshold. The remaining place went to the Liberal Democrats. Tommy Sheridan's Scottish Socialist Party made a brave showing (just under 40,000 votes) but, assuming their votes would otherwise have gone to the Labour Party, their main effect was to cost Labour a fourth seat. In Wales, Labour's dismal showing in the 6 May Welsh Assembly elections was followed up by the loss of what should normally have been its third seat to a resurgent Plaid Cymru. In Northern Ireland none of the expected upsets occurred. Ian Paisley (DUP) just beat John Hume (SDLP) for the first seat. Jim Nicholson (UUP) took the third; in effect, there was no change on 1994.

In the 1984 Euro-election Labour gained 15 seats from the Conservatives. In 1989, they gained a further 13 seats, and in 1994 another 19. It seemed inevitable therefore that the party would lose some

© Steve Bell 1999

1288·15·6·99·

Guardian (15 June) (Steve Bell)

The ...... Labour's poor performance was universal

seats in 1999. But it was the scale of the retreat, from 62 to 29 seats, which was so unexpected. Moreover, if the election had been held under the old first-past-the-post system with single-member constituencies, the 1999 Euro-elections would have given Labour only 29 seats to the Conservatives' 50, and the Liberal Democrats would have got none (see p. 253). As Paddy Ashdown pointed out, PR had reduced Labour's humiliation, rather than enhanced it. Indeed, if the same votes had been cast in a traditional General Election, the Conservatives would have won 352 seats to Labour's 261, and the Liberal Democrats three. The best excuse for Labour seemed to lie in the turnout. Only 24 per cent of those on the register cast a ballot, which meant that only 9 per cent of the full electorate actually voted for the Conservatives (though only 7 per cent voted for Labour).

Ironically, media interest in the consequences of the Euro-elections grew as the elections themselves faded into the distance. There was much speculation about William Hague's forthcoming frontbench reshuffle. What would he do with his newfound authority? Meanwhile, it was learnt that Mr Blair had organised a first post-mortem meeting on Friday 11 June at which he told Downing Street and Millbank officials that he wanted to know as soon as possible how the disaster had occurred. The meeting had already considered a number of rectificatory measures, including the possibility of appointing Peter Mandelson to a senior campaigns position within the government.

The Liberal Democrats became increasingly embroiled in their leadership campaign, with Charles Kennedy – the frontrunner – and Don Foster officially launching their campaigns. Meanwhile, the ten Liberal Democrat MEPs, meeting for the first time on 15 June 1999, elected Graham Watson as their leader, as expected. Mr Watson, a member of the European Parliament since 1994, had been Secretary-General of the Liberal International's youth movement and one of the founders of the European Communities' Youth Forum. The ten MEPs represented the largest national contingent within the Liberal group in the European Parliament, and were accordingly expected to gain in influence.

As Box 7.1 shows, the distortions caused by low and differentiated turnout and a regional list system threw up a large number of unexpected losers and winners. No less than 13 sitting Labour MEPs who could normally have been fairly confident of re-election lost their seats, as did the second Liberal Democrat in the 1994–99 Parliament, Robin Teverson. In addition, Christine May (Labour, Scotland) and Sharon Bowles (Liberal Democrat, South-East) had generally been expected to win but did not. On the other side of the coin, eleven Conservative candidates won unex-

Table 7.2 The 1999 European elections – detailed results in seats (S) and votes

	T/out %	Con S	Con %	Lab S	Lab %	Lib Dem S	Lib Dem %	Nat S	Nat %	UKIP S	UKIP %	Green S	Green %	Other S	Other %	Total S	Total %
E. Mid.	22.6	3	9.5	2	28.6	1	12.8	–	–	–	7.6	–	5.4	–	6.2	6	100
Eastern	24.5	4	2.7	2	25.2	1	11.9	–	–	1	8.9	–	6.2	–	5.1	8	100
London	23.0	4	32.7	4	35.0	1	11.7	–	–	–	5.4	1	7.7	–	7.6	10	100
N.E.	19.5	1	27.4	3	42.1	–	13.5	–	–	–	8.8	–	4.7	–	3.4	4	100
N.W.	19.5	5	35.4	4	34.5	1	11.7	–	–	–	6.6	–	5.6	–	6.3	10	100
S.E.	24.7	5	44.4	2	19.6	2	15.3	–	–	1	9.7	1	7.4	–	3.5	11	100
S.W.	27.6	4	41.7	1	18.1	1	16.5	–	–	1	10.6	–	8.3	–	4.8	7	100
W. Mid.	21.0	4	37.9	3	28.0	1	11.3	–	–	–	5.8	–	5.8	–	11.1	8	100
Yorks & H.	19.6	3	6.6	3	31.3	1	14.4	–	–	–	7.1	–	5.7	–	4.8	7	100
England	22.7	33	38.6	24	7.7	9	13.3	–	–	3	7.9	–	6.6	–	5.9	71	100
Wales	28.1	1	22.8	2	1.9	–	8.2	2	29.6	–	3.1	–	2.6	–	1.9	5	100
Scotland	24.7	2	19.8	3	28.7	1	9.8	2	27.2	–	1.3	–	5.8	–	7.5	8	100
G.B.	23.1	36	35.8	29	28.0	10	12.7	4	4.5	3	7.0	2	6.3	–	5.8	84	100

Northern Ireland turnout 57.0 per cent; UK turnout 24.0 per cent.

pectedly, together with the three successful UKIP candidates and the two Green, as well as the second of the Plaid Cymru MEPs.

The new British contingent was consequently among the least experienced to be returned to the Parliament. Only 40 of the 87 were, or

---

Box 7.1 Unexpected 'victims' and 'victors'

'Victims'	*'Victors'*
The South-West	
Ian White, MEP (Lab)	Neil Parish (Con)
Robin Teverson, MEP (Lib Dem)	Michael Holmes (UKIP)
The South-East	
Anita Pollack, MEP (Lab)	Nirj Deva (Con)
Sharon Bowles, (Lib Dem)	Caroline Lucas (Green)
	Nigel Farage (UKIP)
London	
Carole Tongue, MEP (Lab)	John Bowis (Con)
	Jean Lambert (Green)
Eastern Region	
Clive Needle, MEP (Lab)	Geoffrey Van Orden (Con)
	Jeffrey Titford (UKIP)
East Midlands	
Angela Billingham, MEP (Lab)	Chris Heaton-Harris (Con)
West Midlands	
Mike Tappin, MEP (Lab)	Malcolm Harbour (Con)
David Hallam, MEP (Lab)	Philip Bradbourn (Con)
Yorkshire and The Humber Region	
Roger Barton, MEP (Lab)	Robert Goodwill (Con)
North-East	
North-West	
Tony Cunningham, MEP (Lab)	Den Dover (Con)
	Jacqueline Foster (Con)
Scotland	
Christine May, (Lab)	John Purvis (Con)
Wales	
Joseph Wilson, MEP (Lab)	Eurig Wyn (Plaid Cymru)

Table 7.3 UK MEPs elected in 1999, by region

	Conservative	Labour	Liberal Democrat	PC/SNP	Other
East Midlands	Roger Helmer William Newton Dunn Christopher Heaton-Harris	Mel Read Phillip Whitehead	Nicholas Clegg		
Eastern	Robert Sturdy Christopher Beazley Bashir Khanbhai Geoffrey Van Orden	Eryl McNally Richard Howitt	Andrew Duff		Jeffrey Titford (UKIP)
London	Theresa Villiers Timothy Tannock Lord Bethell John Bowis Martin Callanan	Pauline Green Claude Moraes Robert Evans Richard Balfe Alan Donnelly Stephen Hughes Mo O'Toole	Baroness Ludford		Jean Lambert (Green)
North-East		Arlene McCarthy Gary Titley Terry Wynn Brian Simpson	Chris Davies		
North-West	Lord Inglewood Sir Robert Atkins David Sumberg Den Dover Jacqueline Foster				
South-East	James Provan Roy Perry Daniel Hannan James Elles Nirj Deva	Peter Skinner Mark Watts	Baroness Nicholson Christopher Huhne		Caroline Lucas (Green) Nigel Farage (UKIP)

Region	Conservative	Labour	Liberal Democrat	Nationalist	Other
South-West	Caroline Jackson Giles Chichester Earl of Stockton Neil Parish	Glyn Ford	Graham Watson		Michael Holmes (UKIP)
West Midlands	John Corrie Philip Bushill-Matthews John Harbour Philip Bradbourn	Simon Murphy Michael Cashman Neena Gill	Liz Lynne		
Yorkshire & The Humber	Edward McMillan-Scott Timothy Kirkhope Robert Goodwill Jonathan Evans	Linda McAvan David Bowe Richard Corbett	Diana Wallis		
Wales		Glenys Kinnock Eluned Morgan		Jillian Evans Eurig Wyn	
Scotland	Struan Stevenson John Purvis	David Martin Bill Miller Catherine Taylor	Elspeth Attwooll	Ian Hudghton Neil MacCormick	
Northern Ireland					Ian Paisley (DUP) John Hume (SDLP) James Nicholson (UUP)

had been, MEPs, including four Conservatives (Christopher Beazley, Lord Bethell, Lord Inglewood and William Newton Dunn) who had lost their Euro seats in 1994. It also included representatives of three parties (the Greens, Plaid Cymru and UKIP) which had never been elected to the Parliament before.[1] Not only was the new British contingent more fragmented, but it was likely to be less predictable.

Of the two largest party contingents, Labour's was by far the more experienced, with 24 of the 29 MEPs elected having been members of the outgoing Parliament. This suggested continuity in terms of the leadership and structure of the EPLP, and was confirmed when Alan Donnelly was re-elected as leader shortly after the election results were known (16 June). By contrast, only 8 of the 36 Conservative MEPs had been members of the outgoing Parliament.

A balance sheet

William Hague

The Leader of the Opposition emerged from the Euro-election an undisputed winner. His choice of tactics had been vindicated, his authority strengthened, and that of his detractors undermined. He had scored a direct hit on the previously untouchable Tony Blair. His reputation for steadiness under fire was also confirmed, as he refused to allow himself to be distracted by the potential threat from disgruntled Europhiles within the party, nor by attempts to play up a 'Hague factor' as a potential vote-loser. On the contrary, having already displayed ruth-lessness in expelling dissidents during the campaign, he asserted his authority over the party, through a major reshuffle of his Shadow team just two days after the Euro-results were announced. The reshuffle would in any case have been necessary, since three senior Conservative politicians – Gillian Shepherd, Michael Howard, Sir Norman Fowler – had already announced their intentions of stepping down from the Shadow team. But Mr Hague created more space by effectively sacking the party's Deputy Leader, Peter Lilley, who paid the price for his misfired efforts to shed the party's Thatcherite image (which had menaced Mr Hague's hold on the leadership). Perhaps most importantly, Mr Hague had recaptured the support of the Euro-sceptic press – the *Sun*, the *Mail*, *The Times* and the *Daily Telegraph* – said by some party insiders secretly to have been the most important objective of the whole electoral campaign.

As the glow of electoral success faded, political commentators increas-ingly pointed to the Achilles' heel in Mr Hague's tactics. In effect, the

Leader of the Opposition had skilfully mobilised a passionately Euro-sceptical minority, predicating his tactics on a low turnout. Yet the vote mobilised amounted to just 9 per cent of the British electorate. In overall terms, the Tories still got only 36 per cent of the total vote, much less than Labour had won in Opposition in 1989 or 1994. Middle England had not yet been recaptured. Some commentators argued that, by concentrating on ideological believers, Mr Hague was repeating the mistakes of Labour in the early 1980s. The broad opinion, shared by virtually all of the British press, was that Mr Hague could not hope to oust Mr Blair on a Euro-sceptical platform alone, even if he succeeded in turning the next General Election into a referendum by proxy on the single currency. Mr Hague had to develop a set of attractive alternative policies, and his post-election reshuffle showed that he implicitly accepted this analysis. A MORI poll for *The Times*, published on 29 July, demonstrated the electoral mountain Mr Hague had yet to climb. On voting intentions, it showed Labour leading the Conservatives by 51 per cent to 28 per cent, and the gloomy outlook was confirmed by Gallup and ICM polls the following week, and again in August and September.

Andrew Lansley

A clear winner on the Conservative side was the party's campaign coordinator, Andrew Lansley. He had only become an MP in 1997, but his surefooted management won him a rich reward in the post-election reshuffle, with Mr Hague appointing him as Shadow minister for the Cabinet office and policy renewal. A clever and personable right-wing loyalist, Mr Lansley was tipped as a future leadership contender. Before entering Parliament he had served for five years at Conservative Central Office as director of research, playing a pivotal role in John Major's 1992 election victory. He came into the party from the civil service, having worked as private secretary to Norman (Lord) Tebbit at the Department of Trade and Industry in the mid-1980s, and a period as deputy director general of the British Chamber of Commerce. His new appointment meant that he would become a key player in the run-up to the next General Election, driving through Mr Hague's policy review.

The Greens

The Greens gained two seats, one in London and one in the South-East, the two regions where it was easiest for small parties to break through and where the party's support was most concentrated. Although far from the heady days of the party's 1989 performance, the result was more significant in that the UK had for the first time elected Green politicians in a national election. As had occurred with the Liberal Democrats' two MEPs from 1994 onwards, the two Green MEPs not only provided an electoral platform on which to build, but would bring resources back to the national party and give it direct influence in the Green Group in the European Parliament. The party acknowledged that its vote had been buoyed by disaffected Labour voters. But the Greens, like the UKIP, were above all major beneficiaries of the new voting system. Potential Green voters were told that their votes now counted (with the simple slogan 'Green votes count') and, with emotive issues such as GM foods to mobilise them, the party was bound to benefit from a low turnout. The party's electoral chances were also helped by the way other smaller party votes lowered the threshold. Moreover, the British Green Party boasted an idiosyncratic, but potentially attractive range of policy positions, combining anti-GM foods with an anti-single currency stance. Despite predicted difficulties because of the party's anti-Euro stance, the British Greens smoothly joined the Greens/European Free Alliance Group in the new Parliament where, controversial though they would sit alongside Plaid Cymru and the SNP.

The United Kingdom Independence Party

The UK Independence Party had a good election, plugging into the layer of passionate Euro-scepticism which even the Prime Minister admitted to exist in the electorate and surfing on the more anti-European atmosphere created by Mr Hague's tactics. The UKIP was the only small party to gain support from across the country, winning one seat in the South-West, one in the South-East, and another in the Eastern region. Its share of the vote exceeded 8 per cent in many areas.

The party's chairman, Nigel Farage, said that in Strasbourg the party would oppose the single currency and ultimately work to free Britain from Europe altogether: 'For us the really important reason for going out there is to find the extent of the fraud, the waste and the corruption, to bring that information back to this country and to expose that' (*Financial Times*, 15 June). He rejected Paddy Ashdown's claims that they were Little England xenophobes: 'We are not nationalists, we are nationists ... We want to keep our own identity' (*The Times*, 15 June).

Jaundiced commentators wondered whether the UKIP MEPs could avoid 'going native', since, if they were to have any influence in the Strasbourg Parliament, they would have to join a political group and hence enter into the mechanics of the ubiquitous d'Hondt system. When the dust settled, it transpired that they had joined a new group, the Europe of Democracies and Differences Group (EDD), idiosyncratically composed of Dutch and Danish Euro-sceptics and six French MEPs elected on a pro-hunting and fishing list. As the *Guardian* reported (23 July), 'Despite the UKIP's antipathy towards the EU, its MEPs now see that the payment of expenses – the gravy train so widely ridiculed by Eurosceptics – may have some purpose after all.' The newspaper went on to point out that the Danish anti-EU movement had financed its activities for years on expenses claimed legitimately for travel and office facilities.

The UKIP members' first political act was to abstain in the vote to elect the President of the Parliament. 'We cannot vote and look as though we are taking part in the system', said Michael Holmes, 'but we will vote on issues affecting British interests.'

Plaid Cymru

One month after the Welsh Assembly elections, the Labour Party was still reeling from the extraordinary results which had seen heartlands such as the Rhondda captured by a newly dynamised Plaid Cymru. With no government at stake, and its supporters tired or demotivated, Labour feared more of the same in the Euro-elections. Plaid Cymru set itself the target of overtaking Labour as the largest party – an unthinkable target even in 1997. In the event, Plaid fell just two and a half percentage points short of its objective but won enough to capture what would normally have been Labour's third seat. Equally significant, as with the Greens in this election and the Liberal Democrats in 1994, the return of two MEPs to Strasbourg not only provided an electoral platform on which to build but would bring resources back to the party and give it direct influence in the Greens/European Free Alliance Group. In the negotiations for committee positions the party was given the welcoming present of a Vice-Chairmanship of the Women's Rights Committee for Jill Evans.

Within little more than a month the Welsh Labour Party had thus gone from effortless dominance to apprehensive vulnerability, while Plaid Cymru had become a serious contender for the crown of largest party. Underneath this achievement lay the possibility that the new electoral systems introduced for the Assembly and European elections might have knock-on effects for voting habits under the traditional first-past-the-post system. Wales, it seemed, was becoming far more pluralist, and Plaid Cymru was well placed to benefit from this development.

Alan Donnelly

Labour had a poor campaign, but some Labour politicians emerged with their reputations enhanced. This was true of Alan Donnelly, the outgoing leader of the EPLP. First elected to the European Parliament in 1989, Mr

Donnelly made his parliamentary name with high-profile reports on the monetary union process and served as Parliament's rapporteur on German unification. As MEP for Tyne and Wear, Mr Donnelly was passionately concerned about the European shipbuilding industry. As Secretary to the EPLP in 1989 and 1990 he was instrumental in modernising the group's structure, and he later became close to the Blair leadership. A long-serving coordinator on economic and monetary affairs for the PES Group, and Chairman of the EU–US parliamentary delegation, he was elected to the leadership of the EPLP in July 1998.

Mr Donnelly was one of a number of Labour MEPs subject to intense press investigations during the campaign. The *Sunday Times* published an article about Mr Donnelly's use of a leased Daimler. A carefully cropped photograph of him quaffing champagne above the *Sunday Times* article was intended to underline the 'champagne socialist' theme. In fact, the photograph had been taken when Wearside celebrated the reopening of the Pallion shipyard – a major boost for jobs in a depressed area.

In political terms, Mr Donnelly unhesitatingly pursued a staunch pro-EU and pro-euro line, and was one of a few Labour politicians who persisted publicly with this line once the results were known and the party's introspection began. He was reported to have 'gone round the Labour leadership trying to pump up morale ... It was time to come out fighting' (*Guardian*, 21 June). On 22 June he made a strongly worded speech urging the government to stress the benefits of EU membership as an indispensable condition for winning the narrower debate about the single currency.

The EPLP met on 16 June, two days after the results, and Mr Donnelly's enhanced stature enabled him to drive through a series of reforms to the EPLP structure. Mr Donnelly was re-elected leader, and the leader's mandate was extended from one year to two and a half years. A basic distinction was made between policy and legislative matters on the one hand, and administrative matters on the other. Philip Whitehead was elected Chair of the EPLP. Linda McAvan was elected Deputy Leader with special responsibility for financial matters; Bill Miller was elected Whip; Robert Evans was elected Bureau member, charged with keeping an eye on the opposition; Arlene McCarthy was put in charge of links with the Labour Party; Eluned Morgan was responsible for best practice of regional teams; and Gary Titley was made responsible for relations with the national delegations within the PES Group – something the old EPLP had badly neglected.

The reforms left Mr Donnelly presiding over a leaner machine whose attention was already clearly focused on the next General Election and the referendum which would follow it.

The Pro-Euro Conservatives

The Pro-Euro Conservatives' hopes of making substantial electoral inroads disappeared like a morning mist. The party won just 1.4 per cent of the vote in an election where it had initially hoped to take seats and later hoped to act as a spoiler and bring down Mr Hague's leadership. To rub salt into the wounds, Jacqueline Foster was returned at number five on the Conservative Party's North-West list, a place which had been turned down by both John Stevens and Brendan Donnelly. The party's leadership had always acknowledged the need for a big name to give the party credibility and visibility, and they believed that they had been cheated of success by the failure of Kenneth Clarke or Michael Heseltine to 'come out' in the party's support. But, far from joining the splinter group, both Mr Clarke and Mr Heseltine objected to the use of their names and pronouncements in the Pro-Euro Conservatives' literature. The party seemed deliberately to court controversy with its PEB, displaying a William Hague lookalike as a xenophobic, bigoted tramp. But the attendant publicity soon died away and the consensus amid the ranks of the Conservative Europhiles was that the PEB had been unnecessarily vulgar and had undermined the Pro-Euro Conservatives' own case. The party's biggest break came on 8 June, when *The Times* carried a supportive letter from a group of nine former Conservative MPs and MEPs and reported that Lord Gilmour would be voting Pro-Euro Conservative. But it was too little too late to shift the party centre stage. There were also underlying hints of distrust of a party rumoured effectively to be bankrolled by one individual, just as there had been with James Goldsmith's Referendum Party in 1997.

Whatever the impact of these factors, they were not the major cause of the Pro-Euro Conservative Party's abject failure. It was, rather, a direct reflection of the success of Mr Hague's Euro-sceptical and anti-euro stance and of the failure to motivate the most pro-euro section of the population – 18–24-year-olds – to turn out. Had Labour run a strong pro-euro campaign, the Pro-Euro Conservatives might have benefited in the same way that UKIP benefited from Mr Hague's tactics. But, as far as the Pro-Euro Conservatives were concerned, there was no rising tide.

To borrow from commercial parlance, one of the Pro-Euro Conservative Party's problems was product differentiation. When the Party had been authorised to use the word 'Conservative' in its title, this was seen as a great victory, but in practice the title proved a disadvantage. On 5 July 1999, Mark Littlewood, the party's national campaign director, announced that the party would be changing its name: 'People hate parties, they hate the Conservatives and they hate the pro-euro cause. We had four of the most unpopular words in the English language. In the circumstances, it perhaps wasn't the most sellable name.' He announced that the party would be fighting the next General Election but would discuss fundamental matters at a mini-conference in London in October. 'We don't see ourselves as a single issue party', he said, 'and we want to move towards becoming a much wider group' (*Financial Times*, 6 July 1999). Whatever the party's future, it could not have got off to a more inauspicious start.

Tory Europhiles who had been tempted to join the Pro-Euros but who had remained within the Conservative Party could feel vindicated in their decision. However depressed they were by Mr Hague's hardening anti-euro rhetoric, the Euro-election results had clearly demonstrated that there was little future for a breakaway pro-European Conservative group – with or without the 'big beasts'.

The Conservative Europhiles

In the aftermath of the election, pro-European Conservatives turned their wrath on Mr Blair, particularly when he seemed to waver in his commitment to the Britain in Europe campaign. They felt that, by default, he had let Mr Hague set the pace during the campaign and that, the more the Leader of the Opposition was encouraged to exploit this tactical advantage, the more he was also damaging the pro-euro and pro-European cause. In part, the senior pro-European Tories kept silent because they expected the party to do badly and did not want to be blamed for contributing to the failure. But more subtle reasoning was also at work. As Chapter 4 showed, the Conservative Party's selection process had thrown up a surprisingly large number of Euro-enthusiastic candidates, and the desire to build up a strong group of instinctively pro-European MEPs was probably a key reason why Tory left-wingers stayed glumly loyal during the contest.

One of the senior pro-European Tories, Kenneth Clarke, put a brave public face on events, arguing on the BBC's *Today* programme and in several newspaper interviews that the Conservative success demonstrated how the party could do well if it avoided public divisions. He also confirmed that he would be joining the Britain in Europe campaign with his leader's blessing. Privately, the Tory Euro-enthusiasts expressed determination to remain within the party and fight against it becoming an out-and-out anti-EU party.

The frustration of senior pro-European Tories was matched by exultation among the Euro-sceptics; an Edward Heathcoat Amory article in the *Daily Mail* was headlined, 'SURELY THIS IS THE END FOR THE EURO DINOSAURS' (15 June). The Euro-sceptics argued that the pro-Europeans' bluff had been called. ('CLARKE'S SNOOKERED AND HE KNOWS IT', wrote Michael Portillo in the *Observer* (1 August)). By staying their hand while Mr Hague's vocabulary became increasingly Euro-sceptical, they had surrendered their weapons without a fight. For, once the election results had consolidated Mr Hague's leadership, there was no way back to the old scenario, and it was broadly expected that Mr Clarke, Mr Heseltine, Lord Howe, and the other pro-European grandees would remain marginalised and diminished forces. For their part, they seemed to accept that they would have to wait until events forced a change in policy – which in effect meant waiting until entry into the euro was approved in a referendum. Not surprisingly, therefore, they immediately brought pressure to bear on the Prime Minister, urging him not to waver in his commitments to an early referendum and active participation in the pro-euro campaign. The more the referendum timetable slipped, and the more opposition to the euro grew in the opinion polls, the less it was likely that the pro-Europeans would be able to mount a successful comeback.

Margaret Beckett

As Labour braced itself for a poor result, the Sunday newspapers on 13 June were openly speculating that Margaret Beckett would take the flak and pay the price in the government's summer reshuffle. She had already been damaged by a 3 June *Times* report, alleging that she had spent a week on holiday during the campaign and that Jack Cunningham, the Cabinet 'enforcer', hoped to spend its last week on a fishing holiday. In reality, she had gone for a bank holiday weekend to France early on in the campaign, but although John Prescott staunchly defended her in an 8 June national press conference, the impression of neglect stuck. At a deeper level, insiders argued that she *was* the campaign coordinator and therefore had to take responsibility for a professionally poor campaign. In response, Mrs Beckett's supporters pointed out that the campaign had been starved of resources, both financial and human, and that she had been deprived at short notice of the participation of the Prime Minister and the Foreign Secretary. But Mrs Beckett was one of the more experienced members of the government front bench, and in 1994 had briefly been temporary leader of the Labour Party, and as *The Times* (10 July) reported, she remained 'Well-respected in the party and could be a threat on the backbenches.'

Pauline Green

Although in 1998 rumours circulated that Pauline Green might become Labour's candidate for the future post of Mayor of London, Mr Blair decided before the elections that he wanted her to continue as leader of the Socialist Group within the European Parliament. Working on the assumption that the Labour contingent would remain fairly large (about 35 members), a provisional 'package deal' was worked out with other European socialist and social democrat leaders which included her re-election to the position. But Mrs Green's renewed candidature was undermined by the events leading up to the resignation of the Santer Commission, when she had seemed at first to support the rapidly dis-integrating college and had then been obliged, very publicly, to reverse her position. In Germany, the Santer Commission's fate became a major domestic political issue, and the German Social Democrat members of the Socialist Group, who all favoured censuring the Commission, were critical of Mrs Green's initial stance. Further, French socialists were incensed by the publication, on the eve of the elections, of the Blair–Schröder policy document. Lastly, Mrs Green's public criticism of the Parliament's failure to vote through a new statute for MEPs angered the German Social Democrats, who felt Parliament should not be rushed by the Council (see p. 43). But the election results themselves dealt the severest blow to Mrs Green's hopes. Although the German SPD had done relatively badly in the elections, it returned 33 MEPs (to Labour's 29), and thus regained its pre-eminent position within the PES Group. Moreover, the French (22 MEPs) and the Spanish (24 MEPs) socialist parties were perceived as having 'won' their elections, while Labour was perceived as having 'lost'.

On 16 June, the leaders of the 15 socialist and social democratic parties met in Brussels under the chairmanship of Rudolf Scharping to discuss, among other matters, the Presidency of the Group. French socialist Pervenche Beres and Spanish socialist (and former President of the Parliament) Enrique Baron Crespo formally tabled their candidatures alongside that of Mrs Green, as did an Austrian social democrat, Johannes Swoboda. Although the leaders were able to confirm former Portugese Prime Minister Mario Soares as their candidate for the Presidency of the Parliament, they could not reach agreement on the Presidency of the Group, and postponed the decision.

When, at a new meeting on Tuesday 7 July, it became clear that Mrs Green had support from only 10 of the 18 parties making up the PES Group, she withdrew her candidacy, pledging her support to the Socialist

Group's new leader, Enrique Baron Crespo. In her last speech as leader, Mrs Green refused to apologise for her staunch support for early reform of the MEPs' statute: 'I believe that the self-inflicted wounds of the present regime have done more damage to the legitimacy and credibility of this parliament in the eyes of our electorate than anything else.' Perhaps in compensation, the PES Group announced that Robin Cook, the Foreign Secretary, would take over as President of the Party of European Socialists when the current President, Rudolf Scharping, stood down, although that might not be until 2001.

The Liberal Democrats

At face value, the Liberal Democrats appeared to have made substantial advances, increasing their Strasbourg representation from two to ten MEPs. But they had lost one sitting MEP, Robin Teverson, and at the outset of the campaign they were widely expected to win twelve seats. Although the party could console itself with its newfound weight at Strasbourg, party strategists knew that these hid a worrying evaporation of the 1997 vote. Indeed, in Westminster terms, the party had done disastrously. Behind the statistics was an apparent paradox; many Liberal Democrat voters switched to the UKIP. Yet, as the Nuffield study of the 1994 Euro-elections showed, grassroots Liberal Democrat supporters tend to be far more Euro-sceptic than the party leadership. The party hierarchy – including Paddy Ashdown – realised this, which was why the party placed so much emphasis on domestic issues during the campaign. At the same time, William Hague's decision to adopt a Euro-sceptical stance and the continuing decline of the euro throughout the campaign forced the Liberal Democrats to play down one of the key elements in the party's manifesto. The more pro-European elements in the party argued vociferously that they had been let down by Labour's failure to engage on the issue of the single currency.

It was known that Paddy Ashdown would resign soon after the Euro-elections and the poor result raised fundamental questions about the attitudes of the candidates to succeed him. Should the party modify its position on the single currency? How should the party respond to its very poor showing in Wales and Scotland? Had the party's voters punished it for getting too close to the government? With the Prime Minister prevaricating on the possibility of PR for national elections, should the party back away from Mr Blair's 'project'?

On 9 August 1999, the results of the Liberal Democrat leadership election were announced. Under the single transferable vote system and on a turnout of 61.6 per cent, voting went to a fourth round before

Charles Kennedy emerged as the successful candidate, taking 28,425 votes (57 per cent) to Simon Hughes' 21,833 votes (43 per cent).

PR for national elections

It was believed within the Labour Party that the introduction of PR for the European elections would cost the party dearly. In fact, as Peter Kellner pointed out in the *Independent* (15 June), it would have done so in 1994, but it did not in 1999. Had the same votes been cast in a first-past-the-post election, Labour would have won one extra seat. The big losers were the Tories, who would have won 13 extra, and the big gainers were the Liberal Democrats, Greens and UKIP, who would have won no seats under the old system. The generalised prejudice against PR persisted, both within the Labour Party and among the public at large. This prejudice consisted in part of rejection of the more 'alien' aspects of the new system (particularly the long ballot papers) and in part of resentment at the imposition of the closed list system. PR, its detractors claimed, was primarily responsible for the woefully low turnout. In addition, many Labour activists resented the fact that PR had given the loutish Conservatives healthy representation in the Edinburgh Parliament and PR in the Euro-elections meant that the Conservatives returned their first Scottish MEP since 1989.

Political commentators sensed that Labour's PR commitment for national elections was slipping and on 16 June, at Prime Minister's Question Time, Mr Hague asked Mr Blair outright: 'If he still thinks PR is a good idea, why does he not stick to his manifesto and give people a chance to reject the further destruction of our tried and tested voting system?' The Prime Minister replied: 'For the reason we gave at the time of the Jenkins Report – a new system could not be introduced in time for the next General Election.' In fact, the report argued that there *was* sufficient time, but Mr Blair had clearly decided that there would be no chance of encouraging the Labour Party to campaign enthusiastically for a change.

This was an important moment in British electoral history. Lord Jenkins of Hillhead, the Chairman of the Commission appointed by the government to examine the issue, wrote in the *Guardian* that he did not 'react violently against postponing the referendum on electoral reform until after the next election. What I do strongly contest is the view that the subject should be buried in the interim' (14 July). But few others believed that Mr Blair would return to the commitment until well into a second term, if ever. The Euro-elections were not the cause of the setback to the PR cause, but they were surely the straw which broke the camel's back.

This was confirmed in a 27 July NEC discussion, based on an internal report on the Euro-election defeat. The NEC reportedly agreed that the closed-list system had alienated voters, angered party activists, and been a big factor in the record low turnout. Ian McCartney, the Industry Minister, was charged with canvassing views for improving the system. He would in particular examine the possibility of small or single-member constituencies. One option would be for groups of single-member seats with top-up members elected by PR (*The Times*, 28 July). It was also suggested that every five years, May's local elections be delayed by a month so that they could be held on the same day as the Euro-elections.

Underlying these discussions was a feeling that the government had engaged in too much constitutional reform and that the electorate and party activists were growing tired of referendums and elections.

The government's Anglo-German initiative

The poor performance of both Tony Blair's New Labour and Gerhard Schröder's SDP was interpreted by many commentators as a rejection by the voters of the two leaders' centrist 'Third Way' and *Neue Mitte* policies, as epitomised in the joint document they had presented on the eve of the elections (the Hombach–Mandelson initiative). The impression was compounded by the fact that in France, where Lionel Jospin had pursued a more traditionally idiosyncratic French left-wing course, the socialist party and allied parties gained six seats. 'Third way or new centre?', asked Mr Jospin during the campaign; 'No! I prefer to follow our path, the path of the modern left … of growth, social progress and modernity' (*Independent*, 11 June). This happened after generous press coverage had highlighted the differences between Mr Jospin's policies and those of Mr Blair and Mr Schröder. At the end of July, newspaper reports stated that leading German Social Democrats had revolted against Mr Schröder for following Mr Blair too closely. Reinhard Klimmt, the premier of Saxony-Anhalt, argued that Blairite positions had resulted in the serious losses of the Euro-elections, and that 'The Government would have been better advised to put its chips on the Bonn–Paris axis rather than on Tony Blair so soon before the European elections' (*The Times*, 30 July).

Leaving aside the report's substance, insiders close to Mr Blair questioned the tactics and timing of its publication. As one senior Labour politician put it: 'the question has to be asked, what was it for? and why was it released at that particular moment?' It got the headlines in Germany and may have helped Hombach's *Neue Mitte* along. It certainly got headlines in France, though of the wrong sort. Social democrats throughout Europe felt it had lost them votes, and it certainly won the party no votes in the UK! Another Labour politician complained that, 'It bore no relation to the rest of the campaign. If, as I suspect, it was published in search of tomorrow's headlines, it went badly wrong.'

Continental social democrats were confused by the potentially contradictory messages from 10 Downing Street. The Blair–Schröder paper was one of a series of bilateral initiatives, including the St Malo agreement on defence with the French government and a similar summit with Italian premier, Massimo D'Alema, on 20 July. But what were social democrats to make of Mr Blair's much-trumpeted summit with the Spanish *Partido Popular* Prime Minister, José-Maria Aznar? Even the more loyal of the party's activists asked whether, in new Labour terms, a 'joined-up' strategy existed.

Confusion about the future of Anglo-German cooperation over the 'Third Way' was exacerbated at the end of June, when the German Chancellor pushed Italy Hombach out of his government and into a diplomatic role in the Balkans. By the end of July, as the euro pulled out of its initial nosedive, the British and German governments were thrown even further out of step. On the one hand, Tony Blair sought to sharpen Britain's profile in Europe while simultaneously playing down the immediate significance of the euro. But at around the same time German politicians and bankers were beginning to place the euro back at the centre of the European project. At the very least, the Anglo-German initiative had lost much of its momentum.

Peter Mandelson

Peter Mandelson had little direct influence on Labour's campaign; yet he stood to gain much from the outcome. The former Trade and Industry minister had been in purdah since Christmas 1998, when he had been forced to resign following the furore over a loan he had received from the Paymaster-General, Geoffrey Robinson. The Prime Minister regretted Mr Mandelson's departure and was soon entrusting him with occasional tasks which suggested Mr Blair would like to see him rehabilitated as soon as possible. These included the drafting with the ill-fated Bodo Hombach of the Anglo-German document, *The Way Forward for Europe's Social Democrats* (see p. 195).

On Monday 14 June, as the scale of Labour's disaster was becoming apparent, the newspapers reported that the Prime Minister was considering bringing Mr Mandelson back into the Cabinet. The idea had apparently already been mooted in Mr Blair's 11 June post-mortem meeting at Downing Street. A rash of articles subsequently appeared, contrasting Mr Mandelson's skills and experience with Labour's inept European election campaign. The speculation was being fuelled somehow. The *Daily Mail* (16 June), reported that: 'the push comes from Mr Blair himself. Downing Street is quietly orchestrating an elaborate operation to test out whether the Premier could get away with calling his closest political confidant back from the wilderness'. In the same newspaper Colin Byrne, Mr Mandelson's deputy at Walworth Road from 1988 to 1991, said: 'Most people will find it surprising that in these European elections, Peter Mandelson, one of our brightest and best strategists, was probably delivering leaflets in Hartlepool rather than directing at the centre.'

Throughout the immediate post-elections period, Mr Mandelson made a number of high profile speeches. In a supposedly private address to his constituents, Mr Mandelson was critical of the campaign and expressed strong pro-euro sentiments. On 28 June he made a powerfully pro-European and pro-euro speech in Brussels which won wide coverage in the next day's press, and on 30 June he gave a similar speech to the Amalgamated Engineering and Electrical Union in Jersey. It was difficult not to see this sudden spurt of speeches as anything other than a comeback campaign.

However, Mr Mandelson had one significant hurdle to leap. On 1 July the House of Commons Committee on Standards and Privileges reported on the April findings of Elizabeth Filkin, the Parliamentary 'watchdog', who had argued that Mr Mandelson's dealings had fallen below the standards expected of an MP. The Commons Committee upheld one complaint that Mr Mandelson should have registered the loan he received from Mr Robinson, but concluded that he acted 'without dishonest intention' and recommended no action be taken against him. It was no more than a mild rebuke, and the setback proved shortlived.

On 10 July, in the context of growing reshuffle speculation, it was reported that the former minister had returned as the Prime Minister's behind-the-scenes 'fixer', and was to be given an influential role in a revamped Prime Minister's office, dubbed 'the power suite', which was being built in the Cabinet Office. A Labour insider was quoted as saying: 'The irony is he is still one of the most powerful five or six people in the country. Not bad for a backbencher.' Nevertheless, it was widely known that Mr Mandelson still hankered after a return to the Cabinet, and there were published rumours that he might replace Mo Mowlam as Northern Ireland Secretary. This led an apparently incensed Dr Mowlam to insist, in an unprecedentedly public fashion, that she wanted to see the peace process through to the end. All eyes turned therefore to the 26–27 July government reshuffle. Allegedly because of Mrs Mowlam's insistence on staying on, Mr Blair decided against major changes at Cabinet level.

Peter Mandelson did not therefore return to the Cabinet in July, but his friends were confident that he would do so soon. For the conclusion Mr Blair was reported to have drawn from flying the Mandelson kite was that the kite had, indeed, flown. To the Prime Minister, the European elections had highlighted how much Mr Mandelson's skills were missed. With the Commons Committee report out of the way, the path was free for Mr Blair to bring his friend back into the governmental fold, and in an October reshuffle Mr Mandelson duly returned.

The Prime Minister

The Prime Minister was both a winner and a loser in June 1999. His personal popularity was undented by the electoral setback, and he seemed to be developing almost Reaganesque qualities of avoiding association with the falling of his administration – perhaps a reflection of the growing 'presidential' phenomenon addressed on p. 10. To the British public, the enduring image of the Prime Minister was not that of a Euro-elections loser, but that of the hawk who had not flinched from his moral crusade in Kosovo and the statesman who was prepared to invest his all in the search for peace in Northern Ireland.

Nevertheless, the Prime Minister had been damaged. As Peter Riddell put it in *The Times*, 'Tony Blair still commands the heights, but a vulnerable flank has for the first time been exposed by William Hague's marauders' (15 June). Or, as Alan Watkins put it in the *Independent on Sunday*, 'Mr Blair once again appears mortal and rejoins the human race, which he left briefly on 1 May 1997 to ascend into heavenly regions' (20 June). Nor could he deny all personal responsibility for what had occurred. As *The Times* reported (15 June), 'There is little doubt that the prime minister encouraged, if not instigated, the low-key campaign in the belief that Labour would glide to victory on the back of its popular support.' In other words, Labour had indeed fallen foul of the complacency which Mr Blair had done so much to avoid in 1997.

Further, the results had knock-on effects on the government's policy commitments, most notably the commitments to referendums on the euro and on PR. Nobody knew how close these commitments were to the Prime Minister's heart, but his uncertainty about one and decision to postpone the other created an impression of vacillation and defensiveness and, by implication, confirmation of Mr Hague's tactics. The effects of the Prime Minister's off-hand remarks in the closing stages of the Euro-election campaign, together with the subsequent briefing from Number 10 on the euro, enabled the Euro-sceptical press to alter the political landscape, implying that Mr Blair was out of step with public opinion. The initial strategy of gently building up public support for the euro was no longer tenable.

Above all, Mr Blair now faced a momentous decision about how to handle the issue of the euro at the next general election. Whereas Robin Cook was reportedly one among a group of senior ministers who believed that Labour would not be able to get through to the election without stating where it would stand in the referendum, the Chancellor of the Exchequer was said to be of the view that the possible date of the referendum should be substantially postponed so as to remove the issue from Mr Hague's armoury. And as the Euro-elections had graphically demonstrated, the party's activists could not necessarily be counted upon in an unpopular and onerous campaign.

A series of prime ministerial speeches at the end of July indicated that, after reflection, Mr Blair had strengthened his pro-euro resolve, but the old certainties no longer seemed to be there.

The consequences for the anti- and pro-euro campaigns in the UK

While the anti-euro campaign had much to hearten it, the pro-euro campaign had to deal with a series of difficult issues and was widely perceived as having fallen into disarray. In the first place, the pro-euros had placed their faith in launching a strong cross-party campaign *after* the Euro-elections. This was predicated on an alleged deal between pro-euro Tory grandees and the Labour government, whereby such personalities as Kenneth Clarke, Michael Heseltine and Geoffrey Howe would refrain from comment during the election campaign but join in a vigorous pro-euro campaign immediately afterwards. The Tory grandees' position was in turn based on a tacit agreement with the Hague leadership, whereby the Conservative Party would stick closely to the compromise position on the euro in return for their loyalty throughout the campaign. However, as described in Chapter 5, the euro rapidly became *the* issue of the campaign.

Whatever the misgivings about the longer-term consequences of Mr Hague's campaign, it proved effective in mobilising the Conservatives' core Euro-sceptic vote. The pro-euro campaign had no response. It badly needed heavyweight spokesmen to launch a counterattack, but none were to be found. Mr Clarke, Mr Heseltine, Mr Howe and other pro-euro

Conservatives stuck faithfully to their self-denying ordinance, while the Prime Minister and Mr Cook were deeply embroiled in the Kosovo war and the Chancellor, Mr Brown, stuck resolutely to domestic matters. Paddy Ashdown's frequent and passionate pro-euro declarations at the Liberal Democrats' national press conferences were swamped by his equally frequent and passionate statements on the Kosovo crisis. The Pro-Euro Conservative Party remained a marginal force throughout the campaign.

By the last week of the election campaign, the government had become more alert to the Tory tactics, and a series of spokesmen reiterated the official line, culminating with Mr Blair's declaration at Labour's last national press conference (9 June) that he 'passionately' believed in the government's stance. But three problems had arisen. First, the government had been forced on to the back foot and, with Mr Hague pressing home his advantage, found it impossible to escape a defensive stance on the issue. Second, this was primarily a reflection of the difficulty of launching an offensive based on a series of hypothetical conditions. Mr Hague's simple slogan of saving the pound contrasted with Mr Blair's stance that the government would consider its position which and if a series of conditions were met. Third, there was a perception that Mr Blair might be in the process of reconsidering his position, particularly with regard to the timing of a referendum. To the lack of a strong political stance during the election campaign was added the euro's downward drift, which enabled its critics to argue that it was fundamentally unsound.

After the elections, speculation mounted about the Prime Minister's commitment to the cause of British membership of the euro. The Prime Minister's 9 June declaration that to enter the single currency straightaway would be 'daft' was read by the Euro-sceptic press as a clear signal of change. Although the Prime Minister meanwhile maintained that his and the government's position remained unaltered, there was an increasing perception of change – a perception that was encouraged by the Prime Minister's own spokesman.

The Britain in Europe organisation had long planned to launch its cross-party campaign in favour of British membership of the euro in July, shortly after the European elections. Its leadership understood that it could count on the active involvement of Kenneth Clarke, Michael Heseltine, Geoffrey Howe and Paddy Ashdown, but also of the Prime Minister. However, after the elections, rumours abounded that Mr Blair was increasingly distancing himself from the forthcoming campaign, and would no longer appear on the podium at its launch. These rumours in turn provoked Kenneth Clarke and Michael Heseltine into threatening to boycott the campaign launch. As Mr Clarke put it, 'it is not my style to march on my own into the sound of gunfire so that Tony Blair can later walk over my body' (*The Times*, 15 June).

The embryonic campaign's cross-party nature reached its nadir on 21 June, when the *Financial Times* reported that 'aides to Tony Blair' had made it clear the Prime Minister would not lead it. 'Mr Blair's official spokesman, said he did not even understand the purpose of Britain in Europe.' On the same day, the euro's value plummeted further after the President-elect of the incoming European Commission, Romano Prodi, was reported to have told an Italian audience that if Italian 'costs diverge and we continue on this path we will not be able to stay in the euro'. Mr Prodi argued that he had been misquoted out of context, but the markets took fright at the apparent admission by a senior European politician that the currency union, so recently created, might fall apart.

However, within a week the atmosphere had changed again, with Downing Street confirming that Mr Blair had after all agreed to put himself at the head of the campaign. Pro-European and single currency elements within the party – including Peter Mandelson – had made protracted efforts to convince the Prime Minister that he should 'come out fighting' and not leave Mr Hague to make all the running. But Mr Blair exacted a 'price' for his involvement. The Britain in Europe campaign would no longer concentrate on the euro *per se*, but would set out to make the more general case for Britain to be at the heart of the European Union. The decisions reportedly came after a week of protracted negotiations between the Prime Minister, Downing Street aides, Lord Marshall, Lord Hollick and Giles Radice, MP. Mr Clarke and Mr Heseltine were also consulted (*The Times*, 28 June). Next day's *Guardian* reported that 'BLAIR STOPS WOBBLING AND BEGINS EURO BATTLE'. It was assumed that the battle would now be joined in July, and the Leader of the Opposition began to dig in.

Accordingly, on 9 July in a speech to the European Research Group's second congress in London, Mr Hague inveighed against the 'undemocratic' euro. In his most Euro-sceptic speech to date, Mr Hague came close to ruling out joining the euro altogether, as he listed eight reasons why sterling should stay out. Keeping the pound, he argued, was 'a battle for democracy itself', and there were good economic reasons – flexible exchange rates, low tax, free-enterprise economy – for remaining outside.

On 13 July 1999, the newspapers carried apparently contradictory information. The *Sun* reported that Mr Blair intended to market his party as 'the referendum party'. Described by a 'senior policy adviser' as a 'brilliant strategy', it was reported that the Prime Minister and his ministerial team would use the phrase whenever questioned about the euro, thus underlining the party's commitment and drawing attention to the contradiction in Mr Hague's stance. But the same newspaper also reported that, following 'organisational problems', the launch of the Britain in Europe campaign had been postponed until October. The news came as the euro edged perilously close to parity with the dollar.

On 20 July the Foreign Secretary, Robin Cook, was asked on BBC Radio 4's *World at One* programme whether it was 'absolutely inevitable' that a referendum on the single currency would be staged quickly if Labour won the next General Election. He replied: 'That is a preposterous question. We have said that we will have a referendum when we judge the criteria to be right.' This was enough for newspapers to run headlines such as 'DOUBTS ON EURO TIMETABLE GROW' (*Guardian*) and 'COOK ADDS TO UNCERTAINTY ON THE EURO' (*Daily Telegraph*).

Towards the end of July the euro's downward spiral halted and it began a slow climb against the dollar, but the precise nature of the government's commitment remained unclear. On Monday, 26 July 1999, the outgoing Commissioner responsible for Economic and Monetary Union, Yves-Thibault de Silguy, made a speech in the City of London in which he argued that Britain's failure to sign up to the single currency was reducing its influence across the EU and could leave it in the slow lane of a 'two-speed Europe'. He warned that Britain would pay not only an economic price for staying out, but also a political one, as the Franco-German axis gained new importance.

On the day of M. De Silguy's speech, the newspapers were full of antic-ipatory pieces about a speech the Prime Minister was to deliver the next day on 'Europe'. The Downing Street press machine had clearly flagged the speech up as the strongest signal to date that the Prime Minister would take a leading role in the reformulated Britain in Europe campaign. But several newspapers reported that the Chancellor of the Exchequer was pressing Mr Blair to delay the referendum on joining the euro by five years (see, for example, *Daily Mail*). Influenced by his 'increasingly anti-euro economic adviser, Ed Balls, the Chancellor was said to be calling for the euro to be removed from political discourse until well after the next General Election on the grounds that the government's good economic record would be obscured by constitutional arguments as Mr Hague sought to turn the campaign into a referendum on the single currency.

The next day Tony Blair, in his speech at the London Business School, said he was determined to be 'a leading partner in shaping Europe's future', comparing the Conservatives' position in 1999 with Labour's 'extremist path' in 1983. Then as now, he argued, 'renegotiation' was 'the codeword for being ready to leave ... To be in or not to be in – that's the question. In the end we have always chosen to be in.' He rejected the 'two ideological and absolute positions on the euro' as the Tory 'No, never' and the 'Yes, now' line of the Liberal Democrats. In contrast, Labour's position was 'conditional. It is not inevitable. Both intention and conditions are genuine ... The political and economic case for positive engagement in Europe is overwhelming.' Mr Blair argued that the true lesson of sterling's embarrassing departure from the European Exchange Rate Mechanism in 1992 was not that the project was doomed but that sterling had gone in at the wrong time and at the wrong rate. Hence his government's insistence on putting the economics before the politics when joining 'an economic mechanism'. But Mr Blair still felt the decision would probably be taken 'early in the next Parliament ... If the policy changes, I'll tell you.' While this last comment was greeted with disappointment by pro-euros who wanted the Prime Minister to commit himself to a fixed date around which they could rally, it was seen as a direct put-down to those in the Chancellor's camp who preferred to see the referendum dispatched to the further side of a second governmental term.

Reactions to the speech were mixed. For Mr Hague it was a 'surrender document'. His Shadow Chancellor, Francis Maude, rejected Mr Blair's claim that there were only two positions on the euro. Malcolm Bruce, the Liberal Democrats' Treasury spokesman, argued that the government's position on the single currency remained ambiguous. Lord Marshall, leader of the Britain in Europe campaign, insisted that 'The Prime Minister has given the leadership that business has been waiting for.' Indeed, pro-Europeans across the party spectrum were delighted with the Prime Minister's speech. In *The Times* Kenneth Clarke wrote: 'TONY, I'M WITH YOU ALL THE WAY', while the next week Mr Heseltine declared that he would stand shoulder-to-shoulder with Mr Blair and join the 'historical alliance' (*The Times*, 2 August).

However, Hugo Young in the *Guardian* (27 July) sounded a more cautious note:

There is still a problem, a certain reserve, an unwillingness on the leader's part to deploy his strength. He continues to have a fateful respect for the very scepticism which has discouraged him from telling the British what they need to be told. He is determined to relegate the euro to the technical realm, as if its only political significance lay in its capacity to destabilise his government, rather than its central import to a political leader claiming as strenuously as he does to be a British European.

A Donald Macintyre piece in the *Independent* the same day suggested that, unlike Mr Cook, the Prime Minister and his Chancellor believed Labour could go through the next election once again without being explicit about when and whether it intended to take sterling into the single currency. But Mr Macintyre argued that 'they need to start now the gradual process of conditioning public opinion to the case for entry. Otherwise they will not so much be keeping their options open, as closing them off.'

The 22 July 1999 Eddisbury by-election

The Eddisbury by-election of 22 July gave a first chance to test whether the Blair government had suffered lasting damage, and Mr Hague any lasting advantage from the European result. The answer to both appeared to be in the negative. The result showed that there had been no recovery in Conservative support since the election of May 1997, which was itself the worst defeat the Conservatives had suffered in over 80 years. Nominally, there was a swing back to the Conservatives of just over 1 per cent, but that was on a lower turnout (51 per cent) which should have been favourable to the Tories. Mr Hague needed to recover 80 or more seats to win the next General Election. Yet, extrapolating from the Eddisbury result, the Conservatives would win just seven seats from Labour and another five at the most from the Liberal Democrats. Worse, detailed analysis showed that most of the apparent increase in the Conservative vote could be attributed to the absence of the Referendum Party (which won 2,041 votes in 1997). If a resurgent UK Independence Party were to stand right across Britain and similarly soak up anti-EU votes, then there would be no 'Referendum Party effect' for William Hague to benefit from. In other words, Eddisbury suggested that, despite the Euro-election result, Conservative fortunes had registered no permanent improvement.

At the European level

Complicated preferential vote systems delayed the official announcement of the results in several continental countries, and it was not until 16 June that the overall picture became reasonably clear (though the final composition of the lists in Italy and Luxembourg did not become available until September). Two major 'stories' emerged. The first was that the European Peoples' Party (EPP) had overtaken the Socialist Group

(PES) to become the largest group in the Parliament. The second was the worryingly low levels of turnout – considered in the next chapter.

Table 7.4 The composition of the incoming European Parliament (October 1999)

	EPP-ED	PES	ELDR	GRE-EN	GUE/NGL	UEN	EDD	NI	Total
Belgium	6	5	5	7	–	–	–	2	25
Denmark	1	3	6	–	1	1	4	–	16
Germany	53	33	–	7	6	–	–	–	99
Greece	9	9	–	–	7	–	–	–	25
Spain	28	24	3	4	4	–	1	–	64
France	21	22	–	9	11	12	6	6	87
Ireland	5	1	1	2	–	6	–	–	15
Italy	34	17	7	2	6	9	–	12	87
Luxembourg	2	2	1	1	–	–	–	–	6
Netherlands	9	6	8	4	1	–	3	–	31
Austria	7	7	–	2	–	–	–	5	21
Portugal	9	12	–	–	2	2	–	–	25
Finland	5	3	5	2	1	–	–	–	16
Sweden	7	6	4	2	3	–	–	–	22
UK	37	30	10	6	–	–	3	1	87
Total	233	180	50	48	42	30	16	27	626

EPP = Group of the European People's Party (Christian-Democratic Group) and European Democrats; PES = Group of the Party of European Socialists; ELDR = Group of the European Liberal, Democrat and Reform Party; GUE/NGL = Confederal Group of the European United Left/Nordic Green Left; GREEN = Group of the Greens/European Free Alliance; UEN = Union for a Europe of Nations Group; EDD = Group for a Europe of Democracies and Diversities; NI = Non-attached members.

The European Parliament's left-wing majority ends

The losses sustained by the left in Germany and the United Kingdom switched the numerical balance of power within the European Parliament from the PES Group (180) to the European People's Party (240). However, the gains made by the Greens and non-socialist left lists in several countries meant that the overall balance between left and right remained practically unchanged. This hid a further paradox. Although much had been made of the left–right divide in the election campaigns, there was a history of cooperation between the Socialist and EPP Groups in order to assert the Parliament's legislative powers, and more of the same could be expected; together the PES and EPP had 420 of the 626 seats in the outgoing Parliament, and 413 in the new one.

Nevertheless, the EPP had become the largest group within the European Parliament for the first time since direct elections began in 1979. Psephologists had predicted that the PES Group would be reduced (see, for example, Hix, 1999), but nobody had expected the Labour Party to do quite so badly. The consequences this had for the alliances between the political groups and the election of Parliament's President and for the appointment of the Commission are considered below. In the broader context of the European Union's institutional politics, the new centre-right majority within the Parliament contrasted with the largely centre-left majority (13 out of 15 governments) in the Council of Ministers, and it was predicted that this could lead to policy clashes between a more conservative Parliament and the Council. Similar contrasts certainly led to tension with the incoming Prodi Commission.

Labour and the PES

An immediate consequence of Labour's reduced representation was the loss of Pauline Green's leadership of the PES Group. However, Labour remained the second largest national contingent within the Group and was able to bargain for a number of influential positions within Parliament's hierarchy. Despite the fraught events leading up to Pauline Green's resignation and the German SPD's cooling towards the concept of the 'Third Way', Mr Blair's stewardship and Pauline Green's leadership of the Group had completely banished any remaining doubts about Labour's commitment to the European Union.

The British Conservatives and the EPP Group

The British Conservatives, on the other hand, had a far more awkward passage. There was considerable press speculation about whether the 36 British Conservative MEPs would continue the old alliance and individual membership of the EPP Group, as William Hague had promised Mr Schäuble in Bonn, or whether, as the more Euro-sceptical tendencies in press and party insisted, the Conservatives should seek an alternative alliance. But where might they go? They could have joined the old Union for Europe Group, but the Italian *Alleanza Nazionale* MEPs had also considered this move – which would have confirmed the hotly denied stories about alliances with 'Italian neo-fascists'. There were rumours of a split, with Tory MEPs belonging to two different groups (as had occurred with the French right in the previous Parliament). Up to six hardline Euro-sceptical MEPs were said to be threatening defection. On 15 June, a *Daily Telegraph* editorial sternly admonished Mr Hague to 'STAND FIRM' and remove his MEPs from the EPP Group: 'it is simply not credible to fight an election on an anti-federalist ticket one week, and then join a federalist bloc the next'. On Friday, 18 June, the British Conservative MEPs met in London to discuss potential alliances. In a hyperbolic slip of the tongue at Prime Minister's Question Time on 16 June, the Prime Minister even stated that a Tory desertion of the EPP Group would be a 'national disaster' (it would certainly have prevented the EPP from becoming the largest political group in the Parliament).

The speculation ended on the evening of 30 June, when a Shadow Cabinet meeting approved a compromise deal negotiated by Mr Hague, Mr Maples and Mr McMillan-Scott. The 36 Tory MEPs would rejoin a re-named EPP Group, now including the French RPR, as well as both the British Conservatives and the Italian *Forza Italia*. The EPP Group's outgoing chairman, Wilfried Martens, had confirmed that Conservative MEPs, as 'allied' members, were free to vote differently from the majority of the group, and Mr Hague could argue that he had won the best of both worlds: membership of the largest grouping within the Parliament, giving access to committee chairmanships and other positions of influence, on the one hand; and political independence for domestic consumption, on the other.

On 7 July Mr Hague signed up to the so-called 'Malaga Declaration', under which centre-right leaders invited the EPP Group to change its name to 'Group of the European Peoples' Party (Christian Democrats) and European Democrats'. It also envisaged a merger between the EPP transnational party and the less ideological European Democratic Union (EDU). The next day in a speech seen as an attempt to placate those Euro-sceptics angered by his decision to stay with EPP membership, Mr Hague warned his MEPs not to 'go native': 'Work with our allies in the European Parliament to fight socialism. Work with each other as a united group to fight for our manifesto. Work with the whole of the Conservative Party to keep the pound.' He also 'demanded' that all of the Conservative MEPs should vote together as a single group for the manifesto – 'No exceptions. No two-way or three-way splits' – a reference to the increasing frag-mentation on sensitive issues in the last year of the previous Parliament. Pro-Europeans within the party pointed out that little of substance had changed (under the previous arrangement, Conservative MEPs had never been bound by the EPP international party manifesto).

Others

The decisions of the Greens, UKIP and Plaid Cymru about political group membership were considered earlier. The two Scottish National Party

MEPs sat with the two Plaid Cymru and two British Green MEPs in the Greens/European Free Alliance Group.

The Commission

The British members

With fresh electoral wind in their sails, parts of the Conservative Party began to call upon Mr Blair to rethink his nominations to the new Prodi Commission (Neil Kinnock and Chris Patten). Mr McMillan-Scott was vociferous in asking the Prime Minister to withdraw his nomination of Neil Kinnock as Britain's senior Commissioner, on the grounds that Mr Kinnock had been a member of the discredited Santer Commission, even if no personal blame attached to him. At the same time, Mr Cash – a noted Euro-sceptic MP – and others called for Mr Blair to withdraw his nomination of Mr Patten, since he was known to be very close to the continental Christian Democrats and this would sit badly with the election result, particularly if the British Conservatives decided not to join the EPP. Mr Prodi and Mr Blair stuck to their guns.

As a whole

Despite the very low turnout in some countries and generally low-key campaigns the Euro-election results were widely represented as a swing to the centre-right, away from the centre-left, which continued to hold or share power in 13 of the 15 Member States. As the new Commission had not yet been appointed, it was speculated that the results might put Mr Prodi and the Member State governments under pressure to nominate to the Commission members who would better reflect the new European political map. Several governments had already effectively made their nominations but others had yet to do so. In Germany, for example, it had been expected that Chancellor Schröder would nominate representatives of the two coalition partners, the SPD and the Greens. But, encouraged by the election results, the CDU and the CSU (particularly Mr Ingo Friedrich, MEP and Deputy Chairman of the CSU), called for the second German nominee to be drawn from the largest opposition party, the Christian Democrats. Since all nominees had to run the dual gauntlet of public hearings and an overall vote, and since Mr Prodi could reject government nominees, these calls, which increased in intensity once Gert Pöttering had been elected EPP leader, had to be taken seriously. Again, Mr Prodi stuck to his guns and, to the chagrin of Mr Pöttering, opted for representatives of the two parties from the governing coalition.

The New Parliament Meets

On 20 July 1999, the new Parliament met in Strasbourg. The plenary session took place in a gleaming new, purpose-built riverside palace, the Louise Weiss building, which had been financed and built by the French government at a cost of about £250 million. The building was immediately subject to a barrage of criticism, on practical and aesthetic grounds, but by the end of the week most of the technical hitches had been smoothed out. Several MEPs pointed to the symbolism of the post-Amsterdam Parliament meeting for the first time in its own building in Strasbourg – previously the Parliament had 'borrowed' the Council of Europe's parliamentary chamber.

The Parliament's first job was to choose its leadership, both of the Parliament as a whole and of its committees. In previous Parliaments, the dominant PES and EPP Groups had bargained between themselves so that a representative from each would enjoy a two-and-a-half-year span as President during each five-year parliamentary term. But the unexpectedly strong EPP Group felt awkward about the coninuance of the old agreement, particularly since the PES Group wanted their candidate, Mario Soares, to sit as President for the *first* half of the term. The EPP leadership had frequently reflected on how it might create a loose centre-right coalition within the Parliament to enable it to muster an absolute majority without the PES Group.

The new EPP Group leader, Gert Pöttering, entered into negotiations with the ELDR Group and concluded a 'technical agreement' whereby the EPP's candidate, the longstanding French MEP Nicole Fontaine, would enjoy ELDR support for the first two-and-a-half-year span, in return for EPP support for the ELDR's candidate (widely expected to be the Irish leader of the Group, Pat Cox) for the second two-and-a-half-year term. On 20 July Nicole Fontaine was duly elected President by 306 votes to Mario Soares' 200 votes. The *Independent* reported (22 July) that Paddy Ashdown opposed the agreement and that Paul Tyler, the Liberal Democrats' chief whip, had called on the ten Liberal Democrat MEPs to think again. However, a majority of Westminster Liberal Democrat MPs reportedly backed the deal. Mr Watson, leader of the British Liberal Democrats' ten-strong contingent, was thought to be well placed to replace Mr Cox as leader of the ELDR Group once Mr Cox was elected President.

David Martin (Labour) and James Provan (Conservative) were among the fourteen Vice-Presidents, and Richard Balfe was again elected one of Parliament's five quaestors.[2] Negotiations between the groups over committee chairmanships continued until Wednesday evening, but when the first confirmations came it became clear that the British had done very well – an unexpected result given the more fragmented nature of British political representation and the smaller number of committee positions available in the new Parliament.

Caroline Jackson (Conservative) became Chairman of the powerful Environment Committee. She had strong positive qualifications: she had been a longstanding member of the Environment Committee and, for many years, a Deputy Chairman. She had won her political spurs in a celebrated clash with the unpopular German Industry Commissioner, Martin Bangemann. Some controversy had surrounded Mrs Jackson's candidature, since she was a Director of the Peugeot (UK) motor car company. But Dr Jackson promptly resigned her consultantship and argued that the problem had been resolved.

Terry Wynn (Labour) became Chairman of the even more powerful Budgets Committee, Parliament's 'star chamber' on all financial questions. Mr Wynn's appointment was a major coup for the British and the EPLP. British members have a predilection for the budgets committee and a disproportionate number of British MEPs have served as general rapporteur on the EU's annual budget, including Terry Wynn, but the Committee Chairmanship had previously been considered a German preserve.

Graham Watson (Liberal Democrat) became Chairman of the Civil Liberties Committee. Though not one of the most powerful committees, this was nevertheless considered a coup for the British Liberal Democrats.

On 21 July the Parliament was addressed by its new President and by the President-designate of the Commission, Romano Prodi, who presented his new team for the first time. There were only five Christian Democrats among the twenty Commissioners-designate. Mrs Fontaine spoke about a Parliament that had come of age, which demanded to be treated as an equal player, and which would hold the Commission closely to account. Mr Prodi argued that he had assembled a 'top quality and well-balanced team'. He recognised that the Commission had been badly damaged by recent events, but:

> I believe that the Parliament has also suffered, a view that is borne out by the low turn-out in the recent elections. The task now facing us is to rebuild the complicity and mutual trust between the two institutions that has traditionally been the driving force of European integration

Most speakers in the ensuing debate accepted that Mr Prodi' Commission and his promised reforms would represent a considerabl improvement, but jarring notes were struck by the new leader of the EPP Group, Gert Pöttering, and by the ELDR leader, Pat Cox.

The hearings with the Commissioners-designate took place from 30 August to 2 September. Mr Kinnock and Mr Patten both acquitted themselves well. Mr Kinnock shrugged off Conservative charges that he was 'tainted' by association with the previous Commission – his protestations gaining credibility from the widely shared knowledge in Brussels that he had privately been a passionate critic of some of the previous Commission's more controversial decisions and practices.

On 15 September in Strasbourg, the Prodi Commission was approved by the Parliament, by 404 votes to 154, with British Conservatives voting against as they had promised (after the vote, the British Conservatives refused to take part in a 'family photograph' of all British MEPs and the two new British Commissioners). All Labour MEPs voted in favour, as did nine of the ten Liberal Democrats (Liz Lynne voted against). Of the other parties, UKIP's three MEPs voted against, the two SNP MEPs abstained, the two Plaid Cymru MEPs voted in favour, while one Green voted against (Caroline Lucas) and one abstained (Jean Lambert).

At last some semblance of normalcy returned to Parliament–Commission relations. Both institutions recognised that they would have to work together to restore their, and the Union's, image.

Notes

1. Although it should be noted that the Greens' Jean Lambert had spent three years as an honorary member of the Green Group from 1989 to 1992 (after the Greens had won 15 per cent in the 1989 Euro-elections), with voting rights within the Group, though not in the Parliament, and had been a member of the Group's Executive.
2. It should be noted that Mr Balfe was not an 'official' PES candidate. His standing broke the d'Hondt understanding between the political groups which would otherwise have given the Greens/EFA a quaestor position.

8
Questions

As the *Independent's* Donald Macintyre observed (20 May), the five-yearly elections to the European Parliament have become 'more famous as an interval than as a political event'. Yet:

> it was not meant to be like this. An election that was to have produced a European parliament with a new sense of authority has instead created a body that may fear for its legitimacy ... Europe's voters have rebuked its politicians. ... people in the fifteen member states have made clear they have little interest in the EU in general, and the European parliament in particular ... The low turnout indicates that European integration remains an elitist project that only excites politicians and others directly caught up in it. (*Financial Times*, 15 June)

Not only was turnout low, but it is getting steadily lower (see Tables 8.1 and 8.2). Thus, European elections have provided a growing paradox: as the Parliament's powers have increased, so popular participation in the elections has decreased. The 1999 Euro-elections in the UK provided a fresh paradox, for the introduction of PR was supposed to have provided an unprecedented choice for the electorate, and yet turnout reached unprecedentedly low levels.

In every European election in the United Kingdom so far, national parties and national party political agendas have remained centre stage. In 1999, in what seemed like a new departure, an important part of each party's policy stance was defined with reference to a *European* issue, the single currency. But although the single currency was by far the most

212

Table 8.1 UK turnout levels in Euro-elections

	Votes cast	Turnout
1979	13,446,083	32.7%
1984	12,998,274	32.6%
1989	15,893,408	36.8%
1994	15,847,417	36.8%
1999	10,681,080	24.1%

Table 8.2 Voter turnout (%) across the EU (1979–99)

	1979	1984	1989	1994	1999
Austria	–	–	–	68 (a)	49
Belgium*	92	92	91	91	90
Denmark	47	52	46	53	50
Finland	–	–	–	60 (a)	30
France	61	57	49	53	47
Germany	66	57	62	60	45
Greece	79 (b)	77	80	71	70
Ireland	64	48	68	44	51
Italy	86	84	82	75	71
Luxembourg*	89	87	87	89	86
Netherlands	58	51	47	36	30
Portugal	–	72 (c)	51	36	40
Sweden	–	–	–	42 (a)	38
Spain	–	69 (c)	55	59	64
UK	33	33	37	37	24
EU (average)	63	61	59	57	49

(a) 1996
(b) 1981
(c) 1987
*mandatory voting
Source: European Parliament, *Election Facts* http://www.europarl.eu/int/election/uk

important issue, this was more for its domestic policy ramifications than because it was a European matter *per se*. The elections could just as easily have been dominated by taxation, say, or the Social Chapter, had Mr Hague thought that his tactical advantage lay there. Thus, as Curtice and Steed argue in the Appendix, the 1999 Euro-elections once again confirmed the second-order national election theory. European elections are expressive, rather than instrumental. Freed from the duty of choosing a government, voters, if they bother to turn out, pass messages which are not limited to governmental considerations. But what, then, were the Euro-elections in the UK about if they were not about Europe? The elections raised many questions for all of the parties, but most of all for Mr Blair and Labour.

Mr Blair and Labour

The Nuffield study of the 1994 European elections, which were held in the shadow of John Smith's death, charted the appearance and rapid rise of the 'Blair phenomenon', which culminated in Labour's massive 1997 General Election win. Mr Blair has ridden high in the popularity polls ever since. Five years on, and with a new set of Euro-elections in view, it was generally expected that the Prime Minister and his party would do unusually, perhaps even unprecedentedly, well for a government in mid-term. Even at the beginning of the campaign, it was assumed that the reduced role of the Prime Minister, as he concentrated on Kosovo and Northern Ireland, would have no negative effect on Labour's performance. On the contrary, it was widely expected that the war would result in a 'khaki election'. Even in the week before the poll, several tabloid newspapers ran a story about how listening to Mr Blair had cured a man's stammer! The Prime Minister, it seemed, was simultaneously above politics and all-powerful. Mr Hague's concentration on the single currency was portrayed as representing no more than a flea bite.

However, on 15 June Mr Blair woke up to read headlines about how he was 'AT BAY' (*The Times*), 'FORCED TO RETREAT' (*Daily Telegraph*), and 'RATTLED' (*Daily Mail*), above all over the euro, while *The Times* implored 'DON'T THROW AWAY ALL YOUR WORK, TONY' (15 June). The Prime Minister's image of apparent impregnability had to end at some stage, but to his supporters it seemed a pity that the end should have come almost by default. Moreover, because of Mr Hague's chosen tactics, critics and friends alike speculated that the campaign and results could have constitutional consequences, leading the *Daily Express* (15 June) to declare 'An election which should have been no more than a timely wake-up call for the Government could have a far deeper impact on Britain's future'.

Post-mortem

As the polls closed, the Labour leadership braced itself for a poor result and the Prime Minister was already demanding explanations. On Friday

11 June, he convened a two-hour meeting at Downing Street. Present at the meeting were Bill Bush, the head of the Number 10 rebuttal unit; Philip Gould, the party's chief poll consultant; Jonathan Powell, the Number 10 chief of staff; Charles Falconer, number two in the Cabinet Office; Nick Peccorelli, the party's head of policy and communications; David Miliband, head of the Number 10 policy unit; Margaret McDonagh, the party's General Secretary; Sally Morgan, the Number 10 political secretary; Phil Murphy, the party's communications chief; and Anji Hunter, Mr Blair's personal assistant and gatekeeper.

The meeting considered a number of pressing questions. Had Labour had a clear campaign message? Was the low vote a sign of 'customer satisfaction', or part of a long-term political disengagement by Labour's traditional working-class base? Were they simply registering their dislike of the euro and disapproval of the much-reported European excess? If so, what implications did this have for the euro? And what of the hypothesis, controversially advanced by Mr Hain, that Labour's traditional activists and working class voters felt neglected, even disowned?

According to press reports of the meeting, the Prime Minister was immensely practical: 'He wanted to know what was to be done, insisting that Labour could not have become a bad campaigning party overnight. He argued strongly that he was not going to break up the coalition that had won Labour such a landslide in 1997' (*Observer*). But the Millbank representatives at the meeting reported that activists were as deeply disillusioned as supporters. Reports from different parts of the country suggested that tons of expensive Labour election material were lying unused because the local parties could not motivate people to go out leafleting. The tendency to 'talk right and act left' was turning off activists. Many of them were unaware of the measures the government had taken to help the 'core vote'.

Plans for a 'delivery time' week during the campaign, in which a group of Cabinet ministers, including Mr Blair, would have championed free eye-tests or increases in child benefit, had been scrapped due to the Prime Minister's preoccupation with Kosovo. The Millbank team also complained that too many senior ministers now regarded themselves primarily as government administrators, unwilling to spend time out of their departments on the campaign trail. Mr Blair accepted this criticism and at a 17 June Cabinet meeting told his ministers that they had to start acting like politicians again, looking for political mileage in what they were doing. Ministers' special advisers underscored the theme at an 18 June meeting, agreeing to simplify the big political messages from their departments and to differentiate themselves from the Conservatives. It was also agreed that Number 10 and the party should coordinate political messages more closely. The Prime Minister voiced criticisms of the Number 10 strategic communications unit, admitting it had become swamped with work and was only thinking a week or two ahead. To overcome 'core vote' suspicions, the Prime Minister was urged to give the party a formal voice in the Cabinet – the equivalent of a party chairman. Ian McCartney, who had been working on plans to revive heartland constituencies by instilling the campaigning activism of marginal seats, was thought to be a frontrunner.

A psephological analysis of the results produced by Millbank's Greg Cook leaked to the press. Mr Cook scorned theories that the election had produced an abstentionist protest by Labour's core vote. The point of departure in any analysis was the extraordinarily low turnout, which could not be regarded as a reasonably representative sample of opinion and was bound to produce distortions. The election was simply perceived 'as of no relevance to large sections of the electorate'. Mr Cook's analysis addressed two fundamental questions: who had and who had not turned out? The evidence suggested that participation was 'most strongly correlated with the two most anti-Labour groups in the electorate – the over-55s and rural dwellers, especially those involved in agriculture'. At the same time, low participation rates were correlated not only with Labour's heartland areas but urban areas generally. The implications were alarming: 'for what we have to envisage is an election in which large groups of the electorate just sat out, and which was effectively the province of a tiny, unrepresentative section of the electorate'.

All was not gloom, however. The polling background to the election was that the Labour lead remained exactly where it was in 1997, suggesting that Labour would do just as well, if not better, in a new general election. The problems Labour had encountered therefore seemed specific to the Euro-election.

Modernisation and the 'project'

In retrospect, one of the most important overall themes in the 1999 Euro-elections would appear to have been the future of Mr Blair's 'project', aimed at creating a new, durable, centre-left governing coalition, based on new constitutional arrangements and a new approach to Europe. The Euro-elections brought together a number of interrelated aspects of the 'project': the successor to Mr Ashdown; the possible resurgence of the pro-European Mr Mandelson; the Continental prevarications about the 'Third Way', particularly in the governing French and German left-wing parties; PR, and the prospects of PR for general elections; the referendum on the single currency and, more generally, the UK's whole relationship with Europe; and, perhaps above all, the change in Labour's electoral support. *The Economist* likened Mr Blair to Napoleon on the march to Moscow and wondered whether he wasn't 'A LONG WAY FROM PARIS', with winter coming on and the troops restive (26 June); 'IS TONY'S COALITION CRACKING UP?', asked Andrew Rawnsley (*Observer*, 20 June). Political commentators argued that Mr Blair had two basic options: to return to a more traditional, party-based power base; or to plough on regardless towards a new model of coalitionary politics.

Mr Blair was not slow in providing an answer. On 22 June in Birmingham, the Prime Minister made a defiant speech in which he denied being out of touch with Labour voters, but also made it clear that there would be no attempt to switch Labour's appeal from the coalition which had ensured the 1997 landslide victory.

A taste of the ideological opposition to Mr Blair's approach came from former Deputy Leader Roy Hattersley, who declared in the *Observer* (27 June):

> On the day he was elected as Labour leader, [Blair] spoke about the people who had voted for him because he was a born winner. Once he loses the aura of invincibility, their allegiance will be in serious doubt … When bad times come, leaders hope the reservoir of affection and shared ideology has not dried up. For Blair, it has never existed … Blair cannot complain. He is the prophet of ideologically footloose politics, the advocate of electoral empiricism who wants people to vote according to their prejudice-free judgement. Yet ideology holds parties together. And I hope he will not come to regret his disdain for loyalty to an idea, and for the people who fought for it over the years.

More pragmatically, Hugo Young argued:

> 1997 cannot happen again. Labour may be odds-on to win, but it will never re-create the galvanic enthusiasm that united a party after two decades of Tory party rule. This time, it will be defending the long, slow march of government without any core of national enthusiasm to plug into. It will be doing so, moreover, in a Scotland and Wales, if not England, that now have credible alternative locations for disenchanted Labour votes. It will actually need the party in 2002 more than it did in 1997. (*Guardian*, 24 June)

'President' Blair?

For Labour Party activists, one of the Prime Minister's more controversial decisions was effectively to absent himself from the campaign. Since Labour's campaign and central message had been predicated on the Prime Minister's popularity and record, his absence voided the campaign of its central protagonist. Moreover, Labour's campaign had been supposed to contrast Mr Blair's leadership with that of Mr Hague. There was a suspicion among some candidates that Mr Blair did not care very much about the European Parliament and its elections, a suspicion they felt was confirmed when it was learnt that the Prime Minister had gone to bed rather than wait up for the results. The *Daily Mirror* was fiercely critical, running a front-page headline entitled: 'THE NIGHTMARE THAT WE ALL COULD LET HAPPEN. WILLIAM HAGUE, ELECTED PRIME MINISTER, MAY 2002, BECAUSE TONY BLAIR WAS TOO BUSY DOING SOMETHING MUCH MORE IMPORTANT' (15 June). Inside, a ferocious Paul Routledge argued that 'BLAIR TOOK HIS EYE OFF BRITAIN', and was even guilty of 'dereliction of duty'.

One old Labour hand ruefully compared Mr Blair with another young, brilliant, centre-left, populist politician, Felipe Gonzalez. Mr Gonzalez, whose personal popularity was for many years his party's most potent electoral weapon, became increasingly detached from the political nitty-gritty, preferring instead to concentrate on the broad sweep, a tendency dubbed 'the Moncloa complex'. Mr Blair, it was argued, had just received a warning from the British electorate not to follow the same tendency. Perhaps of more practical relevance to future electoral contests was the way in which Mr Blair's personal popularity and standing failed to translate into voter and activist support. In presidential systems of governance the distancing of presidents from their administrations is a well known phenomenon. Some political commentators wondered whether a similar trend was emerging in the UK. For example, writing in the *Financial Times* (16 June), Philip Stephens argued that:

> There are many advantages to Mr Blair's presidential style of premiership. It allows an intensity and focus ... denied to more collegiate governments. But there are weaknesses too. An obvious one is that the bursts of energy alternate with periods of drift ... when the prime minister is not driving European policy, there are precious few others willing or able to step into the vacuum ... As long as Mr Blair's immediate preoccupations are elsewhere, the field lies open for his opponents.

Shortcomings

This was Labour's second poor Euro-campaign in a row. 'Thank God it didn't matter', said one activist in 1994 (Butler and Westlake, 1995, p. 298). It did not matter then because John Smith had tragically died, the Blair phenomenon was already gathering momentum, and John Major's Conservative Party was in increasing disarray. But in 1999, it surely *did* matter. As Paul Routledge wrote in the *New Statesman* (20 June), 'In effect, calculating that turnout would be low, Mr Hague and his tacticians focussed all of their energies on encouraging the anti-euro Conservatives – by definition a passionate group – to turn out. This election mattered deeply to Mr Hague and, because it mattered to him, it should have mattered to Labour.' In *The Times* (15 June), Peter Riddell argued that Labour had ignored 'the lesson of the Tory failures in 1989 and 1994 that half-hearted campaigns always fail'.

Several candidates complained that Labour had expected Conservative divisions over the euro. When these did not occur, the party seemed at a loss as to how to manage its campaign. Nor, it seemed, had anybody in Millbank thought through the implications of a really low turnout, despite the fact that many were speculating on a figure of around 25 per cent. Labour complacently believed that high standings in the opinion polls would automatically be translated into a similar vote at the elections, but ignored such factors as the lower level of motivation among party activists. Nor was the party very adroit at adapting to the system. As one candidate put it:

> as a party we were not able successfully to meet the challenges posed by a regional election system. It was as though we assumed that the same method of campaigning as used in other elections would be successful under this form of PR. There must be lessons we can learn from other countries where a regional list system has been used repeatedly.

The party's election broadcasts concentrated on the achievements of the government, with very little reference to Europe or the European Parliament. Candidates, particularly incumbent MEPs, believed there was an untapped agenda which could have been highlighted and could have been registered more strongly with the electorate. The absence of such a message meant the party had nothing to counterbalance the claim by the critics and the disenchanted that the Labour government was 'responsible' for the ills of the EU.

The decision to issue an election address, rather than a specific national manifesto, opened the party to both ridicule and criticism. As Neil Kinnock, responsible for Labour's European manifesto in 1994, laconically declared: 'manifestos are there because they are there'. The absence of a national manifesto in itself gave the media a story and the opposition ammunition. The story, argued activists, could have been positive if the party had chosen to present it that way. But in the end there was no such presentation and by default the advantage passed to the opposition.

London – a special case, or an example for the future?

Amid all the clouds for Labour, there was one possible silver lining – London, a region which seemed to buck the trends. In particular, turnout fell less (diminishing the effects of turnout differential) and, although the party lost sitting MEPs lower down the list, the fall in the Labour share and the increase in the Conservative vote were both proportionately the smallest of any region in the country. The party was only a half of 1 per cent short of gaining a fifth seat. Most encouragingly, if the same results had been obtained in the 2000 Greater London Assembly elections, Labour would have won nine out the fourteen constituencies and one additional seat from the 'top-up' list.

In his leaked analysis, Millbank's Greg Cook posited a number of possible interrelated explanations for the London phenomenon: a different and distinct political attitude in London; a possible region-wide demographic feature, such as the generally younger age profile (though this would have run against the turnout pattern elsewhere); the more cosmopolitan nature of the electorate and the higher participation rate among some ethnic communities; the fact that London is an almost entirely urban region; and a generally higher level of political competitiveness and organisation than elsewhere.

Of these factors, perhaps the last was the most significant. As Greg Cook's analysis argued, since the proportion of habitual voters in the electorate has fallen, 'more and more, electoral success may depend upon effective local organisation', and the London party prided itself on having been relatively well organised. Moreover, as one insider declared, 'the team of ten candidates ... was probably the strongest and most united of any team in the country. We had a credible list balanced by gender, race and experience. The team were ready and working together long before other regions had sorted themselves out.' Perhaps of most interest to party organisers, London Labour's carefully formulated, four-stage strategy was predicated on the assumption of a low turnout:

We concentrated all of our efforts on motivating the Labour vote, focussing our campaign on those wards where there was substantial, identified Labour support and getting the team of candidates out and about as much as possible to increase the recognition factor.

Perhaps this strategy explains the very different perception of the campaign offered by George Parker in Chapter 7.

Mr Hague and the Conservatives

The Euro-elections answered the questions about the future of Mr Hague's leadership, but not about the future of the party. A strong Euro-sceptic message mingled with jingoistic language about sterling had won the support of only 9 per cent of all electors. This, clearly, would not be enough to win a General Election. Mr Hague's tactics had produced not so much a verdant spring as a short Indian summer. As the glow of the Euro-elections 'victory' faded, Mr Hague and his new policy henchman Andrew Lansley were faced with the challenge of coming up with a distinctive and original policy mix which would put the Conservative Party back in serious electoral contention. Ironically, Mr Hague's Euro-sceptical short-term tactics may well have taken the party further away from the centre ground it would need to recapture. Mr Hague's chosen tactics were predicated on the euro's failure, but its success was an intuitive expectation – it was so important that the European political and economic elites could not allow it to fail. Yet, if the euro did succeed, pressure on the UK economy to join the single currency would rapidly increase. As Peregrine Worsthorne, an old Tory journalist, put it:

> In resting their nationalistic pitch so much on the continuing unpopularity of the euro, the Conservative right is relying most imprudently on very shifting sands, rather as it did in the 1930s by relying overmuch on the perpetual popularity of the Empire. (*New Statesman*, 16 August 1999)

This observation led several commentators to argue that Mr Hague's tactics risked condemning the Tories to becoming a 'natural party of opposition' (for example, John Gray, *Guardian*, 1 June).

Mr Kennedy and the Liberal Democrats

Mr Ashdown's predominance in the Liberal Democrats' national campaign was described in Chapter 5. There were a number of parallels between the circumstances of the Liberal Democrats' campaign in 1999 and the Labour campaign in 1994. In particular, Labour's 1994 campaign had been similarly overshadowed by a 'phoney' and distracting leadership race, and Menzies Campbell's decision to stand down in June 1999 strongly echoed Gordon Brown's decision to defer to Mr Blair in June 1994. Thereafter, Mr Kennedy became the clear favourite – just as Mr Blair had been in 1994. But there was one important difference from 1994. Although June 1999 was Paddy Ashdown's swansong, the Liberal Democrats could never have hoped for the strong wave of sympathy from which Labour benefited following the death of John Smith. In 1994, Labour's – poor – campaign did not matter. In 1999, the Liberal Democrats' poor campaign, particularly at the regional level, did.

The electoral implications of June 1999 were disastrous for the Liberal Democrats. At the Euro-constituency level, the party apparently did well, but the success was marred by the defeat of an incumbent MEP, Robin Teverson, in what should have been a Liberal Democrat stronghold and by the way in which the party leadership had allowed itself to be talked up. In 1994, Mr Ashdown had been wise to this risk. He seemed less so in 1999, perhaps because his advisers were so adamant about the prospect of victory in twelve seats. At the Westminster constituency level, the results were exceedingly grim, with just one seat – Orkney and Shetland – held. Party activists might be tempted to put the blame on a combination of the new system and low, differentiated turnout, but the probable explanation is simultaneously more worrying and more reassuring for the Westminster party.

Four particular aspects of the Euro-election results should provide food for thought for the newly ensconced Liberal Democrat leader. The first, as the Appendix argues, is that under a PR system voters no longer feel the need to vote in the tactical way that gave the Liberal Democrats so many Westminster seats in 1997. This trend was probably exacerbated by the fact that no government was at stake and that the Conservatives as yet provide no credible alternative to Labour. Nevertheless, for a party which has made PR for Westminster elections one of its chief aims, the Euro-election results provide a simple and self-evident message; under PR, parties win seats on their merits and not on other parties' de-merits.

The second, a message for all of the parties, is that in a low-key regionally organised election, a strong national message and strong local campaigning are important factors in success. Both were noticeably absent from the Liberal Democrat campaign, and the party will need to reflect on why it was unable to build on its 6 May successes in the local elections. Certainly the party will rue its failure to turn out 2,121 more of its voters in the North-East – the difference between one and no seats.

A third aspect which confronts Mr Kennedy is the strong showing of the UKIP in the South-West, apparently at the expense of the Liberal Democrats, and on higher-than-average turnouts. The ten Westminster constituencies with the highest UKIP vote (Table 8.3) share one common theme: the fishing industry. Several candidates campaigning in the South-West reported a generalised wave of Euro-scepticism merged into opposition on particular issues such as the single currency and the Common Agricultural Policy. The Liberal Democrats have always campaigned on a strong reforming basis, but it is also well known that the Liberal Democrats' grassroots support is far more Euro-sceptical than its leadership.[1] It could be that the UKIP was able to siphon off the Liberal Democrats' more passionately Euro-sceptical support in the South and particularly the South-West. If so, the leadership may ponder whether the party should sound a more Euro-sceptical note in 2004. But Conservatives in the South West also saw encouragement in the Liberal Democrats' poor performance, attributing it more to the indifference of party activists and, allegedly, growing public resistance to Liberal Democrat rule on local councils.

The last aspect concerns the Liberal Democrats' participation in Mr Blair's 'project'. As a result of the 1999 Euro-elections, several elements in the 'price' Mr Ashdown charged for Liberal Democrat participation – firm commitments to referendums on PR for Westminster and the single currency, for example – would appear to have been postponed. Certainly PR was discredited on the Labour backbenches. At the same time, many Liberal Democrat activists felt that the party's poor Euro-election showing was a shot across its bows. Advisers to both Mr Kennedy and Mr Blair would be pointing to these considerations, Mr Blair not being in a position to give satisfaction to the Liberal Democrats on their policy demands, and the Liberal Democrats not being in a position to make such demands. One of the few areas for future concessions might be the introduction of PR for local elections, but given the strength of feeling on Labour's backbenches, delivery on this would be hard for the government and, as with the 6 May Assembly elections, the immediate advantages unclear. The situation led political commentators to predict that the 'project' would be reduced to a hard core of 'manageable' constitutional reforms.

The United Kingdom Independence Party

Whether achieved by riding on the back of Mr Hague's Euro-scepticism or because of its own distinctive stance, the UKIP now enjoys political representation in Strasbourg. Its three members of the European Parliament will bring financial and staffing resources to the party. The fundamental question raised for the UKIP is, where to from here? Though the UKIP MEPs have joined an EP political group, they continue to insist on an essentially negative strategy of abstention and voting against integrationist measures, yet their small numbers make this a Pyrrhic policy at most, and raise doubts as to whether it can continue for long in its purist form.

Seasoned Parliament watchers have seen such policies weaken and founder before, with the French *Front National* and various Continental anti-integration parties. Membership of a political group brings with it the right to rapporteurships on reports. Will the UKIP members take up their right? Which reports might they win, given that the choice of rapporteurships will not be in their gift? Will they opt for potentially controversial rapporteurships on integrationist measures? Will they bow to the traditionally consensual working methods of rapporteurs or will they choose an adversarial stance?

The UKIP's performance at the 2004 European elections may well depend on the answer to these questions, for the challenge facing the party is that of retaining a distinctive character which can survive after Mr Blair's promised referendum has settled the issue of the single currency in one way or another. Moreover, in 2004 the Liberal Democrats in the South-West can be expected to be wise to the risk of losing Eurosceptical voters. (Table 8.3 shows the UKIP's ten highest votes in Westminster constituencies.) If it can meet these challenges, the UKIP may become as regular a part of Britain's political representation in Strasbourg as the Danish June Movement.

Table 8.3 The UKIP's ten highest votes (in Westminster constituencies)

Constituency	Percentage of total vote
Torridge and West Devon	19.2
North Cornwall	16.9
North Devon	16.4
Totnes	16.1
Teignbridge	16.0
Bognor	15.8
Torbay	15.6
St Ives	15.5
Chichester	15.5
Falmouth	15.1

The Green Party

The Greens' success similarly raised many questions. The party's campaign was carefully targeted on London and the South-East (the near-miss in the South-West – fruit of Liberal Democrat voters' dissatisfaction – was a surprise). The focus was on efficient organisation and a professional approach, perhaps best characterised by the party's much-praised PEB, which largely eschewed policy messages in favour of strong images. Nevertheless, the party's idiosyncratic policy mix – anti-Kosovo intervention, anti-single currency, anti-GM foods – was well suited to the particular circumstances of June 1999. As Jean Lambert, the party's co-leader and one of its two successful candidates put it: 'At one point we were wondering whether it was official Labour policy that their supporters should vote Green' (*Evening Standard*, 9 June). The party's targeted advertising in the Labour-sympathising press was certainly shrewd, although Peter Kellner later argued in the *Evening Standard* that, without the boost from the government's controversial handling of the GM foods issue, the Greens would probably have won no seats (14 June 1999). London Labour insiders regretted the failure to turn out the half of 1 per cent of the electorate which would have denied the Greens their London seat.

Given the prevalence of the euro as a campaign issue, some party activists later regretted not making more of the party's Euro-sceptical, anti-single currency stance, though this might have brought them into conflict with their Continental allies. Indeed, activists were surprised at the depth of Euro-sceptical feeling.

On the positive side, the party won representation at Strasbourg for the first time. Recruitment of new members was only modest but, perhaps most importantly, the party now knew where better to target its efforts in the next General Election. Table 8.4 shows the ten Westminster constituencies which returned the highest Green votes in the Euro-elections.

In 1999, the Green movement was on a roll in Europe. Greens were part of the governing coalitions in Italy, Finland, France and Germany and, in a new departure after the 10 June General Election, in Belgium. Participation in government had generated a new, less anti-establishment, image for the Greens and the British party could well benefit from this change in perceptions (*cf.*, 'GREENS GROW UP', *The Economist*, 7 August).

However, the party's success raised classic questions about its strategies and tactics. Was the party's message or its electoral success the more important? Should it continue to target its electoral strongholds and use these as bridgeheads, or should it adopt a broader campaigning front for the next General Election? In terms of the next European elections, what could the party do to keep the support of the disaffected Labour voters it won this time around?

Table 8.4 The ten highest Green votes (in Westminster constituencies)

Constituency	Percentage of total vote
Brighton, Pavilion	19.0
Islington, North	17.9
Oxford, West and Abingdon	17.0
Hackney, North	16.5
Lewisham, Deptford	15.1
Hornsey	14.7
Bristol, West	13.8
Edinburgh, Central	13.9
Holborn and St Pancras	13.5
Edinburgh North	13.3

The Scottish National Party and Plaid Cymru

Through the doughty services of Winnie Ewing, the SNP had been represented in the European Parliament since the inception of direct elections in 1979. The much-loved Allan Macartney had won a second seat in 1994, and the party had been reasonably confident of making further progress in 1999. The failure to capture a third seat was therefore a disappointment, leaving rueful party strategists to contemplate where the required 18,000-plus votes might have been harvested.

For a delighted Plaid Cymru, on the other hand, the post-elections questions were much more positive. The twin effects of the introduction of PR and the disgruntlement of traditional Labour voters had gifted the party a firm electoral basis and fresh electoral horizons which may represent a sea change in the nature of Welsh politics.

Although, thanks to PR, the Conservatives now enjoyed political representation in Scotland again, the chief message which the national parties could take away from the Euro-elections was that it was now they, and not the Conservatives, who provided the main opposition to the Labour Party.

The dog that didn't bark

Britain's ethnic communities could be much reassured by the BNP's failure to make any substantial electoral inroads, despite the PR system and the low turnout. There had been much apprehension prior to the elections, particularly in view of the broadcasters' decision to allow the BNP an electoral broadcast.

Low turnout

The UK's record low turnout triggered off considerable reflection in the British media and political establishment. Among the reasons initially advanced for such unprecedented apathy were: the fact that normal domestic politics had been overshadowed for more than two months by the war in Kosovo; the suspension of the House of Commons for roughly five weeks over the previous three months; the cumulative weariness induced by the Scottish, Welsh and local elections in May; the concomitant draining of party finances and fatigue of party activists.[2]

The political journalist, Paul Routledge, put the blame squarely on the political parties – particularly Labour – for failing to convince their voters there was a reason to turn out (BBC TV, 20 June). While partly agreeing, a (successful) Labour Party candidate spread the blame further:

> For the last five years (and longer) there has been no serious effort by the Labour Party, the British press or the media in general, to understand the European Parliament and to give it the status it is afforded in other European countries. This meant that the MEPs and the elections were either not understood, not considered very important, or both.

Other commentators – particularly in the Euro-sceptic press – argued that, through its apathy, the electorate had been expressing basic hostility to European integration and either the single currency or the European Parliament in particular. In similar fashion, those within the Labour Party opposed to its modernisation or heavy-handed centralisation argued that Labour's traditional voters had stayed at home in protest. Still others within the party argued that it had been 'punished' for the government's slow pace of delivery on its policy commitments.

Labour's internal reflection papers acknowledged a degree of truth, supported by qualitative evidence, for all three of these arguments, but did not accept that any had been decisive. Rather:

> By far the most rational explanation … is that the European Parliament is an institution which is perceived to have no relevance, which is tainted by folklore about bureaucracy and minor corruption, and in

which voters find it difficult to distinguish the reasons for voting for one party rather than another. (Cook, 1999, p. 8)

Punctual, specific activities, such as 'Operation Black Vote' and the cross-party operation 'Get Out The Vote', seemed to make little impression on turnout figures. A GOTV/Institute for Citizenship operation in Halton which encouraged children to accompany their parents to the polling stations seemed to have made little, if any, difference. On the other hand, Barnet Council undertook as an experiment a wide advertising campaign to recruit postal voters. This was clearly successful, with nearly 13,000 postal votes issued, of which 7,322 were returned.

Chapters 5 and 7 examined the way in which the media was alleged to have created the impression that PR was an 'alien' and complex system. Some close Blairite allies argued that PR had not worked: 'It was supposed to get people to polling stations, but it failed dismally' (Sir Ken Jackson, *The Sun*, 14 June). At a purely impressionistic level, it seems that few voters stayed away for this reason. On the other hand, the media also did much to encourage prejudice against the closed list system. Again, at an impressionistic level, candidates reported some prejudice in the electorate against an election which denied them the right to vote for 'their' candidate.

Notoriously low though turnout has traditionally been in Euro-elections, electoral participation has been in general decline in the United Kingdom, as demonstrated by the 1997 post-war low of 71.4 per cent. The new Labour government subsequently established a Home Office working party to consider structural ways of encouraging greater electoral participation. The working party continued its considerations apace. On Tuesday, 13 July, George Howarth, the Home Office Minister responsible for electoral law, published an interim report from a group of electoral officers and representatives from the other main parties which discussed *inter alia* the establishment of pilot schemes to use the Internet for local elections. Other ideas considered included mobile polling stations, polling booths in supermarkets and railway stations, postal balloting, telephone voting and possible weekend voting. The *Sunday Telegraph* (11 July) reported that the government was 'determined to rush through permanent reforms in time for the next general election'. In the *Daily Express*, Richard Heller launched a heartfelt plea: 'FOR THE SAKE OF OUR KIDS, LET'S VOTE ON A SUNDAY' (10 June). 'There is', he argued, 'no law behind Thursday voting and certainly no logic. The habit became established in 1935. The 1931 election fell on a Tuesday, 1922 and 1924 on Wednesdays and 1918 on a Saturday … .' In its electoral post-mortem, Labour's NEC speculated whether shifting local elections forward to June in Euro-elections years might encourage higher turnout. It also decided to conduct a series of consultations within the party on the idea of returning to single-member constituencies with additional 'top-up' MEPs to ensure proportionality. But Peter Riddell took a more sceptical view. The Home Office's proposals, he argued, classically mistook symptoms for causes – 'VOTERS MUST HAVE REASON TO TURN OUT' (*The Times*, 18 June).

The Appendix provides a detailed analysis of the effects of low turnout.

The new electoral system

PR systems can be capricious. In the North-East, 30.5 per cent of the votes cast were 'wasted', going to parties which did not win a seat. But in the South-East, 96 per cent of the votes went to parties which elected MEPs. The d'Hondt system of allocating seats notoriously favours the larger parties. This was most sharply demonstrated in the South-West region, where the Conservatives, with only 42 per cent of the vote, secured four of the seven seats. With 27.2 per cent of the vote to Labour's 28.7 per cent, the SNP could legitimately argue that it had been unlucky not to have won a third seat.

As the first regional results came in at the European Parliament in Brussels, a senior British official observed that the d'Hondt system's effects were difficult to understand: 'They read out the voting figures and then announced that "X is therefore elected, Y is therefore elected," and so on. It was difficult to follow exactly why X and Y had been elected.'

The new system was capricious, then, and difficult to understand but, despite the media Cassandras, no major difficulties were encountered in its application. Counting went smoothly and the few recounts reportedly passed off without event.[3] Jaundiced local government officials said that all had gone well administratively at the local level 'despite the Home Office'. The ballot papers caused little difficulty, notwithstanding their size (13 inches wide in some regions). There were 25,812 spoiled papers in Great Britain (0.26 per cent of the votes cast). This compared with 32,316 (0.21 per cent) in 1994 and 90,288 (0.28 per cent) in 1997. In an exit survey of over 17,000 voters across 300 polling stations, over 90 per cent were satisfied with the management of the election and only 10 per cent had questions about the ballot paper (*Euroelection*, Issue 8, July 1999 – published by *Solace*).[4] Yet, to the frustration of those who favoured PR, it proved impossible to counter the generally negative media campaign. This even led one candidate to argue that PR for the Euro-elections should only have been introduced *after* it had already been introduced for Westminster elections !

The Appendix considers the psephological implications of the new system in detail, but some more general matters are worth emphasising.

First, there were plenty of grumbles from activists and candidates in the two major parties about the system having been introduced too soon, and the major parties clearly encountered problems in adapting to the novel dynamics. There was, it seems, a collective failure of imagination by the British political establishment and certainly no discernible efforts to discover how Continental political parties fought under the same or similar systems.

Second, all of the parties were in unknown electoral territory. Most of the parties, their resources depleted by the May elections, neglected local campaigning and all of the parties realised – too late – that a little extra effort, judiciously directed, could have made a big difference to them or to their ideological opponents. Parties will presumably be wiser to the system (assuming it remains unchanged) in 2004.

Third, as the high vote for Christine Oddy demonstrated, PR makes possible the new phenomenon of the local protest vote.[5] This experience, together with Dennis Canavan's success in the Scottish Assembly elections, underlined the potential risk to the Labour Party of a maverick candidature by Ken Livingstone in the 2000 London mayoral elections. Indeed, the experience also implicitly reveals another possibility, so far only briefly experienced through the fleeting and expensive participation of the late Sir James Goldsmith in the 1997 General Election. PR brings British politics into the world of politicians such as Bernard Tapie and Silvio Berlusconi; that is, strong, charismatic individuals with high recognition factors and access to resources and/or local support. It is no coincidence that both Mr Tapie and, less contro-versially, Mr Berlusconi, have been members of the European Parliament. Another current high-profile example is provided by the French/German Green, Daniel Cohn-Bendit (notorious as the 'Danny the Red' of the 1968 Paris Uprisings). The media's preference for known and charismatic candidates probably explains why, on a rough calculation, the failed Italian candidate Gina Lollobrigida received more British media coverage than any British candidate.

Fourth, the dire level of participation in the Euro-elections led to a number of specific calls for reform. Chapter 5 noted the generalised media introspection about the electorate's democratic 'obligations'. In a 14 June *Guardian* article, Peter Preston speculated as to whether it might be appropriate to introduce compulsory voting: 'We have the power, but we don't care. We can't be bothered to use it.' Preston argued: 'The key benefit of compulsion … is not what happens at the end of the electoral process. Its force is the vital earlier stages of registration and inclusion. It obliges the state to find the poor and the mobile young and indigent.' Anthony King more pragmatically wrote in the *Daily Telegraph* that, 'Whatever else it does, Thursday's paltry turnout should make the Government pause before it inflicts yet more elections and referendums on an increasingly unwilling public.'

Fifth, all of the major parties professed themselves to be content with their candidate selection procedures. The Liberal Democrats were proud of an efficient and democratic system. The Conservatives were proud at the popular system they had devised and disappointed at low participation levels. By far the most controversial were the Labour Party's approach. But there was open acknowledgement that the selection procedure was transitional, and had respected the three guiding principles the party had set itself; managing the transition from 60 to far fewer MEPs, ensuring quality and diversity, and involving the membership. A key consideration was a virtual guarantee of a place on the list to all incumbent MEPs who wished to present themselves again.

In addition to its partisan critics, several incumbent Labour MEPs were critical of the closed list system. The most high-profile of these critics was David Martin, a Vice-President of the European Parliament, who called in a 14 June *Times* interview for the closed list system *per se* to be scrapped.

The Home Office and *that* ballot paper

A minor *cause célèbre* of the 1999 Euro-elections was the Home Office's information leaflet about the new system and the mock ballot paper it contained. The leaflet, published in 13 languages including Urdu, Hindi, and Welsh, was part of a £3.5 million publicity campaign. It was criticised from all angles: for minimising all but the three largest political parties (*Daily Telegraph*, 4 June), for mixing genuine parties with fictitious ones, for looking like a Conservative leaflet (because of the deep blue cover) and for excluding parties with genuine hopes of election (it was this last which led the UKIP and Greens to write a joint letter of protest). The *Daily Express* (5 June) reported that a government help-line to deal with requests for a multi-language leaflet on the Euro-elections had been condemned because it was staffed only by English speakers.

All of these protests must have been slightly galling to the civil servants who had acted in good faith in order to inform and reassure the electorate about the new system. It should be pointed out, however, that one of the most probable reasons why the Home Office leaflet received so much attention was that it was the *only* one. It was the modest scale, as much as the detail, which caused frustration. Allied to this was the lack of any attempt to counter the media-led apprehensions about the system. As one disgruntled candidate put it, 'If the Government was so hot about the new system why didn't they do more to defend it?'

The Post Office

In comparison with many other democratic countries, British elections are regulated in a quaint and idiosyncratic way (see, for example, Chapter 5 on election broadcasts). The Post Office plays a key part in the dissemination of electoral material, both paid and unpaid. In the 1999 Euro-elections, for example, the regulations provided that parties were entitled to one free delivery to each address or, if the material was personally addressed, one free delivery to each elector. In addition, the Home Office leaflet explaining the new electoral system was also to be distributed by the Post Office.

During the campaign, the BNP complained that Edinburgh Post Office workers were refusing to deliver its Euro-election material. A Post Office spokesman insisted that the material would be delivered in accordance with its obligations (*Daily Telegraph*, 28 June). But, at an anecdotal level at least, the BNP was not the only party to believe that its electoral material had failed to arrive at all destinations, and many also claimed not to have received the Home Office leaflet. Such allegations are notoriously hard to prove: was the material not delivered, or did the household throw the material away inadvertently? The allegations underlined the importance, given the UK's *sui generis* electoral system, of efficient and universal distribution mechanisms.

On the other hand, the Post Office was able to play an entirely positive role in the London Borough of Barnet, where it participated fully in the Council's successful experiment in encouraging the postal vote.

Britain and Europe

Writing in the *Financial Times* (18 June), Philip Stephens argued that 'the significance of the European elections lies in the fact that Mr Hague's eurosceptics did manage to step into the vacuum left by the Prime Minister. If Mr Blair is not prepared to engage, then the electorate will stick with its instincts.' For the time being, as the opinion polls demon-

EUROPEAN ELECTIONS 1999

BLAIR · SCHROEDER · JOSPIN

O'Brien

Jospin was the only socialist leader to be happy at the results

Independent (15 June) (Steve O' Brien)

strated and the Prime Minister acknowledged, a roughly two-thirds majority would prefer to stick to sterling. However, as Mr Stephens went on to argue:

> The fine print of these surveys carries a more optimistic message for Mr Blair. Whatever their own preferences, about three-quarters of the electorate believe Britain will join the single currency. The contradiction points to a nation waiting to be led.

More pessimistically, Hugo Young, writing in the *Guardian* (10 June), observed that:

> The state of things resolves itself into an appalling paradox. So long as Britain remains outside the euro, a broad and open debate about the future of Europe will be impossible to hold. As long as the euro argument it is not concluded its ferocity will banish all other discussion from the field … We await the referendum. It should be the high point of the British people's engagement with Europe. But this is the paradox. Only after the referendum is over is an honest debate about European Britain likely, at last, to begin.

Perhaps not all would agree that resolution can come only after the euro-referendum, but many on the pro-European side felt that the strongest message of the Euro-elections was the need to proselytise and evangelise a little more. EPLP leader Alan Donnelly, interviewed on BBC 2's *Newsnight* and on BBC Radio Four's *Tonight* programme (Monday 21 June) argued passionately that what was required was a 'structured dialogue' on all things European. Carole Tongue, a London Labour MEP from 1984 to 1999, believed that the malaise went deeper:

> In order to make a European representative democracy work, we need to foster, at European level, the kind of empathy which citizens of one country currently have with each other… The EU will never be a proper democratic entity until European citizens know more about each other. (Carole Tongue, 'Democratic Deficit? Cultural Deficit!', January 1999)

Mark Leonard, a noted Blairite think-tanker, wrote in the *New Statesman* (21 June) that, 'They have tried to sell us Europe with lofty rhetoric about federalism, but it's the wrong pitch and it's confusing us … .'

Underlying all of these analyses was genuine disappointment that the 1999 Euro-elections had not, as many had expected, marked a genuine new departure in the UK's relationship with Europe.

The European Parliament

Reflection on 'what went wrong' among the political parties and groups was matched by similar reflection within the European Parliament's hierarchy. Where had the *'introuvable peuple européen'* (*Le Monde*) gone? On Wednesday 23 June, the outgoing Parliament's Bureau decided to launch a detailed study of the reasons which led to the record rate of abstention. The decision was taken after the presentation of a first analysis by outgoing Vice-President Giorgios Anastassopoulos, a former journalist, and an interim report by the Secretary-General, Julian Priestley. In his report, Mr Anastassopoulos pointed out that low turnout was neither an isolated phenomenon nor necessarily a delegitimising factor. In the 1998 Congressional elections in the United States, for example, turnout was just 36 per cent. Moreover, the European elections had taken place in what Mr Anastassopoulos described as 'hostile circumstances'.

According to his analysis, the first of these 'hostile circumstances' was the ongoing war in Kosovo, which squeezed out the electoral campaigns whilst simultaneously underlining the Parliament's impotence and relative weakness compared with, say, the American Congress. The second was the dioxin scandal in Belgium, which probably strengthened the positions of the Greens and the radicals but also encouraged feelings of disillusionment. The third was the ongoing institutional crisis. 'It is my firm belief', wrote Mr Anastassopoulos, 'that, in the end, it discredited Community Brussels in general and all of the institutions, including the Parliament.'

To this generally hostile climate, Mr Anastassopoulos added three general political factors. The first was what he described as a 'global crisis' for participatory politics. He cited a Dutch study which demonstrated that 17.7 per cent of voters said they had not voted because they had lost all interest in politics, and 13.8 per cent because they did not have time. The second was the absence of grand designs, manifestos or projects capable of stirring voters' imaginations. The third was the lack of presence of MEPs and of 'Europe' in general in the campaigns, which focused more or less exclusively on domestic debates.

Mr Anastassopoulos concluded that election laws needed to be radically reformed, notably through the introduction of electoral regions and preferential voting. He also argued that the next elections should be pushed forward to May, and that wherever possible they should be combined with national or regional elections. It was time, he argued, for the British and the Dutch to vote at weekends.

In his analysis, Mr Priestley felt that the media had played to the full its role in relaying and mirroring the political debate, and that where there had been coverage of the European Parliament, its new roles as co-legislator and 'monitor of the Executive' had been stressed. In addition to the distractions of Kosovo and the dioxin scandal, he also listed a number of factors which, in his opinion, had contributed to low turnout. These included: political parties' low commitment to the campaign in terms of human and financial resources; the electorates' sense of distance and powerlessness; the negative image of the Commission (poor management) and of the Parliament (members' statute); the perception of the EU as an economic rather than political entity; and the voting methods (lists blocked at national level, hence allowing no trans-European element).

The French President of the European Movement, Jean-Louis Bourlanges, who was also re-elected as an MEP, expressed 'alarm, but not surprise' at the the high rate of voter abstention. He argued that the low turnout had demonstrated how European elections had 'not yet really found their place in our public life'. Ironically, in the particular case of France, his conclusion was the need to 'create a real link between voters and elected officials through the creation of regional constituencies' – exactly the system which had produced a record low level of voter participation in the UK.

On the continent, more radical ideas about how to encourage greater popular participation circulated. Jacques Delors had once floated the idea of a 'European president', directly or indirectly elected through the European elections. National governments clearly disliked the idea, with its implication of an overarching leader with a popular mandate, but the suggestion was revived by an influential German MEP, Elmar Brok, in the immediate aftermath of the 1999 Euro-elections. 'Parliament has got to get a bigger profile with our voters in the future, and has got to be part of the political debate in which people know they are voting for something real', said Mr Brok. 'That means the political parties putting forward their candidates to be president' (*Guardian*, 16 June).

As an upbeat *Financial Times* editorial put it: 'Trying to create democracy from the top down, rather than bottom up, does not generate great popular enthusiasm ... Low turnout may be inevitable and it is certainly not a disaster ... and is still, continent-wide, higher than that in any recent US Congressional election … Creating a democratic control system in the EU is certainly a long and slow process.'

The continued search for legitimisation

At a more fundamental level, the poor levels of participation in the 1999 Euro-elections dashed the hopes of those who had continued to believe that a directly elected Parliament was the best means of legitimising not only the Parliament itself, but the European integration process in general. As the resignation of the Santer Commission and the solid (now uncontested and generally praised) legislative and budgetary work of the Parliament showed, MEPs had been successful in developing and fulfilling the Parliament–Executive side of their role. It was the popular, legit-imising electoral link which continued to elude them.

Through the provisions relating to national Parliaments, the draftsmen of the Maastricht Treaty and, even more, the Amsterdam Treaty, had indicated their realisation that the European Parliament was, by itself, a necessary but insufficient part of the EU's democratisation process. The 1999 Euro-elections will surely have confirmed the draftsmen of the next Treaty (scheduled for 2000) in this view.

Yet the Parliament could rightly feel aggrieved at such a characterisa-tion of the EU's political arrangements. To use an old saw, people do not vote for parliaments, they vote for parties. If only 23 per cent of the British electorate felt motivated to turn out on 10 June 1999, political parties must also contemplate why they were unable to mobilise more of their supporters for an election which, in retrospect, will almost certainly be seen as having been highly influential in determining the course of the UK's future relationship with the European Union, and hence its future in general.

The 1999 European elections provided a brief interruption in the flow of British politics, and one that was little noticed by the public. As one party official put it, the election had been 'a tactical exercise without troops'. Despite the unexpected setback, the Blair government sailed on, high in the opinion polls and unfrightened by the opposition, despite its success on 10 June. But the election, and the use of PR, released forces into the political scene – the Greens, the United Kingdom Independence Party – which would reverberate into the future. Moreover, Mr Hague's successful short-term tactics had important consequences for the Blair 'project' and, perhaps, for Britain's relationship to the single currency. The election also taught the parties lessons about campaigning and structure from which, if they chose to, they could learn much for the politics of the new millennium.

There were differing perceptions of the attitudes of Labour' Leader and Deputy Leader towards the party's 'core vote'

The Times (9 July) (Peter Brookes)

Notes

1. As one candidate put it, 'In 1974 there were about 25,000 members, of whom about 20,000 were committed federalists. Today, membership is at about 100,000, of whom about 30,000 are committed federalists. The party is simply less European than it used to be.'
2. *10 highest turnouts*
   40.2   Carmarthen East
   39.4   Merionydd
   39.2   Brecon & Radnor
   38.6   Caernarfon
   37.8   Ceredigion
   36.4   Ynys Mon
   34.7   Cotswold
   34.4   East Devon
   34.3   Monmouth
   33.9   Leominster
   10 lowest turnouts
   10.3   Liverpool, Riverside
   10.7   Liverpool, Walton
   11.2   Liverpool, West Derby
   12.1   Manchester, Central
   12.6   Hull, East
   12.6   Bootle
   12.8   Walsall, North
   12.9   West Bromwich, West
   13.0   Barnsley Central
   13.0   Manchester, Gorton
3. Where recounts occurred they were sometimes caused by the regional returning officers' scrupulous anxiety about the discrepancy between the exact party totals and the verified ballot papers.
4. Though the tellers at the counting stations in London complained that they had had to stand up to deal with the lengthy ballot sheet. They also complained of cuts and of 'election finger'. Some party activists pointed out that, on the London ballot paper, the text said 'put your cross in one of the boxes', but the arrow pointed directly to the BNP box.
5. *10 highest other votes*
   24.9   Coventry NE   Oddy
   24.5   Coventry NW   Oddy
   22.6   Coventry South   Oddy
   15.8   Glasgow Pollok   S. Lab.
   12.3   Nuneaton   Oddy
   11.6   Glasgow, Springburn   S. Lab.
   11.4   Warwickshire N.   Oddy
   11.4   Glasgow Shettleston   S. Lab
   11.3   Glasgow Baillieston   S. Lab
   10.8   Rugby & Kenilworth   Oddy

Appendix: An Analysis of the Result

John Curtice and Michael Steed

One of the original aims of holding European elections was to strengthen the links between the European public and the European Union. Yet in practice the elections are widely regarded as having failed to secure that aim. Largely uninterested in the European Union, relatively few voters go to the polls. Those that do vote do so on the basis of matters domestic rather than issues European, using the occasion as an opportunity to send a (often adverse) message to the national government of the day. And because the future of the national government is not at stake, voters feel less inhibited about voting for smaller parties. Together these three characteristics have led commentators to describe Europen elections as second-order elections (Reif and Schmitt, 1980; Reif 1984; van der Eijk and Franklin, 1996; Heath *et al.*, 1999).

At first glance, many of these symptoms of a second-order election are evident in the outcome of the 1999 European election in Great Britain. At 23.1 per cent, turnout was not only lower than in any of the four previous European elections (as indeed it was across the EU as a whole), but Britain regained the ignominious position it had lost to the Netherlands in 1994 as the country with the lowest turnout in the EU.

The election was a disappointment for the incumbent Labour government. The party was outpolled in a nationwide contest for the first time since 1992; the Conservatives on 35.8 per cent were even slightly further ahead of Labour than they were in 1992. At 28.0 per cent, Labour's share of the vote was lower than in 1983, its worst ever performance in a general election since 1918. Moreover its vote was only just better than the 27.9 per cent to which the previous Conservative government fell in the last Euro-election in 1994.

Meanwhile, smaller parties did well. No less than 18.9 per cent of the vote was secured by parties not currently represented at Westminster, a record haul. Both the United Kingdom Independence Party (UKIP) and the Greens won well over 5 per cent of the vote, putting them well ahead of the Scottish National Party and Plaid Cymru combined in the Britain-wide vote.

But can we regard the 1999 European election as simply more of the same? Take Labour's drubbing, for example. It came at a time when the party was still very high in the opinion polls. True, those poll ratings had not been fully reflected in recent domestic mid-term elections. Even so, the party had, for example, remained ahead of the Conservatives in local elections held only just the previous month, something that neither Margaret Thatcher nor John Major ever achieved two years into a Parliament (Curtice, 1999a). If voters were using this election to send a message to their national government we might have expected them to proffer a bouquet of flowers rather than a crown of thorns.

Meanwhile, how do we explain why the smaller parties did better than at any previous European election? Even more importantly, how do we account for the fact that, while the UKIP and Greens won 7.0 per cent and 6.3 per cent respectively, no other party currently unrepresented at Westminster won more than the 1.4 per cent secured by the Pro-European Conservatives? The second-order model gives us little apparent guidance as to why two of the smaller parties should have done well while the remainder barely made their presence felt at all.

The second-order model may have become the prism through which European elections are mostly viewed, but it is not wholly unchallenged. In Denmark, like Britain one of the more sceptical members of the EU, voters have long since voted on the basis of European issues rather than just domestic ones (Nielsen, 1996; Worre, 1996). Indeed, the country has spawned not just one but two anti-European movements that fight European but not national elections. In France, both the 1994 and 1999 elections saw voters lend considerable support to explicitly anti-European rebel party lists, and in 1999 they gave significant support to strongly pro-European lists too.

Perhaps it is now time to ask whether European issues are coming to matter in Britain's European elections also. Perhaps the Conservatives', UKIP's and the Greens' successes and Labour's failure happened because electors were voting on the basis of their views about Europe. The anti-single currency pitch of the Conservatives certainly chimed with poll evidence on the unpopularity of the euro (see Curtice, 1999b). And there are already signs that Europe may have taken on an added importance in the country's domestic elections (Heath *et al.*, 1998; Evans, 1999).

This is the first of two main themes explored in this appendix. Did the low turnout simply confirm voter disinterest in Europe? Should the Conservative success and Labour failure be put down to the appeal of the Conservatives' anti-euro campaign or to disillusionment with New Labour? How do we account for the successes of the UKIP and the Greens?

We also have to bear in mind that the 1999 European election was fought under a regional closed party list system of proportional representation, the first time any system of proportional representation had been used in an election throughout Great Britain. This gives rise to the second main theme to be explored. What impact did the new system have? Did voters behave differently than they would have done under the old system? How did the new system work? How far was the outcome really proportional? And how did it compare with might have happened if the old system had still been in place?

For evidence we analyse the election results themselves. Although the new voting system used only eleven separate regions, the votes were counted and published separately for each of the 641 British constituencies. So we can compare how the parties fared in 1999 with the outcome two years earlier in the 1997 General Election in each constituency. Given the wide diversity in the political and social characteristics of parliamentary constituencies this enables us to gain vital clues about who might have voted for which party and why. But it should be borne in mind that some of the issues we explore can also be illuminated by analysing survey data on the behaviour and attitudes of individual voters. Doubtless subsequent analysis of such data will help establish the validity or otherwise of the inferences that we make here.

Turnout

Does the record low turnout simply tell us that the British electorate now has even less interest in Europe in general and its Parliament in particular than ever before? Perhaps not. This was but the latest in a sequence of low turnouts. In the 1997 General Election, turnout was lower than in any previous post-war election. In the 1998 annual round of local elections, just 30 per cent went to the polls (Rallings and Thrasher, 1998), lower than in any other recent annual round of local elections (Rallings and Thrasher, 1997). In England, at least, turnout proved to be similarly low in the 1999 local elections held just a month before the European elections. Equally, the relatively low proportions voting in the 1997 Welsh referendum (50.1 per cent), the 1998 London referendum (34.1 per cent) and the 1999 Welsh Assembly elections (46.3 per cent) also raise questions about whether the public is becoming disengaged from conventional politics.

Turnout has always been lower in European elections than in contemporaneous local elections. A turnout below 30 per cent was thus to be expected even if the importance people attach to Europe relative to Westminster or their local council has not fallen. Why the public's willingness to turn out and vote has dropped generally at recent elections is far from clear; explanations offered include the absence of political competition (Taylor and Heath, 1999) and a decline in trust in the political process (Curtice and Jowell, 1995). Whatever the cause, we can reasonably assume that it accounts for much of the drop from 36 per cent in the 1994 European elections to 23 per cent this time.

Nevertheless, a seven point gap between local and European turnout is as large as the difference has ever been. A suggestion widely made was that voters were suffering from a surfeit of elections. True, in London, the only region where no elections had been held at all a month earlier, turnout fell by just 44.0 percentage points, less than anywhere else in Great Britain. But the fall in turnout was also somewhat below the overall British figure in Scotland (–46.7 per cent) and Wales (–45.3 per cent), in both of which significantly more voters had participated in the previous month's elections than had been the case anywhere else in England.[1]

Table A.1 Variation in Turnout

| | Turnout | | % of total vote cast | | |
| | Mean % | Mean change | | | |
Lab % vote1997	1999	since 1997	1999	1997	
0–30%	27.8	–46.7	26.1	30.1	(155)
30–50%	24.5	–49.1	28.2	29.0	(171)
50–60%	21.5	–49.7	25.5	23.6	(166)
60%+	18.2	–46.9	20.2	17.2	(148)
All seats	23.1	–48.2	100.0	100.0	(640)

Table excludes Tatton, which was not contested by Labour in 1997.

There is another explanation as to why some people at least stayed at home that is better supported by the evidence: it is that Labour voters were less inclined to vote than were supporters of other parties. As Table A.1 shows, in seats where Labour's share of the vote was below 30 per cent in 1997, turnout averaged 28 per cent. In contrast, in constituencies where Labour won more than 60 per cent in 1997, turnout was on average as little as 18 per cent.

Turnout is, of course, usually lower in constituencies where Labour is relatively strong. Indeed, as Table A.1 also shows, the fall in turnout compared with the 1997 General Election was no higher in seats where Labour was particularly strong than where it was weak. But this reflects the impact of floor effects; turnout was already so low in some safe Labour seats in 1997 that it could not fall much more than it actually did. Even so, turnout did fall more heavily in seats where Labour was moderately strong in 1997 than where it was weak.

In any event a ten point difference in the level of turnout between a party's strong and weak seats will clearly have a more adverse impact on its vote tally when turnout is just 23.1 per cent rather than the 1997 level of 71.4 per cent. As the final column of Table A.1 shows, the proportion of the total vote that was cast in seats where Labour won over 50 per cent of the vote in 1997 fell from 46 per cent in 1997 to 41 per cent in 1999. Even if party shares of the vote in each constituency had remained the same as in 1997 – and thus by implication the fall in turnout had been the same among Labour and non-Labour supporters within each constituency – Labour's share of the overall vote across Britain as a whole would still have fallen by two points.

In practice it also seems likely that, within each constituency, Labour voters tended to stay at home more than non-Labour supporters. In those seats where turnout was down by more than 50 points compared with the 1997 election, Labour's vote fell on average by 17.8 per cent; elsewhere, Labour's vote fell by just 14.4 per cent. More complex analyses discussed below that take into account some of the other influences on Labour's performance broadly confirm this pattern.[2]

Why were Labour supporters more likely to stay at home? One much-mooted possibility is that they were disenchanted with their party's policy on Europe. The Labour party itself was more inclined to offer a domestic explanation, suggesting that it reflected contentment rather than disillusion with the government. It is impossible to refute or confirm either account by looking at the election results themselves. But it should be noted that the gap in turnout between areas where Labour is weak and those where it is strong had already widened at the two previous General Elections, well before there was any Labour government to be content about (Curtice and Steed, 1997; Denver and Hands 1997). Moreover, survey analysis of the last election suggests that abstention grew particularly amongst traditional working-class Labour supporters who no longer thought that Labour looked after their interests (Taylor and Heath, 1999). It thus seems most likely that the pattern of Labour abstention reflected a continuing and perhaps even growing lack of enthusiasm amongst some of the party's traditional supporters for Labour's repositioning towards the centre.

So far as turnout is concerned, the 1999 European election would appear then to have been a second-order election. True, the fall in turnout may not have been occasioned by any growing disinterest in matters European. But interest was certainly insufficient to overcome a variety of domestic influences that meant that voters were disinclined to go to the polls. But what picture do we obtain when we look at party performances?

Labour and the Conservatives

The pattern of Labour's performance clearly confirms that voters in areas of traditional Labour strength were reluctant to support the party. Labour's share of the vote consistently fell more, the better it had polled in a constituency two years previously. Thus, for example, as Table A.2 shows, in seats where Labour won less than 30 per cent of the vote in 1997, its share of the vote fell by less than 5 points.[3] In contrast, in seats where it had won over 60 per cent two years ago, its vote slumped by well over 20 points.

Table A.2 Labour strength and party performance

| Lab % vote 1997 | Mean change in % vote for | | |
	Con	Lab	Lib Dem
0–30%	+3.0	–4.1	–14.8 (155)
30–50%	+2.6	–15.7	–2.9 (171)
50–60%	+4.0	–20.2	–0.3 (166)
60%+	+5.6	–22.6	+0.3 (147)
All seats	+3.7	–14.4	1.1 (639)

This might be thought to be no more than could be expected when a party suffers a double-digit fall in support, as Labour did on this occasion. After all, in some of its weakest seats, Labour did not have 20 per cent of the vote to lose in the first place. If Labour were everywhere losing the same proportion of its 1997 support, that would mean that its share of the vote would fall more where its vote was previously highest.

However, previous research has suggested that there is no necessary reason why a party's support should fall in proportion to its previous strength (McLean, 1973). Moreover, Labour's support did not fall more heavily in its strongest seats in the 1983 General Election, when its support fell to a similar level as in the 1999 Euro-election (Curtice and Steed, 1984). Indeed, comparing Labour's performance in each constituency in 1999 with that in 1983, reveals that in seats where it scored less than 30 per cent of the vote in 1983, its vote was on average no less than six points higher in 1999. In contrast, in seats where it had secured more than 40 per cent of the vote in 1983, its share in 1999 was typically nearly 6 points lower.[4] In short, although Labour's share of the overall vote was almost the same in 1999 as in 1983, the distribution of that support was very different.

So we have here another sign that Labour had particular difficulty in securing the support of some of its more traditional adherents. In contrast, there is no evidence that it had any particular difficulty in retaining support where it had done particularly well under its New Labour banner between 1992 and 1997. In seats where Labour's share of the vote had risen by over 12 points between 1992 and 1997, the average fall in Labour support was, at 17.1 per cent, almost identical to the 17.0 per cent drop in seats where it only gained between 7 and 12 point between 1992 and 1997.

As a result of these patterns, the geography of Labour's vote took on an ever less traditional character than it had in 1997 (Curtice and Steed, 1997; Curtic and Park, 1999). Its vote fell far less in the South of England than in Wales, the North of England or the Midlands.[5] Equally, as we show further below, its vote fell less, the less middle class the seat. Reorientating the party's support in this way is clearly one of the aims of Tony Blair's rebranding of the party as 'New' Labour (Radice, 1992). The 1999 Euro-elections confirmed that aim was being achieved, but raised doubts as to whether doing so would necessarily ensure electoral success.

Who were the beneficiaries of Labour's difficulties in its heartlands? In part, it would appear to have been the Conservative Party. On average, its share of the vote rose most strongly in those seats where Labour had won over 60 per cent of the vote in 1997. As a result the best Tory performance was across all three regions in the North of England, where its share of the vote rose since 1997 by between 7.6 per cent and 8.7 per cent. But the more striking feature of Table A.2 is how different the pattern of the Conservative performance appears to have been from Labour's, varying far less from one type of constituency to another. (At 3.6, the standard deviation of the change in the Conservative share of the vote was far less than the equivalent figure of 8.1 for Labour.)

Moreover, the pattern of such variation as there was in the Conservative performance was rather different than in the case of Labour. We can see this in Table A.3, which shows the change in the two parties' share of the vote since 1997, according to the class and educational composition of each constituency. The Conservatives clearly performed less well in those constituencies in which a relatively high proportion of people have a degree. Once allowance is made for this, the class composition of a constituency made little difference to how well the party did. But in Labour's case the exact opposite appears to be true. As we noted above, the party performed less badly in middle-class seats than in working-class ones. Once allowance is made for this, the educational composition of the constituency made much less difference to how well the party did.

Table A.3 Class, education and party performance

	Mean Change since 1997 in % voting			
	Conservative		Labour	
	% with degree		% with degree	
% employers and managers	Low	High	Low	High
Low	+5.3	+2.3	−20.0	−19.1
High	+4.4	+2.2	−13.2	−10.6

Constituencies with a low % of employers and managers are those with less than 19.0% of economically active heads of households in socio-economic groups, 1, 2 or 13 as measured by the 1991 Census. Constituencies with a high % are those with more than 19%.

Constituencies with a low % with a degree are those where less than 13% of the population aged 18+ have a degree as measured by the 1991 Census. Constituencies with a high % are those with more than 13% in that category.

This gives us a vital clue to the reasons for the two parties' contrasting fortunes. Analysis of survey data indicates that attitudes towards Europe in general, and the single currency in particular, are more strongly related to education than they are to social class. Those with a degree are far more likely to favour Britain's adoption of the euro than are those without any educational qualifications at all. Once we allow for this, there is no significant relationship between social class and attitudes towards the euro.[6] In short, while the pattern of Conservative performance is consistent with the proposition that the party's campaign against the euro attracted voters, Labour's performance is more consistent with an explanation that argues the party lost ground because of disillusion amongst some of its traditional supporters with its domestic policy repositioning.

The contrast in the pattern of the two parties' performances can also be seen in the regional variation. Although the Conservatives did relatively well in the North of England, they did not do so well in other parts of Britain where Labour is relatively strong. Most strikingly, in London the Conservatives' share of the vote rose by just 1.2 per cent. Support for European integration is unusually high in the capital even after we take into account its relatively high proportion of persons with a degree (Curtice, 1996); it thus seems likely that the Conservatives' anti-euro campaign was less attractive to Londoners. Meanwhile, in Scotland and Wales, the Conservatives' share of the vote increased by just 2.3 per cent and 3.2 per cent, respectively. Perhaps here the Conservatives' anti-euro campaign reinforced the impression already created by its anti-devolution stance that it has become an English party. Certainly within Wales the party's vote rose most in the more English parts of the principality, where opposition to devolution had been strongest, where the party performed best in the Welsh Assembly election and where adherence to Britishness rather than Welshness is at its highest (Taylor and Thomson, 1999).[7] In all, the weak Conservative performances in London, Scotland and Wales suggest that the nationalism of the Tory campaign resonated most among provincial English voters.

One other feature of the Conservative performance was that the party failed to reverse one of the key patterns of its 1997 defeat. This was that its vote fell most where it had previously been strongest. Not only did this help bring about the landslide defeat in terms of seats, but it also potentially leaves the Conservatives at a serious disadvantage in future (Curtice and Steed, 1997). As we might already have anticipated from Table A.2, at this election Conservative support rose, if anything, a little less in the party's traditional strongholds than it did elsewhere. In seats where the Conservatives had over 50 per cent of the vote in 1992 Conservative support was up on average by just 2.4 per cent.

Thus there is some evidence to suggest that the 1999 Euro-election may not simply have been a second-order election. It looks likely that the Conservatives did gain support on the basis of their opposition to the euro and that this was at least part of the reason for the party's largely unexpected success. But at the same time, some of Labour's traditional supporters seemed to have been sending a message to their national government too. Not only did Britain's two main parties fight very different election campaigns, but they also appear to have secured very different results that had very different underlying messages.

The Liberal Democrats and the electoral system

For the Liberal Democrats, the party most in favour of Britain's further integration with Europe, this was the fifth time in a row that its share of the vote in

European election was less than its share at the previous General Election. Indeed, at 12.7 per cent, it was its second worst performance in any general or European election since 1970; only the outcome in the 1989 Euro-election held soon after the disastrous merger between the Liberals and the Social Democrats was worse. The party's vote was also markedly weaker than it was the previous month in the local elections in England and in the devolution elections in Scotland and Wales.[8] While the party's local election performance in particular now regularly outstrips its current level of Westminster popularity, this result appears to confirm that the party tends to underperform in European elections (Curtice and Steed, 1995).[9] This is evidently one party whose support in European elections does not simply fit a second-order model.

However, there was, arguably, good reason to expect the Liberal Democrats to have performed better on this occasion than at previous European elections. At last it was free of the fear that a Liberal Democrat vote would be a wasted vote. But, as in the Scottish and Welsh elections in May, the party discovered that introducing proportional representation did not suddenly transform its electoral prospects.

Nevertheless, the change of electoral system did make a difference to the way that people voted. Under the new proportional system, voters did not have the incentive to vote tactically that existed under the single member plurality system. Under the latter, some voters, perhaps as many as one in ten, vote for their second preference party because the party they like most has no chance of winning in their constituency and they want to secure the defeat of the party they like least. In 1997 in particular, a significant number of voters made the tactical switch (in both directions) between Labour and the Liberal Democrats in order to unseat the local Conservative (Curtice and Steed, 1997; Evans *et al.*, 1998). It would appear that many of those voters returned to their first preference in 1999.[10]

Table A.4 Party performance and tactical position

1st/2nd party 1997	Mean change in % vote since 1997		
	Con	Lab	Lib Dem
Con/Lab	+2.5	–12.6	–5.2 (92)
Con/Lib Dem	+2.9	–4.2	–14.6 (73)
Marg. Lab/Con	+2.7	–17.7	–0.9 (117)
Marg. Lab/Lib Dem	+6.8	–15.9	–9.4 (7)
Safe Lab/Con	+5.1	–21.4	+0.1 (223)
Safe Lab/Lib Dem	+5.9	–23.2	–1.2 (23)
Lib Dem/Con	+4.3	+0.8	–23.0 (39)
Lib Dem/Lab	+6.3	–7.7	–17.8 (6)

Table excludes seats where Nationalists or Others came first or second in 1997.
Marg. Lab seats where Labour's majority was less than 20% in 1997.
Safe Lab seats where Labour's majority was greater than 20% in 1997.

Table A.4 shows how each of the three main parties fared, according to which came first and second in 1997. If tactical voting did unravel in this election, we would expect to find that each party did best where it was third in 1997;[11] and this largely proves to be the case.

First, the Liberal Democrat vote barely declined at all in seats that Labour won ahead of the Conservatives in 1997. Their performance in seats where the Conservatives were first and Labour second in 1997 was also far better than it was where the Liberal Democrats shared first and second place with the Conservatives.

Second, Labour's vote actually held up at its 1997 level in those seats that the Liberal Democrats had won from the Conservatives, and its vote fell less in seats where the Conservatives were first and the Liberal Democrats second than it did in any other category of seat. Finally, the Conservatives also recorded their largest advances in seats where the party was third in 1997.

These patterns have two important implications. First, just as some proponents of change have argued (Linton and Southcott, 1998), it appears that voters are more likely to vote sincerely for their first preference party under a proportional system. Future assessments of the impact of using proportional representation for elections to the House of Commons will evidently need to take this prospect into account.

Second, the results illustrate just how important tactical switching now is to the fortunes of Labour and the Liberal Democrats under the current electoral system. Support for the Liberal Democrats fell by no less than 22 per cent on average in the 46 constituencies that they won in 1997, ensuring that they failed to come first in all but one of them. Equally, Labour's support also came tumbling down by 22 per cent in the 418 seats they captured two years previously.[12]

Yet it would be a mistake to presume that all of the patterns in Table A.4 simply reflect the impact of a reduction in tactical voting. Note, for example, that Labour's vote fell more in its safe seats than in those where its hold was more marginal. Note also that the Liberal Democrats did better in seats where they were a poor second to Labour than in seats where they were third behind a first placed Conservative. And we should also bear in mind that the Conservatives did better in seats where they were a long way behind Labour in 1997 than where they were closer.

None of these necessarily are easily accounted for by a reduction in tactical voting. After all, voters have more incentive to vote tactically in marginal seats than in safe ones; so we might have expected both Labour and the Conservatives to have done less well in marginal Labour seats than in safe ones, to the benefit of the Liberal Democrats. Equally, there seems no good reason why the Liberal Democrats' vote should hold up better in many seats where the party was second to Labour than it did in those where it was second to the Conservatives.

We have already seen that Labour's vote fell more, the stronger the party was in 1997. This remains true even if we take into account the tactical situation in a constituency. In fact, the same is also true of the Liberal Democrats.[13] In other words, while some significant unravelling of tactical voting may have taken place we should not assume that it was the only reason for the Liberal Democrats' difficulties in their stronger seats (just as it was not the only reason for Labour's in its). It is more likely that, with many of the party's strongholds being the product of significant local campaigning, the party suffered heavily from the virtual absence of such activity in a low-key regionally organised contest.

One of the reasons advanced as to why party activists appear to have been reluctant to campaign locally is that under the closed list system they had no local candidate to sell to voters. If so, this was to ignore the potential to attract votes through the popularity of the candidate at the top of the list, a potential that is commonly exploited in other countries. That voters could be attracted in this way was demonstrated by the unusually good performances recorded in some Westminster constituencies by lists whose leading candidate had a connection with the area. Thus for example, the presence of Jonathan Evans, former Conservative MP for Brecon & Radnor, at the head of the Conservative Welsh list was accompanied by the second largest increase in the Conservative vote in Wales in that constituency. Meanwhile, the presence of Chris Davies, former Liberal Democrat MP for Littleborough and Saddleworth, at the head of the Liberal Democrat list in the North-West saw the party in the successor constituency secure its second highest share of the vote anywhere.[14]

The Small Parties

The Scottish National Party and Plaid Cymru once again did substantially better in the European election than they had done in the previous Westminster election (Curtice and Steed, 1995). Of the two, Plaid Cymru made the more progress. At 29.6 per cent, its share of the vote in Wales was a full 19.7 per cent higher than in the 1997 General Election. In contrast, the SNP's 27.2 per cent of the Scottish vote was up only 5.1 per cent on the General Election and was as much as 5.4 per cent lower than in the last European election in 1994.

Neither performance was surprising, given the outcome of the Scottish Parliament and Welsh Assembly elections in May. Both parties' share of their nation's vote fell between their score on the constituency vote in the earlier domestic contest and their tally on the list vote. Moreover, in both cases the geographical pattern of the parties' performances was similar to that five weeks earlier.[15] In Wales, Plaid Cymru repeated its sweeping performance in the valley constituencies of South Wales. In Islwyn and Rhondda their advance brought about the largest Labour drops in support anywhere in Britain (these two traditional Labour strongholds having been won spectacularly by Plaid Cymru the previous month).

There seems little reason to believe therefore that the nationalists' European stance had much effect on their performance. And, given that in both countries they have now replaced the Conservatives as the principal opposition to Labour, there is perhaps no longer any strong reason to expect them to benefit from the second-ordered quality of a European election.

Neither of these statements applies to the UKIP who with 7.0 per cent just pipped the Greens (6.3 per cent) as the most successful of the parties not currently represented at Westminster. For the most part the UKIP's performance confirmed the evidence of the UKIP and Referendum Party vote in 1997 as to the character of anti-European support. As in 1997, the party's vote was highest in the South of England outside London, though the party also did surprisingly well in the North-East. In contrast, the party's British, and thus perhaps to many a Scottish and Welsh eye, English, nationalism had relatively little appeal outside England. Once again, the party tended to do relatively well in constituencies with larger numbers of older people and especially in seaside resorts and rural areas.

The pattern of the UKIP's vote was very much what would be expected if the party were securing support on the basis of its anti-European stance. Opposition to greater European integration tends to be higher in the South of England outside London and among older people (Curtice 1996; Evans, 1995). Meanwhile, as Table A.5 shows, while the party did relatively well in middle-class constituencies, it also did relatively well in constituencies with fewer persons with a degree, just the kind of territory where, as we argued earlier, we might expect an anti-European campaign to flourish. There seems every reason to conclude that the UKIP vote was the result of voters casting their ballots on the basis of their views about Europe.

The particular success of the UKIP in middle-class England naturally raises the question, did the party do particular damage to the Conservatives? However, as was also true in 1997, this is not evidently the case (Curtice and Steed, 1997; Heath *et al.*, 1998). There is no apparent relationship between the strength of the Conservative performance and either the increase in anti-European support since 1997 or the level of UKIP support in 1999. Superficially, there would seem to be a stronger case that the UKIP might have done more harm to the Liberal Democrats, as it secured its highest votes in the Liberal Democrats' far south-western strongholds in Cornwall and Devon. But once we allow for the general tendency for the Liberal Democrat vote to fall most where the party was previously strongest, even this supposition finds little support. Given that anti-European sentiment is still to be found among the supporters of all the main parties we should perhaps not be surprised that the UKIP seems to hurt all of them about equally (Evans, 1999), even if the views of many candidates were to the contrary (see Chapter 6).

Table A.5 Class, education and UKIP and Green support

| | Mean % UKIP | | Mean % Green | |
| | % with degree | | % with degree | |
% employers and managers	Low	High	Low	High
Low	5.9	3.8	5.7	7.9
High	8.8	7.4	5.8	6.9

For definitions see Table A.3.

The Green Party's pattern of support was very different from that of the UKIP. They did relatively well in London for example, and were not particularly strong in rural areas. However, they also performed best in middle-class constituencies (particularly in the South of England) but, as Table A.5 above shows, these were a very different kind of middle-class constituency from those where the UKIP did best. As might be expected from previous research on patterns of support for Green parties and from theories of post-materialism (Inglehart, 1977; Burklin, 1985), the Greens did particularly well in constituencies where there are relatively large numbers of people with a degree. In short the Greens appealed where there was a substantial professional, rather than business, middle class and did so even though people in these kinds of constituencies were least likely to share the Greens' opposition to the euro.

On the face of it then, Europe appears to have had little to do with the Greens' success. Their performance could be accounted for by the proportional electoral system, a classic second-order willingness on the part of voters to support a small party, together with an underlying sympathy among a particular section of society for its cause. Yet we should remember that this is not the first time European elections have proved to have been a particularly happy hunting ground for Greens. In 1989 the party won no less than 14.9 per cent of the vote, overtaking the Liberal Democrats. Moreover, as in 1989, its share of the vote at this election was far higher than could have been anticipated from its performance in local or parliamentary by-elections. It may be that the presence of Greens from other countries in the European Parliament gives its European election campaigns a vital credibility they otherwise would lack.

Certainly, none of the other small parties were able to capitalise on the nature of the election or the opportunities afforded by the electoral system. This was the first time that voters throughout Britain had the opportunity to vote for parties of the far left and (with the exception of Wales) the far right. The British National Party was able to secure just 1.0 per cent of the vote while the Socialist Labour Party secured just 0.9 per cent, in both cases even less than the percentage obtained where they fought under first-past-the-post in 1997. Fears that the introduction of proportional representation would lead to a fracturing of the British party system or encourage extremism would appear to have been exaggerated.

The operation of the electoral system

The electoral system was one that was known not to be particularly kind to small parties. By dividing the country into eleven separate regions and then using the d'Hondt method to allocate seats, it effectively imposed a high threshold before a party could be sure of winning a seat. Even in the largest region, the South-East, the percentage required to be guaranteed a seat was as much as 8.3 per cent. Although, in practice, the actual thresholds proved to be somewhat lower (thanks to the incidence of votes for parties with no hope of securing representation), even the lowest, 7.1 per cent in the North-West, was still a significant barrier to any small party's hopes of a breakthrough.

Indeed, just how disproportional the outcome still proved to be is clear from Table A.6. In the first row of this table we show to two decimal places the number of seats to which each party would have been entitled if seats had been allocated in strict proportion to shares of the overall vote in Great Britain. In practice, no electoral system is able to allocate parts of a seat, but the calculation provides a benchmark of 'pure proportionality' against which to evaluate both the system that was actually used and a number of alternatives. The result of the new system is shown in the second row labelled Regional d'Hondt, while the outcome that would have been produced by alternative systems is shown in succeeding rows.

It can be seen immediately that the Regional d'Hondt system proved to be more disproportional than any of the alternative party list systems that might have been chosen. We summarise the overall degree of disproportionality by adding across all parties the absolute differences between each party's pure proportionality entitlement and the number of seats it actually won and dividing by two (as any party's 'over-representation' has to be counterbalanced by another's 'under-representation').[16] By this measure, the regional d'Hondt system 'misallocated' as many as eleven seats. Both the Conservatives and Labour won five or six more seats than their entitlement. While they did secure some representation, both the UKIP and the Greens were under-represented. Meanwhile, all of the remaining small parties failed to secure any seats at all.[17]

Table A.6 Comparing electoral systems

	Con	Lab	Lib Dem	UKIP	Green	Nat	Others	Deviation
				Seats				
Pure Proportionality	30.05	23.55	10.65	5.85	5.25	3.82	4.83	0
				Regional party list				
d'Hondt	36	29	10	3	2	4	0	11.58
Sainte Lagüe	31	24	11	7	7	4	0	4.83
Modified SL	34	29	11	4	2	4	0	9.48
Largest remainder	30	24	11	8	7	4	0	4.88
				National party list				
d'Hondt	37	28	11	6	3	4	1	4.18
Sainte Lagüe	30	24	11	6	5	4	4	1.13
				Single-member				
Plurality	50	29	0	0	0	5	0	21.13

Of particular note is the degree to which the system proved to be more dis-proportional than the Sainte Lagüe system of allocation. The relative merits of d'Hondt and Sainte Lagüe were the subject of some debate during the course of the passage of the European Elections Act, not least because the Home Secretary initially argued in the second reading debate that the former could be expected to be more proportional than the latter, a claim that he had later to retract (Curtice and Range, 1998; see also p. 34). Table A.6 shows that the Sainte Lagüe method would indeed have produced a far more proportional outcome, with neither the Conservatives nor Labour significantly 'over-represented' at all. Indeed, because of the much higher proportion of the vote cast for smaller parties, the difference between the outcome produced by the two methods was notably greater than had been found by simulations of the two methods based on the outcome of the 1994 European and 1997 General Elections (Curtice and Range, 1998). A largest remainder system would also have produced a more proportional outcome.[18]

However, the Sainte Lagüe method would result in a potentially important anomaly; the disproportionality that it does produce works to the advantage of the UKIP and the Greens, who prove to be beneficiaries of the somewhat lower effective thresholds that Sainte Lagüe produces. This ability of Sainte Lagüe to favour small parties is over-ridden in some Scandinavian countries by using a modified version that effectively raises the threshold required to win an initial seat (Carstairs, 1980).[19] As Table A.6 shows, this modified Sainte Lagüe method would not have over-represented either the UKIP or the Greens, and although this outcome would be achieved at the expense of less overall proportionality the result would still have been more proportional than that produced by d'Hondt

Even so, none of these variants of a regional party lists system would have produced as proportional an outcome as would a national party list system using either the d'Hondt or the Sainte Lagüe method without any formal threshold. The former indeed would have allowed the Pro-Euro Conservatives to win a seat while the latter would also have given representation to the British National Party, the independent Liberal Party and the Socialist Labour Party.[20] Whatever the gain in proportionality, many would regard encouragement of small extreme parties as a disadvantage.

At the same time, even the regional d'Hondt system produced a far more proportional result than would have been obtained under the old single-member plurality system. As it happens, prior to the government's decision to change the electoral system, all of the Boundary Commissions had published at least provisional recommendations for new single member constituencies for use in the 1999 European elections. If we simply add up the total votes cast in each of these proposed constituencies we find that the Conservatives would have won as many as 50 Euro-seats while Labour would have been left with exactly the same tally as they actually won, 29. The Liberal Democrats, UKIP and Greens would have won no seats at all. Our earlier analysis suggests that some voters would have voted differently under a single-member plurality system and this might have affected the seats outcome somewhat. Even so, it seems safe to conclude that far from costing the party a significant number of seats, the switch of electoral system enabled Labour dramatically to reduce the impact of the Conservatives' victory.

At the same time, the new system ensured that Labour's new delegation was far more regionally representative than it otherwise would have been. Under the single-member plurality system, Labour would have failed to win any seats in the South-East, South-West or Eastern regions, compared with the five that they actually won. Doubtless such a result would have resulted in claims that Labour was once again losing the southern voter. Equally, the Conservatives would still have been bedevilled by claims that it was an English party. It would have failed to win any seats in Wales, and while it came first in one Scottish single member Euro-constituency, its lead of 0.7 per cent might well have disappeared in the event of anti-Conservative tactical voting.

Conclusion

At the beginning of this appendix we remarked that, to date, European elections have largely failed to strengthen the links between the public and the European Union. Voters have tended to regard European elections as unimportant and in most Member States at least have seen them primarily an opportunity to cast a judgement on their current national government; they and have sometimes lent their vote to a smaller party they would not think of supporting in a national election. One consequence has been that the European Parliament has tended to be dominated by parties that are out of national office, a fact which in itself has not helped to raise the status of the Parliament in the eyes of national governments.

Some features of the 1999 European election in Britain still fit that model, most notably the apparent message that stay-at-home Labour voters were sending to their government. But other features fit a different model. In this, the minority of voters interested enough in the election to turn out include a significant proportion who use the chance to vote about Europe, and their preferences help to shape the way that national and European voting differs. But this is not necessarily good news for those who believe in European integration. Pan-European Union issues still play very little role; rather, those voters for whom Europe matters are rewarding or punishing parties according to how they regard the position of their country in relation to the European Union.

In Britain in 1999 the main beneficiaries of this were the Euro-sceptically repositioned Conservative party and the United Kingdom Independence Party. In contrast, the Pro-Euro Conservatives failed to make any real impact, while the most pro-European of the established parties, the Liberal Democrats, failed to match their contemporaneous national level of support. In other countries which seem to fit our alternative model in 1999, such as Denmark and France, centrist parties did mange to prosper by emphasising their pro-European credentials. It remains to be seen whether such a strategy can be made to work in Britain.

The first nationwide British trial of proportional representation also posed problems for the advocates of electoral reform. True, they can point to a politically more representative delegation of British MEPs than first-past-the-post would have delivered, a geographically more representative group of MEPs within both the two major parties, and clear evidence that more people voted sincerely and fewer tactically. But the new system is now indelibly associated with the record low turnout. While it is not clear (as some reformers would like to believe) that it was the particular type of system used that was responsible for the dull campaign or the low turnout, the introduction of proportional representation clearly failed to encourage more people to vote. This was evidently an election that raised as many questions as it answered both about Britain's stake in Europe and about electoral reform.

Notes

1. Survey data collected from those who actually did vote fails to give credence to the argument that potential voters were discouraged by the closed list system. An ICM survey conducted for the BBC's election results programme found that 58 per cent preferred to vote for a party list while only 34 per cent wanted to vote for an individual candidate.
2. For example, we show below that Labour's vote fell more where it was previously strongest. This pattern holds true irrespective of the level of turnout drop. Even so, among seats with similar levels of Labour vote in 1997, Labour's vote tended to fall a little more where turnout fell most.
3. Note that in this and in all other analyses of change in party vote shares we exclude Tatton and West Bromwich West where not all of the parties put up candidates in 1997.
4. The constituency boundaries used in 1983 are different from those used in 1999. We have constructed an estimate of the 1983 outcome on the 1999 boundaries using the notional results of the 1992 election produced by Rallings and Thrasher (1995) and constructing a 1983–92 swing based on what happened between those dates in the component old constituencies.

5. By the South of England here we mean London (–14.4 per cent), the South-East (–9.5 per cent), the South-West (–8.4 per cent) and Eastern (–13.4 per cent) regions. We would note that this pattern appears to be the byproduct of the correlation between prior Labour strength in 1997 and performance in 1999. The average fall in Labour's support was similar in every region for seats with a similar level of Labour support in 1997. The one exception is London where Labour's support on average fell rather less than might have been expected. As we noted earlier there was also a below average drop in turnout in the capital, lending further weight to our argument that Labour voters were more likely to stay at home (see also further below).

6. We undertook a logistic regression of whether someone was in favour of Britain adopting the euro as measured by the 1998 British Social Attitudes survey (Jowell *et al.*, 1999), using a sixfold measure of education and a sevenfold measure of social class. The former had a Wald statistic of 49.2 and was significant at the 0.1 per cent level. The latter had a Wald statistic of 7.9 and was not even significant at the 10 per cent level.

7. Conservative support rose by 4.4 per cent in those seats where less than 15 per cent speak Welsh but by only 1.4 per cent where more than that do so.

8. The Liberal Democrat vote was on average 14.0 per cent down on its local election performance in a sample of 81 constituencies where all the parties fought all the component wards. Meanwhile, its share of the vote in Scotland was 4.7 per cent lower than in the second vote in May while in Wales it was 4.3 per cent lower.

9. The party's share of the vote ranged between 13 per cent and 19 per cent in regular opinion polls undertaken by Gallup, ICM and MORI in the period immediately before and immediately after the European election.

10. It is true that even under the first-past-the-post electoral system, tactical voting has previously been less common in European elections than at Westminster ones. But by the time of the 1994 election, tactical voting had also become apparent in European elections (Curtice and Steed, 1995).

11. The outcome in 1997 is of course an imperfect measure of the extent to which voters have had an incentive to vote tactically. For example, in some seats where Labour came second to the Conservatives in 1997, the Liberal Democrats will have been second at previous elections. Here, fewer voters may have switched from the Liberal Democrats to Labour than in a seat where the Liberal Democrats have usually been second. However, if tactical voting did unravel at this election, we should still see the pattern identified here.

12. Note also that in contrast to the Conservatives, Liberal Democrat performance did vary as much as Labour's did. The standard deviation of the change in Liberal Democrat support was no less than 7.6. The extent to which the Liberal Domocrat and Labour performances tended to be the mirror image of each other is clearly shown in Table A.2 above.

13. These two patterns are of course related to each other, as Labour tended to be weak where the Liberal Democrats were strong in 1997, and vice versa. But regression analysis suggests that the Labour and the Liberal Democrat performances were both independently associated with prior Labour and prior Liberal Democrat strength. So the pattern of Liberal Democrat performance is not simply a mirror reflection of Labour's (or vice versa).

14. Christine Oddy, previously Labour MEP for Coventry and Warwickshire North, who stood as an Independent, also demonstrated that individuals could attract votes under the new system by winning 4.3 per cent of the vote in the West Midlands, with much of her vote coming from her former constituency.

15. In Scotland the correlation between the SNP performance in these elections (as measured by the change in support since 1997) and the party's performance in the Scottish Parliament election (as measured by the change in support since 1997 on the first vote) was as much as 0.68. For Plaid Cymru, the equivalent statistic is no less than 0.89. Unsurprisingly, similar correlations are also found for the Labour performance in the two countries.

16. This is in effect the Loosemore–Hanby index of deviation from proportionality (Loosemore and Hanby, 1971), a widely used measure of disproportionality (Lijphart, 1994; Dunleavy *et al.*, 1997) expressed in terms of actual seats rather than as a percentage of seats.

17. We might further note that both the seats won by the Greens were the last seats to be allocated in those regions, indicating how perilously close they were to not being represented at all.

18. The calculation in Table A.6 is based on the Hare quota.

19. This is done by treating the first divisor 1.4 rather than 1.

20. The votes cast for these parties were

Pro-Euro Conservatives	138,097	(1.4%)
British National Party	102,644	(1.0%)
Liberal Party	93,051	(0.9%)
Socialist Labour Party	86,749	(0.9%)

Bibliography

Anderson, S.S. and Eliassen, K.A. (eds) (1996), *The European Union: How Democratic Is It?'* (London: Sage).

Banchoff, T. and Smith, M.P. (1999), *Legitimacy and the European Union: the contested polity* (London: Routledge).

Beetham, D. and Lord, C. (1998), *Legitimacy and the EU* (London: Longman).

Blackman, R. (1999), *European Parliamentary Elections 1999* (London: Federal Trust).

Blair, T. (1999), 'Europe: The Third Way', transcript of speech, London.

Blondel, J., Sinnot, R. and Svensson, P. (1999), *People and Parliament in the European Union*, (Oxford: Oxford University Press).

Britain in Europe (1999), *Britain in Europe* (London: Britain in Europe).

Burklin, W. (1985), 'The Split between Established and the Non-established Left in Germany', *European Journal of Political Research,* 13: 283–93.

Butler, D. and Kavanagh, D. (1997), *The British General Election of 1997* (London: Macmillan).

Butler, D. and Westlake, M. (1995), *British Politics and European Elections 1994* (London: Macmillan).

Carstairs, A. (1980), *A Short History of Electoral Systems in Western Europe*, (London: Allen & Unwin).

Conservative Party (n.d.), 'Kitchen Table Conservatives – A Strategy Proposal', internal Conservative Party document.

Corbett, R., Jacobs, F. and Shackleton, M. (2000), *The European Parliament* (London: John Harper Books).

Curtice, J. (1996), 'One Nation Again?', in R. Jowell, J. Curtice, A. Park, L. Brook and K. Thomson (eds), *British Social Attitudes: The 13th Report* (Aldershot: Dartmouth).

Curtice, J. (1999a), 'All Claim Victory, But They are Wrong', *Guardian,* 10 May.

Curtice, J. (1999b), 'Can Britain Join the Euro? Political Opportunities and Impediments', in D. Cobham and G. Zis (eds), *From EMS to EMU: 1979 to 1999 and Beyond* (London: Macmillan).

Curtice, J. and Jowell, R. (1995), 'The Sceptical Electorate', in R. Jowell, J. Curtice, A. Park, L. Brook and D. Ahrendt (eds), *British Social Attitudes: The 12th Report* (Aldershot: Dartmouth).

Curtice, J. and Park, A. (1999), 'Region: New Labour, New Geography?', in G. Evans and P. Norris (eds), *Critical Elections: British Parties and Voters in Long-Term Perspective* (London: Sage).

Curtice, J. and Range, M. (1998), 'A Flawed Revolution? Britain's New European Parliament Electoral System', *Representation*, 35: 7–15.

Curtice, J. and Steed, M. (1984), 'Appendix 2: An Analysis of the Voting', in D. Butler and D. Kavanagh, *The British General Election of 1983* (London: Macmillan).

Curtice, J. and Steed, M. (1995), 'An Analysis of the Results', in D. Butler and M. Westlake, *British Politics and European Elections 1994* (London: Macmillan).

Curtice, J. and Steed, M. (1997), 'Appendix 2: The Results Analysed', in D. Butler and D. Kavanagh, *The British General Election of 1997* (London: Macmillan).

Denver, D. and Hands, G. (1997), 'Turnout', *Parliamentary Affairs*, 50: 720–32.

Duff, A. (1994), 'Building a Parliamentary Europe', *Government and Opposition*, 29.

Dunleavy, P., Margetts, H., O'Duffy, B. and Weir, S. (1997), *Making Votes Count: Replaying the 1990s General Elections under Alternative Electoral Systems* (Colchester: Democratic Audit).

Dunleavy, P. *et al.* (1998a), *Ready Reckoner for the 1999 European Elections* (Brussels: Adamson Associates).

Dunleavy, P. *et al.* (1998b), *Counting on Europe* (London: LSE Public Policy Group).

Evans, G. (1995), 'The State of the Union: Attitudes towards Europe', in R. Jowell, J. Curtice, A. Park and L. Brook (eds), *British Social Attitudes: The 12th Report* (Aldershot: Dartmouth).

Evans, G. (1999), 'Europe: A New Electoral Cleavage?', in G. Evans and P. Norris (eds), *Critical Elections: British Parties and Voters in Long-Term Perspective* (London: Sage).

Evans, G., Curtice, J. and Norris, P. (1998), 'New Labour, New Tactical Voting?', in D. Denver, J. Fisher, P. Cowley and C. Pattie (eds), *British Elections and Parties Review, Vol. 8 (London: Frank Cass).*

Gaffney, J. (ed.) (1996), *Political Parties and the European Union* (London: Routledge).

Gardner, David, 1998, 'The Selectors', *Tribune*, 16 October.

George, S. (1990) An Awkward Partner: Britain in the European Community (Oxford: Oxford University Press).

Gould, Philip, 1999, *The Unfinished Revolution* (London: Little, Brown).

GPC (Government Policy Consultants) (1999), 'Proportional Representation in the UK for the European Elections – Impact on the Political Landscape' (Brussels: GPC).

Hayward, J.E.S. (1995), *The Crisis of Representation in Europe* (London: Frank Cass).

Heath, A., Jowell, R., Taylor, B. and Thomson, K. (1998), 'Euroscepticism and the Referendum Party', in D. Denver, J. Fisher, P. Cowley and C. Pattie (eds), *British Elections and Parties Review, Vol. 8* (London: Frank Cass).

Heath, A., McLean, I., Taylor, B. and Curtice, J. (1999), 'Between First and Second Order: A Comparison of Voting Behaviour in European and Local Elections in Britain', *European Journal of Political Research*, 35: 389–414.

Hedges, A. and White, C. (1999), 'New Electoral Systems: What Voters Need to Know' (London: The Constitution Unit, Social and Planning Research).

Hix, S. (1999), 'The 1999–2004 European Parliament: A Forecast for the June 1999 Elections, and Its Implications' (Brussels: Adamson BSMG Worldwide).

Hix, S. and Lord, C. (1997), *Political Parties in the European Union* (London: Macmillan).

Inglehart, R. (1977), *The Silent Revolution: Changing Values and Political Styles among Western Publics* (Princeton, NJ: Princeton University Press).

Jowell, R., Curtice, J., Park, A. and Thomson, K. (eds) (1999), *British Social Attitudes: The 16th Report. Who Shares New Labour Values?* (Aldershot: Ashgate).

Katz, R.S. and Wessels, B. (eds) (1999), *The European Parliament, the National Parliaments, and European Integration* (Oxford: Oxford University Press).

Labour Party (1998), *Selecting Labour's European candidates for 1999: A Step-by-Step Guide to the Selection Procedure* (Millbank: Labour Party).

Leonard, M. (1998), *Making Europe Popular – The Search for European Identity* (London: Demos) February.

Lijphart, A. (1994), *Electoral Systems and Party Systems: A Study of Twenty-Seven Democracies 1945–90* (Oxford: Oxford University Press).

Linton, M. and Southcott, M. (1998), *Making Votes Count: The Case for Electoral Reform* (London: Profile Books).

Loosemore, I. and Hanby, V. (1971), 'The Theoretical Limits of Maximum Distortion: Some Analytic Expressions for Electoral Systems', *British Journal of Political Science*, 1: 467–77.

McLean, I. (1973), 'The Problem of Proportionate Swing', *Political Studies*, 21: 57–63.

Marquand, D. (1979), *Parliament for Europe* (London: Jonathan Cape).

Marsh, M. and Norris, P. (eds) (1997), *Political Representation in the European Union*, Special Issue of the *European Journal of Political Research*, 32.

Morgan, R. and Tame, C. (eds.) (1996), *Parliaments and Parties: The European Parliament in the Political Life of Europe*, (London: Macmillan).

Nielsen, N. (1996), 'Denmark', in J. Lodge (ed.), *The 1994 Elections to the European Parliament* (London: Pinter).

Norton, P. (ed.) (1996), *National Parliaments and the European Union* (London: Frank Cass).

O'Neill, N. (1998), 'Regional MEPs: Free Floating Elites or Integrated Regional Teams?' *Regional Review*, 8(2).

O'Neill, N. (1999), 'Closed Lists and the European Election,' *Renewal*, 7(2) Spring.

Prag, D. (1999), *Democracy in the European Union* (London: Action Centre for Europe).

Radice, G. (1992), *Southern Discomfort* (London: Fabian Society) Pamphlet 555.

Rallings, C. and Thrasher, M. (eds) (1995), *Media Guide to New Parliamentary Constituencies* (Plymouth: Local Government Chronicle Elections Centre).

Rallings, C. and Thrasher, M. (1997), *Local Elections in Britain* (London: Routledge).

Rallings, C. and Thrasher, M. (1998), *Local Elections Handbook 1998* (Plymouth: Local Government Chronicle Elections Centre).

Reif, K. (1984), 'National Electoral Cycles and European Elections 1979 and 1984', *Electoral Studies*, 3: 244–55.

Reif, K. (1985), 'Ten Second-Order National Elections', in K. Reif (ed.), *Ten European Elections: Campaigns and Results of the 1979/81 First Direct Elections to the European Parliament* (Aldershot: Gower).

Reif, K. and Schmitt, H. (1980), 'Nine National Second-Order Elections: A Systematic Framework for Analysis of European Elections Results', *European Journal of Political Research*, 8.

Schmitt, H. and Thomassen, J. (1999), *Political Representation and Legitimacy in the European Union* (Oxford: Oxford University Press).

Smith, J. (1999), *Europe's Elected Parliament* (Sheffield: UACES/Sheffield Academic Press).

Taylor, B. and Heath, A. (1999), 'Turnout and Registration: New Sources of Abstention?', in G. Evans and P. Norris (eds), *Critical Elections: British Parties and Voters in Long-Term Perspective* (London: Sage).

Taylor, B. and Thomson, K. (1999), *Scotland and Wales: Nations Again?* (Cardiff: University of Wales Press).

van der Eijk, C. and Franklin, M. (1996), *Choosing Europe? The European Electorate and National Politics in the Face of Union* (Ann Arbor: University of Michigan Press).

Westlake, M. (1994), *A Modern Guide to the European Parliament*, (London: Pinter).

Westlake, M. (1997), 'Mad Cows and Englishmen – The Institutional Consequences of the BSE Crisis', *Journal of Common Market Studies, Annual Review of Activities 1996*, 35, September.

Westlake, M. (1998), 'The European Parliament's Emerging Powers of Appointment', *Journal of Common Market Studies*, 36(3) September.

Worre, T. (1996), 'Denmark: Second-order Containment', in C. van der Eijk and M. Franklin, *Choosing Europe? The European Electorate and National Politics in the Face of Union* (Ann Arbor: University of Michigan Press).

Internet references

(Note: It is in the nature of the Internet that pages are liable to move or to disappear over time. These references are correct as of 10 January 2000.)

European Elections Project <http://www.european­elections­projects>
House of Commons Library Research Papers <http://www.parliament.uk/commons/lib/research/rpintro.htm>
European Commission <http://europa.eu.int/comm/index_en.htm>
European Parliament <http://www.europarl.eu.int/sg/tree/en/default.htm>
European Union <http://europa.eu.int/index-en.htm>
Federal Trust <http://www.fedtrust.co.uk>
Register of Political Parties <http://www.party-register.gov.uk>
Home Office <http://www.homeoffice.gov.uk>
Statutory Instrument 1999 No. 1214 (European Elections) <http://www.legislation.hmso.gov.uk/si/si1999/19991214.htm>
European Parliamentary Elections Act 1999 <http://www.hmso.gov.uk/acts/acts1999/19990001.htm>

Websites of political parties which have MEPs

Labour Party <http://www.labour.org.uk>
Conservative Party <http://www.conservative-party.org.uk>
Liberal Democrats <http://www.libdems.org.uk>
UK Independence Party < http://www.independenceuk.org.uk>
Green Party < http://www.greenparty.org.uk>
Scottish National Party <http://www.snp.org.uk>
Plaid Cymru <http://www.plaidcymru.org>
Ulster Unionist Party <http://www.uup.org>
Democratic Unionist Party <http://www.dup.org.uk>
Social Democratic and Labour Party <http://www.sdlp.ie>

Index